7 DAY

Studies in Diplomacy and International Relations

General Editors: **Donna Lee**, Senior Lecturer in International Organisations and International Political Economy, University of Birmingham, UK and **Paul Sharp**, Professor and Head of Political Science at the University of Minnesota Duluth, USA

The series was launched as *Studies in Diplomacy* in 1994 under the general editorship of G.R. Berridge. Its purpose is to encourage original scholarship on all aspects of the theory and practice of diplomacy. The new editors assumed their duties in 2003 with a mandate to maintain this focus while also publishing research which demonstrates the importance of diplomacy to contemporary international relations more broadly conceived.

Titles include:

G.R. Berridge (*editor*)
DIPLOMATIC CLASSICS
Selected Texts from Commynes to Vattel

G.R. Berridge, Maurice Keens-Soper and T.G. Otte
DIPLOMATIC THEORY FROM MACHIAVELLI TO KISSINGER

Herman J. Cohen
INTERVENING IN AFRICA
Superpower Peacemaking in a Troubled Continent

Andrew F. Cooper (*editor*)
NICHE DIPLOMACY
Middle Powers after the Cold War

Mai'a Davis Cross
THE EUROPEAN DIPLOMATIC CORPS
Diplomats and International Cooperation from Westphalia to Maastricht

David H. Dunn (*editor*)
DIPLOMACY AT THE HIGHEST LEVEL
The Evolution of International Summitry

Brian Hocking (*editor*)
FOREIGN MINISTRIES
Change and Adaptation

Brian Hocking and David Spence (*editors*)
FOREIGN MINISTRIES IN THE EUROPEAN UNION
Integrating Diplomats

Michael Hughes
DIPLOMACY BEFORE THE RUSSIAN REVOLUTION
Britain, Russia and the Old Diplomacy, 1894–1917

Gaynor Johnson
THE BERLIN EMBASSY OF LORD D'ABERNON, 1920–1926

Christer Jönsson and Martin Hall
ESSENCE OF DIPLOMACY

Donna Lee
MIDDLE POWERS AND COMMERCIAL DIPLOMACY
British Influence at the Kennedy Trade Round

Donna Lee, Ian Taylor and Paul D. Williams (editors)
THE NEW MULTILATERALISM IN SOUTH AFRICAN DIPLOMACY

Mario Liverani
INTERNATIONAL RELATIONS IN THE ANCIENT NEAR EAST, 1600–1100 BC

Jan Melissen (editor)
INNOVATION IN DIPLOMATIC PRACTICE
Soft Power in International Relations

THE NEW PUBLIC DIPLOMACY
Soft Power in International Relations

Peter Neville
APPEASING HITLER
The Diplomacy of Sir Nevile Henderson, 1937–39

M.J. Peterson
RECOGNITION OF GOVERNMENTS
Legal Doctrine and State Practice, 1815–1995

Gary D. Rawnsley
RADIO DIPLOMACY AND PROPAGANDA
The BBC and VOA in International Politics, 1956–64

TAIWAN'S INFORMAL DIPLOMACY AND PROPAGANDA

Karl W. Schweizer and Paul Sharp (editors)
THE INTERNATIONAL THOUGHT OF HERBERT BUTTERFIELD

Paul Sharp and Geoffrey Wiseman (editors)
THE DIPLOMATIC CORPS AS AN INSTITUTION OF INTERNATIONAL SOCIETY

Ronald A. Walker
MULTILATERAL CONFERENCES
Purposeful International Negotiation

A. Nuri Yurdusev (editor)
OTTOMAN DIPLOMACY
Conventional or Unconventional?

Studies in Diplomacy and International Relations
Series Standing Order ISBN 0–333–71495–4
(outside North America only)

You can receive future titles in this series as they are published by placing a standing order. Please contact your bookseller or, in case of difficulty, write to us at the address below with your name and address, the title of the series and the ISBN quoted above.

Customer Services Department, Macmillan Distribution Ltd, Houndmills, Basingstoke, Hampshire RG21 6XS, England

---

The Diplomatic Corps as an Institution of International Society

Edited by

Paul Sharp
Professor and Head of Political Science
University of Minnesota Duluth, USA

and

Geoffrey Wiseman
Professor of the Practice of International Relations and Public Diplomacy
University of Southern California, USA

First published 2007 by
PALGRAVE MACMILLAN
Houndmills, Basingstoke, Hampshire RG21 6XS and
175 Fifth Avenue, New York, N.Y. 10010
Companies and representatives throughout the world

PALGRAVE MACMILLAN is the global academic imprint of the Palgrave
Macmillan division of St. Martin's Press, LLC and of Palgrave Macmillan Ltd.
Macmillan® is a registered trademark in the United States, United Kingdom
and other countries. Palgrave is a registered trademark in the European
Union and other countries.

ISBN 13: 978–0–230–00165–7   hardback
ISBN 10: 0–230–00165–3   hardback

This book is printed on paper suitable for recycling and made from fully
managed and sustained forest sources. Logging, pulping and manufacturing
processes are expected to conform to the environmental regulations of the
country of origin.

A catalogue record for this book is available from the British Library.

A catalogue record for this book is available from the Library of Congress.

10   9   8   7   6   5   4   3   2   1
16   15   14   13   12   11   10   09   08   07

Printed and bound in Great Britain by
Antony Rowe Ltd, Chippenham and Eastbourne

Adam Watson (1914–2007)
In Memoriam

Contents

Acknowledgements

The genesis for this book was an idea proposed by Professor Iver Neumann in a conversation with the editors at the 2004 annual convention of the International Studies Association (ISA) held in Montreal, Canada. The three of us were meeting as a working group on diplomacy, part of an international scholarly networking initiative on Reconvening the English School of International Relations Theory. Subsequently, the editors organized panels at the 2005 ISA annual convention conference held in Hawaii and at the 2006 convention in San Diego. The book emerged from those panels as a spontaneous international collaborative enterprise, involving both scholars and former practitioners from a range of countries. We are very grateful to all our contributors for their collaborative spirit in driving this book project.

The editors would like to express their gratitude to Alison Howson and Gemma d' Arcy Hughes for their support at Palgrave Macmillan. Geoffrey Wiseman would like to thank the faculty and staff in the School of International Relations at the University of Southern California for their support of his work. Paul Sharp also wishes to acknowledge the University of Minnesota Duluth, the College of Liberal Arts and its Dean, Linda Krug, for all their support and encouragement.

Notes on Contributors

Adam Watson, former British ambassador and visiting professor, University of Virginia

James Mayall, formerly LSE and University of Cambridge

G. R. Berridge, professor emeritus, Leicester University

Sasson Sofer, Hebrew University, Jerusalem

Alan K. Henrikson, The Fletcher School, Tufts University

Peter Lyon, formerly the Commonwealth Institute, London

Halvard Leira, Norwegian Ministry of Foreign Affairs

Iver B. Neumann, University of Oslo

J. E. Hoare, British Foreign and Commonwealth Office (ret.)

Kishan S. Rana, DiploFoundation, Malta; former Indian ambassador

Humayun Kabir, Bangladeshi Ambassador to Nepal, 2003–06

Joyce E. Leader, University of Georgetown, former US ambassador

Paul Sharp, Head, Department of Political Science, University of Minnesota, Duluth

Mai'a Keapuolani Davis Cross, Colgate University

Geoffrey Wiseman, University of Southern California

Foreword

This collection of essays on the diplomatic corps as an institution is very welcome. The diplomatic corps is by its nature a protean and many-sided institution, which needs to be studied from many angles. This book looks at the different forms and functions which the corps has assumed at various times and places, and also enables us to see it as a whole.

The diplomatic missions in a country not only represent their own individual governments: they are also *colleagues*, with certain interests in common. Together they protect the immunities and privileges necessary for their work more effectively than when they act alone. Professional solidarity is particularly useful to consular corps, whose members have to deal with regional authorities less familiar with diplomatic practice. More important, embassies collectively symbolize and indeed represent the international system or society to which their governments and the host governments belong. The diplomatic corps is, like all diplomacy, part of the lubricating oil of an international society. For some three centuries now, in Europe and those countries that have adopted the European system, the diplomatic dialogue has been continuous and all-embracing; whereas the use of force is sporadic and localized. War, and even strong disapproval, breaks off the direct dialogue with the enemy; but contact often continues discreetly and indirectly through third parties. Here again a neutral embassy, acting for international society as a whole, provides a line of communication.

The discussions between embassies, at all levels, and especially between heads of mission, help to broaden each embassy's perception of the host country. A competent embassy can learn much from colleagues who represent governments with very different objectives from their own. Such exchanges also enable an ambassador to nudge his or her colleagues towards a greater understanding of their (that is, their government's) view of the host government and its policy; and so affect what they report back to their governments. Professional diplomats understand the usefulness of the corps more clearly than non-career appointments and embassy officers representing other departments of government, who tend to concentrate on bilateral relations with the host government.

The diplomatic corps functions very differently from one capital to another. Extra elasticity is needed with dictatorships. When I was British Ambassador in Havana in the early 1960s, the embassies constantly needed to act collectively on matters like the right to bring in and out unexamined material; but the doyen by seniority of the corps was the North Korean, with whom most of us did not have relations. After some discussions, the Cuban Government agreed to my proposal that the doyenship should be tripartite, with the senior Western ambassador to act for those embassies that could not deal through the Korean. In many other posts the longer residence of the doyen in the host country makes his experience and advice especially valuable to more recent arrivals.

I hope that this book will appeal not only to academic and diplomatic specialists, but also introduce a wider public to some of the realities of diplomatic practice.

Adam Watson

Introduction

James Mayall

Should the man on the Clapham Omnibus encounter a diplomat, he would be likely to regard him as a member of a different species. Even those who are aware of their existence seldom have a clear idea about what they do beyond possessing an enviable capacity to avoid paying parking fines. And it is true that much as dog-owners are said to resemble their dogs, diplomats often seem to have more in common with each other than with those they allegedly represent. In popular imagination they belong to a caste set apart, collectively as well as personally.

When the diplomatic corps first made its appearance as an institution within the European society of states – with the establishment of resident missions, rules of precedence and procedure etc. – the distance between diplomats and others was perhaps not so great. Or rather it was not so great between diplomats and other members of the social class from which they were drawn. European society was itself stratified and hierarchical. More importantly, the vast majority of society enjoyed neither civil nor political rights, in the modern sense of these terms. They were not involved, even symbolically, in issues of representation and negotiation between states. Diplomacy was conducted on behalf of sovereigns and between courts.

Like much in contemporary international society, the modern diplomatic corps and the practice of diplomacy that has grown up both within and alongside it owes much to its European origins and evolution from the Renaissance onwards. But its successful export to the rest of the world, and its survival into our own globalized age, is not to be explained merely in terms of the European enclosure of the world by western imperialism and industrialization, important as these seismic events are. There were structural reasons for the development of diplomacy, which cut across cultures. Those who represented

1

their sovereigns in foreign lands originally had to overcome the difficulties of long distance communication. Without the telegraph, telephone or internet, they were on their own.

In such circumstances trust was all important. Plenipotentiaries had to have the authority to represent their sovereign and be taken seriously where they did so. Hence the extravagance of the gifts carried by diplomatic missions: splendour provided *prima facie* evidence of authority and seriousness of intent, as did the high status of those who travelled abroad on official business.[1] There is no reason to believe that this logic was confined to Europe, otherwise early European missions to non-European courts – to India and the Far East for example – would not have been recognized for what they were. In the western Sudan the institution of the embassy was well established by the 13th century. As Thomas Hodkin noted, the ambassador 'might be a member of the ruling family,...or he might be a permanent official, or a scholar...or a wealthy citizen. In all cases he stood in close relations with the ruler, who would normally keep – or try to keep – effective control over foreign relations.'[2] I have also been told that amongst the pre-colonial Tswana chieftains diplomacy followed essentially the same logic: the business was too important to be handled by anyone other than aristocrats, generally close kinsmen of the chief. Indeed, it may be not too fanciful to see in the work of Malinowski, Marcel Mauss and many other anthropologists the lineaments of diplomacy viewed as a universal response to a perennial human problem.[3]

The problem itself can be simply stated: how best to manage mutually beneficial relations between separate political communities? The institutionalization of diplomacy and the establishment in each capital of a diplomatic corps is the most evolved solution to the problem that has been devised so far. The essays in this book examine its operation from different angles, in different places, and in response to a series of different challenges. In the remainder of this introduction I should like to examine three questions, which in one way or another can be said to inform them. These questions are respectively: Can the diplomatic corps properly be regarded as an institution of international society and why? Can it move with the times or is it progressively becoming an anachronism? How well can it handle ideological conflict? Before turning to these questions it may be helpful to raise two preliminary observations about my formulation of the problem itself.

First, it is political pluralism that necessitates both diplomacy and its institutionalization, not a particular kind of society, be it monarchy, empire, republic or modern nation-state. The relations of pastoral, acephelous and other stateless societies with outsiders are admittedly problematic. Such groups have no difficulty in dealing with other countries on an individual basis as the often spectacular commercial success of Somalis since their state disintegrated in the late 1980s demonstrates. The problem is not theirs but the outside world's. Since they have difficulty in maintaining a central authority amongst themselves for any length of time, with whom do outsiders deal and how do they establish an orderly and stable framework for reciprocal relations. It is perhaps for this reason that as the world has become increasingly integrated by modern communications over the past 150 years such societies have become progressively marginalized in world affairs. Most probably this trend is set to continue although it is possible that the individualist bias of the computer age, especially of the internet, may paradoxically give them a new lease of life.

The second observation is that although the world is anything but peaceful, diplomacy is fundamentally about maintaining peaceful relations. No doubt even had Hobbes' state of war not been a description of the State's *propensity* to war, but an account of the day to day reality of relations between sovereigns in a state of nature, there would still have been a need for negotiators with diplomatic skills.[4] 'When we have destroyed the land, then we will make peace.' These words put into the mouth of the Protestant General Wallenstein, by Schiller in his play about the Thirty Years War, point to the recognition that even war, in Clausewitz's famous definition, is 'politics with an admixture of other means.' He could just as well have said diplomacy.

But while diplomats certainly occupy a world that Hobbes would recognize, and have a responsibility therefore to pass on political intelligence to their home governments, they are not spies. Many diplomatic missions have Intelligence Officers masquerading as attaches of one sort or another. Everyone knows that this goes on – indeed as we shall see it is a reflection of the schizophrenic nature of international society – but it does so on the general if implicit understanding that if found out its existence will be denied. This is necessary if the legitimate work of the mission is to continue. Indeed, the diplomatic corps demonstrates the essentially peaceful mandate of the diplomatic profession whenever an espionage scandal leads to a rupture of relations between states. In such circumstances it is customary for the corps to arrange for a section to be opened in another embassy to look after the interests of the accused state until the row blows over and formal relations are restored.

The diplomatic corps and international society

Within the cannon of the oddly named 'English School', international order is generally understood to be a product of international society. This society is said to have emerged in its modern incarnation from the Treaty of Westphalia, which finally brought the European wars of religion to a close in 1648, and its predecessor, the Treaty of Augsburg. In his influential book, *The Anarchical Society*, Hedley Bull differentiated international society from an international system. All that was necessary for the latter to exist was a pattern of relations of sufficient regularity to ensure that rational governments would factor in probable external reactions to their calculations of state interests and how best to achieve them.[5]

By contrast, international society was based on a commitment to common values. These values – sovereignty, mutual recognition, territorial integrity, non-interference and so on – were embedded in a string of supporting institutions. The most important and least contentious were international law and diplomacy, without which international cooperation would be impossible. Liberal realists such as Bull maintained that the values of international society were also upheld by three other institutional practices: the balance of power, the role of the great powers in maintaining the balance and hence international order, and most contentiously of all, war itself. It was only through accepting war as a social institution – and until the 20th century it was accepted that the sovereign had a right to go to war for any reason of state – that the international hierarchy could be periodically shifted and the membership of international society changed.

The merit of this account is that it can accommodate the cooperative as well as the conflictual dimensions of international life within a single scheme. It is of course a useful historical metaphor not an accurate historical record of how the contemporary world developed from its early modern origins. But it is truer to human experience than either of its main theoretical rivals, realism and liberalism (in either their pure or their fashionably 'neo-realist and neo-liberal' manifestations). The former tends to seal the State at its borders, which can be pushed outwards or inwards by wars of conquest and expansion, but finds it harder to account for the extent to which international life is regulated by law and characterized by cooperative ventures. The latter tends towards utopian schemes for international reform, regarding all clashes of interest as both irrational and misperceived.

These advantages, however, are secured at a price. To examine the relations of human beings through the concept of a society is to self-consciously opt for an abstraction. Its justification must be that it allows us to identify behavioural and other patterns that would be invisible if we employed a more microscopic or individuated approach. But international society is a society of states not people, so it might reasonably be objected that to view international relations through this prism commits us to relying on an abstraction of an abstraction, ensuring that the analysis remains at two removes from reality. Since I have advanced the claim that the English School is truer to experience than its rivals, this is a troublesome objection.

Fortunately, at this point the diplomatic corps rescues the English School from what might otherwise be dismissed as just another flight of academic fancy, 'nonsense on stilts' as Jeremy Bentham would probably have described it. Diplomats are real people, who do a practical job, and the diplomatic corps, which protects their collective identity and professional integrity, is the most tangible expression of international society that exists. It is admittedly a strange kind of social institution, which echoes the schizophrenic character of international society to which I referred earlier. This is because diplomats are, so to speak, rivals for influence at a foreign court, and colleagues with common interests to protect there. But, in the final analysis, and despite such idiosyncrasies, it is the institution of diplomacy that translates international society from a theoretical proposition into some kind of practical reality.

The diplomatic institution performs both practical and symbolic roles in international society. We live at a time when most diplomats probably see themselves as functionaries doing a practical job – securing trade deals or investment opportunities, organizing ministerial visits, seeking the support of the host government on issues of particular concern of their own etc. – rather than the dignified representatives of a society of sovereign states. Yet the recognition of this symbolic role by the host is what gives diplomats their right of access and is therefore a necessary precondition for them doing their job properly. The diplomatic corps is the guarantor of this sovereign representational role.

It may be that recognition and participation in the corps is more important for small states that may be less able to secure access on demand to advance their interests on their own than for the major powers, whose representatives often prefer to deal with as many issues as possible on a purely bilateral basis. But ignoring the representative role of the Ambassador is still ill advised. In *DC Confidential*, Christopher Meyer argues persuasively that the work of Britain's Washington Embassy was compromised by the attempt of the Prime Minister's Office to deal directly with the White House during the Iraq crisis. Since the Prime Minister visited Washington only at intervals, without the Ambassador's input, he could not always be sensitized to the fast moving currents of Washington politics. In other words a breach of protocol can have practical as well as symbolic consequences. In this case, Meyer argues it led to Britain having less influence with the Bush Administration than might otherwise have been the case.[6]

I suggested earlier that the underlying rationale of the diplomatic profession is to facilitate orderly and peaceful relations amongst states. Sometimes the corps is called upon to play a collective role in managing, or even resolving, international crises. The essays on its role in Macedonia and Kathmandu examine this aspect of its work. In other cases, as during the Arusha Peace Talks prior to the Rwandan genocide, the corps, or at least a cross section of its members, may try to play a proactive role but fail.

But despite its normative bias, diplomacy is not always a fair weather profession. Nor is it necessarily always appropriate for it to be constantly engaged in promoting change and reform. Indeed, one of its most important roles is passive, 'keeping the show on the road' when the diplomatic weather turns foul. As Paul Sharp has written elsewhere, it does not actually matter whether rogue states actually exist. In the end, their roguishness is, after all, in the eye of the beholder. What matters is that major powers believe such states to exist and fashion their foreign policies on this assumption. It falls to the diplomats to try and contain the damage.[7] What Sharp calls diplomacy as a holding action – while a crisis blows itself out – will in some circumstances be a worthy end in itself. It is also one that provides as clear evidence of the role of the diplomatic corps as an institution of international society as those rarer occasions on which it briefly grabs the international spotlight.

The challenge of technology

The answer provided by the essays in this book to the second question raised earlier is again I believe affirmative. The diplomatic profession has by and large succeeded in moving with the times and so avoided the charge of anachronism, 'an outdoor relief system for the upper classes', as the European Left persisted in viewing it for many years after 1945. Ernest Renan once described a nation as a community bound together by collective amnesia.[8] It takes what it regards as useful from the past, reinterprets it to suit present purposes and moves on. And in a real sense for any society, flexibility and adaptability are the price of survival. International Society is no exception.

Flexibility was certainly required to accommodate the steady expansion of international society from the 51 states that signed the UN Charter in 1945 to the current membership of 192. This expansion was also accompanied by the increased cultural heterogeneity of the membership on the one hand and the widening of the number and kind of issues requiring international negotiation on the other. Depending on the country and the context these developments introduced a degree of caucusing into the life of the diplomatic corps, the creation in some countries of inner and outer groups (for example the local neighbours and the G8), and the growth of specialized negotiators who tend to concentrate on specific issues such as trade or arms control.

Such functional divisions of labour within the profession were reinforced by the broader East-West and North-South divides. Apart from the UN itself where the forging of unlikely alliances on particular issues bears witness to the continued vitality and flexibility of the diplomatic community, a few intergovernmental organizations such as the Organisation for Security and Cooperation in Europe (OSCE) and the Commonwealth have specialized in bridging the gap. The OSCE, for example, has played the leading role in seeking creative solutions to the problem of minorities and its potential as a breeding ground for ethnic conflict. There was also some truth (and perhaps still is) in the former Commonwealth Secretary-General Shridath Ramphal's claim that because of its membership that straddles the North–South divide, while 'the Commonwealth cannot negotiate for the world, it can help the world to negotiate.'[9]

When we turn to the impact of technology, however, there can be no denying the strength of the challenge. The world may still be politically plural but it is integrated into a single system at so many levels by modern technology that direct communications between governments, if necessary in real time, have indeed made many of the traditional functions of diplomacy redundant. In the modern world – so the argument runs – there is simply no need for a separate profession, a caste set aside from the people they represent, as I suggested at the beginning of this Introduction. I believe this view to be mistaken for one very important reason.

From a philosophical point of view pluralism, as Ernest Gellner was one of the few modern thinkers to grasp, is a problem not a solution.[10] And if philosophy seeks the truth through a holistic understanding of the world should not this quest inform our social arrangements as well? Throughout most of history, and in most places, men have sought a single truth and preferred conformity to diversity. Whether this desire to make social reality conform to philosophical aspiration has its origins in aesthetic sensibility or, more probably, in human insecurity and fear of the stranger, is immaterial. Fortunately perhaps the monist solution has proved unobtainable and sooner or later people of different faiths and customs have settled for co-existence and sought to make a virtue out of necessity.

Diplomats, who were originally formed into a kind of craft guild to manage this historic compromise may these days have different functions than their predecessors, but their management role has not fundamentally changed. Indeed, in two important respects it has become more not less important. In the first place, the rise of nationalism and the doctrine of popular sovereignty had the inevitable, if not always intended consequence, of bringing popular passions to bear on foreign policy and relations. For the diplomatic profession it increased their schizophrenia: anyone who stayed too long in one post, or became too familiar with the customs and practices of the country to which he or she was accredited, was likely to be viewed with suspicion at home. In the 1960s I worked for a diplomat in the British High Commission in New Delhi. As a former member of the Indian Civil Service he had unrivalled access to the upper echelons of its successor, the Indian Administrative Service, as a result. Sadly, one could almost hear the official scepticism crackling down the wires in response to his weekly telegrams home. To some extent the diplomatic corps and its collective *esprit* can still provide protection for the hapless official caught between sympathy for his host and the need to advance the interests of his home country. 'Going native' remains the kiss of death for a successful diplomatic career.

The second reason why the strategic role of diplomacy has been reinforced is oddly a consequence of globalization. We live at a time when the ease of electronic communication has changed the nature of international migration. In the great population movements of the past, the vast majority of migrants had no opportunity to stay in close contact with the communities from which they came. The pattern varied in different parts of the world but assimilation was a much less controversial (although probably no less painful) process than it is today. These days the impact of globalization, and more particularly of high speed Information Technology, has paradoxically been to sharpen the political salience of religious and cultural differences. Diasporas not only send remittances back to their families, they often help to fund political parties in their home countries and even import some of their local political battles into their countries of adoption. This phenomenon was observable in the West well before the attack on the Twin Towers in September 2001, the subsequent 'war on terror' and the Afghan and Iraq invasions. The combined impact of all these events has been growing intolerance in world affairs. If the world order is to be restored to something like stability modern diplomats will need not merely to reinforce their commitment to the values of their corps, but also to 'go native' at least to the point of demonstrating the international communities' toleration of cultural and political diversity.

Ideological tension

Extreme ideological conflict – the juxtaposition of two mutually exclusive versions of the truth – is arguably the greatest enemy of diplomacy. The clash between liberal capitalism and communism sometimes strained diplomatic relations nearly to breaking point. Yet, in the recent as in the more distant past, the diplomatic corps has proved itself remarkably resilient. It worked fairly effectively even during the coldest parts of the Cold War when the Americans kept a diplomatic back channel open to the Chinese regime that it did not recognize through the good offices of a third party. Relations between the United States and the Soviet Union were largely bilateral, and were institutionalized with the establishment of the hot line between the Kremlin and the White House following the Cuban missile crisis in October 1962.

It may seem strange that the diplomatic fall-out from the ideological conflict occurred as much within the blocs, particularly the Atlantic Alliance, as between them. Strange that is, until one recalls that collectively the diplomatic profession exists to preserve the values of a pluralist international society. Several American allies, usually led by Britain, disagreed with the United States over the appropriateness of waging economic warfare against China, Cuba, the Soviet Union and its Warsaw Pact partners. Arguments over the scope of the strategic embargo and the definition of so called dual-use items was a perennial bone of contention within the Alliance, as were the periodic attempts by US administrations to flex their economic muscles in order to extend the reach of American domestic law beyond their own borders.

As late as 1985, the British Prime Minister and French President had to intervene personally to ensure that the Friendship Pipeline was completed after the US had threatened to prevent French and British suppliers fulfilling their contracts by sanctioning any subcontractors with American participation. In such circumstances, the ritual politeness of diplomatic convention is useful in smoothing ruffled feathers on both sides. Again, the work falls naturally to a profession whose ultimate *raison d'être* is to uphold sovereign immunity from outside interference.

It is more difficult to be sanguine about the ability of international society to accommodate the ferocious ideological disputes that have flared up since 1989. The triumph of one side, albeit by default, revealed a fracture that had been concealed by the icy stability of the Cold War. The belief that popular sovereignty should logically result in a democratic world order was not new. It had been around at least since the Paris Peace Conference following the First World War. Once fascism had been defeated, the grand alliance broke apart with both east and west proclaiming rival visions of a democratic world order. Pluralism survived because neither side could prevail.

There is a beguiling and slightly comic theatricality about diplomatic life: in New Delhi, for instance, until mid-2006, the Dean of the Corps was the Somali Ambassador who had remained stranded there since 1989, shortly before the State he represented comprehensively failed. For all that, most diplomats would subscribe to the realist dictum that in any international system it is the great powers that necessarily determine its overall shape and trajectory.[11] It is not surprising, therefore, that despite their outward commitment to the pluralist rules of diplomacy, both Cold War super powers penetrated deep inside other countries to advance their rival visions of the democratic future of humanity. So long as two versions of this project were on offer, there was space not only for some states to sit the contest out, (or as the non-aligned always insisted they were doing, to decide their own policies on the merits of the case and in their own interests) but also for the diplomats to display their healing skills.

The playing field was never in fact as level as this account implies. Well before the end of the Cold War, the western powers had begun to shape the 'developing' world to their own design by attaching economic conditions to their bilateral loans and debt relief and imposing structural adjustment programmes through the International Monetary Fund and the World Bank. The collapse of communism left the liberal democratic powers in command of the field. For the first time, moreover, International Society was dominated by a single hegemon. Under unconstrained American leadership the pressure for democratic reform quickened, whether it was appropriate or not. Good governance, democratization and human rights criteria were added to the economic conditionality of the early 1980s.

It is a reasonable surmise that diplomacy works best when change, however fervently it may be desired, is slow enough to be largely invisible. It was not merely the violent events, attributed to Islamist terrorism, in New York in 2001, followed by those in New Delhi, Bali, Madrid and London that shifted the political furniture around so dramatically that the impartiality on which diplomacy depends became suspect to those who saw themselves as targeted by malignant forces and rogue states. The over zealous attempt first to establish a single standard of world civilization and then to promote it through diplomatic channels has had a similar, and possibly more insidious, effect.

Indeed, despite western disclaimers, we cannot be sure that the resurgence of terrorism (a phenomenon with which diplomats have periodically had to contend for centuries) is not partly a reaction to the over energetic pursuit of liberal internationalism. It rests on a solidarist rather than pluralist conception of international society and must therefore subject the diplomatic profession to a formidable test, even if the diplomats themselves do not always recognize it. To the ardent enthusiast for global democracy and civil society, Talleyrand's famous quip, 'above all not too much zeal' will have little appeal. Collectively the essays in this volume suggest, however, that it is still the best advice if international society is to restore its equilibrium.

Notes

1 This practice has not only survived into the modern world, but flourished even under socialism during the Cold War. I am grateful to my colleague, Dr Nikolai Ssorin-Chaikov, for sharing with me the role that gifts played in the Soviet Union. See, Olga Sosnina and Nikolai Ssorin Chaikov, 'Archaeology of Power: Anatomy of Love', the introduction to their catalogue of the fascinating Moscow exhibition, *Gifts to Soviet Leaders* (Moscow, 2006).

2 T. Hodkin, 'Diplomacy and diplomats in the Western Sudan', in K. Ingham (ed.) *Foreign Relations of African States*, Colston Papers No 25 (London: Butterworths, 1974) p. 19.

3 Bronislaw Malinowski, *Magic, Science and Other Essays* (Westport: Greenwood Press, 1992), and Marcel Maus (translated by W. D. Halls), *The Gift: the form and reason for exchange in archaic societies* (London: Routledge, 1990).

4 'But though there had never been any time, wherein particular men were in a condition of war one against another; yet in all times, Kings and persons of sovereign authority, because of their independency, are in continual jealousies, and in the state and posture of gladiators,...' Thomas Hobbes, *Leviathan* (numerous editions) Chapter 13.

5 Hedley Bull, *The Anarchical Society, A Study of Order in World Politics*, 1st edn (Houndmills, Basingstoke: Macmillan, 1977) Parts I and II.

6 Christopher Meyer, *DC Confidential* (London: Weidenfeld and Nicolson, 2005).

7 Paul Sharp, 'Rogue States, International Theory and the Diplomatic Tradition of International Thought', Unpublished paper presented at the International Studies Association Annual Convention. San Diego, 2006.

8 Ernest Renan, *What is a Nation?* Paper presented at the Sorbonne, 1882.

9 Shridath Ramphal, 'Empires of the Mind: Canada and the Commonwealth', in C. Turner, Frank and Tim Dickson (eds), *The Empire Club of Canada Speeches 1986–87* (Toronto: The Empire Club Foundation, 1987).

10 His position is succinctly presented in *Postmodernism, Reason and Religion* (London: Routledge, 1992) and also in *Conditions of Liberty: Civil Society and its Rivals* (London: Penguin Books, 1994).

11 For a classic statement of this doctrine, see Raymond Aron, *Peace and War, A Theory of International Relations* (London: Weidenfeld and Nicolson, 1966). 'The structure of international systems is always *oligopolistic*. In each period the principal actors have determined the system more than they have been determined by it.' p. 95.

Part I

The Diplomatic Corps from the Past to the Present: Historical and Conceptual Background

1
The Origins of the Diplomatic Corps: Rome to Constantinople

G. R. Berridge

It appears to have been about the middle of the 18th century before the term 'diplomatic corps' was used to refer to the body of diplomats resident in one capital and about the same time before the corporate existence of these envoys – by *any* name – was remarked upon in a general work on diplomacy.[1] It was even later before individual courts began to issue diplomatic lists and thereby crystallize the group by formally identifying the boundaries of its membership.[2] Nevertheless, according to Garrett Mattingly, the diplomatic corps originated in Rome a full three centuries earlier.[3] This chapter will begin by elaborating briefly on this but proceed swiftly to an emphasis on the development of the diplomatic corps in Ottoman Constantinople, especially during the early 17th century. Here many special circumstances caused the resident envoys to close ranks (however reluctantly in some cases), and it would be surprising if this did not strengthen the development of the diplomatic corps in the European states-system as a whole. This is because vigorous and influential men were drawn to Constantinople, and many of them presumably took the lessons they learned there to other posts.

Rome

It is hardly surprising that the origins of the diplomatic corps should be found in the middle of the 15th century since it was at precisely this juncture that the recognizably modern resident mission itself first appeared. While diplomacy was conducted by special envoys staying for only brief spells at foreign courts, the usual preoccupation was with discharging tasks and returning home as quickly as possible; such envoys had little incentive and less opportunity to create a body with a code of practice, periodic meetings, and a rolling agenda. This all began to change with the invention of the resident mission. Doomed to a stay which could be anything from one year to ten, or occasionally even longer, resident envoys had much to gain from regular collaboration with their professional 'colleagues'. Since they appeared first in the Italian peninsula and above all in Rome, it is also here that the diplomatic corps was first created. '... [I]t is at Rome, and during the Renaissance only at Rome,' continues Mattingly, 'that we find the first signs of something like an organized diplomatic corps, developing a rudimentary sense of professional solidarity, exchanging social courtesies, codifying their mutual relationships, and even, in certain emergencies, acting together as a body'.[4]

Apart from well known common interests – for example in sharing information and maintaining observance of special privileges[5] – a number of practices adopted by the popes heightened the *esprit de corps* among the diplomats who found themselves at the papal *curia*. For one thing, they tended to be addressed collectively, not least because the popes had discovered that this was a most valuable means of 'spreading important announcements, or initiating new lines of negotiation'.[6] For another, 'regulations for their common governance' were periodically issued to them.[7] And finally, they were usually assigned 'places together at all important ceremonies'.[8] The last practice appears to have been particularly encouraged by Pius II, pope from 1458 until his death in 1464, himself a former career diplomatist, and the only pontiff to have left memoirs. Pius II is well known for his special love of Roman ceremonial and the choreography essential to it, and was perhaps especially disposed to see that ambassadors were a prominent group on such occasions because they were 'a marvelous sight with their foreign dress and ways'.[9] In his *Germania*, which he wrote shortly before assuming the pontificate himself, Pius noted of the formal occasions at which the pope presided that 'Bishops, Abbots, Protonotaries, *ambassadors*, all have their place'.[10] Of course, since these men were also the representatives of Christian princes, it seems likely that he was also anxious to see them publicly stand shoulder to shoulder in order to symbolize the unity of Christendom. This is because he was anxious to promote this as a precondition of driving the Turks back into Asia.[11]

There seems no reason to doubt that Mattingly is right to assign the greatest importance to Rome in any account of the origins of the diplomatic corps. This becomes doubly persuasive when he reminds us of its central importance in spreading Italian practice to the rest of Europe.[12]

However, any account at least of the early evolution and strengthening of the diplomatic corps would surely be remiss if it did not also attach importance to diplomatic life in Constantinople, a great city which after 1453 was the capital of the Ottoman Empire. Much information can be gleaned about this from a source that is now readily accessible. This is a collection of the despatches of Sir Thomas Roe, formerly English ambassador to the Great Moghul, close confidante of Elizabeth Stuart (eldest daughter of James I of England, and Queen of Bohemia), and from 1621 until 1628 English ambassador at Constantinople.[13] It is chiefly on this collection that I shall draw in order to explore the evidence for corporate activity among the diplomats in Constantinople at this time and suggest the reasons for it.[14] In the process, it should be instructive to compare them with the reasons for the original emergence of the diplomatic corps, in Rome.

Constantinople: 'A Concourse of All Nations'

'No other capital', observes Philip Mansel in his outstanding thematic history of Constantinople, 'welcomed so many embassies. ... Power was the draw. The Ottoman Empire was at once a European, Middle Eastern, African, Black Sea, Mediterranean and Indian Ocean power. It had more neighbours – more matters for dispute or negotiation – than any other state.'[15] And the sultans welcomed ambassadors as guests, permanent as well as extraordinary, because they flattered their power and invariably came bearing rich gifts. They were also indispensable sources of intelligence as well as of great value in negotiations because until 1793 the Ottoman Empire was unwilling to stoop to establishing abroad any permanent embassies of its own.[16] As with Rome, Constantinople also required – and by at least the late 16th century attracted[17] – able and resilient men. In addition to questions of high politics with which to deal, there were trading colonies to protect, Christians to rescue from the galleys, and 'marbles' to buy or steal for grateful aristocratic patrons at home. There was also a great deal of money to be made on the side for those with the necessary energy and acumen. 'Here are many ambassadors, all experienced and tried in other parts, before they arrive at this trust', wrote Sir Thomas Roe in 1624. 'Here is a concourse of all nations, great and many varieties, important to Christendom.'[18]

For the Ottomans, the 1620s was a decade marked in the west by the Thirty Years' War, in relationship to which their attitude was of great interest to all of the major players. In the east it was marked by the resumption in 1623 of fighting in their endemic conflict with the Persians. Against this background, numerous special ambassadors came to Constantinople, often with vast retinues,[19] and if their purpose was to conclude a peace with the sultan they were sometimes detained for months as hostages. Among the extraordinary embassies to arrive were ones from Poland, Austria, Muscovy, Venice, Transylvania, Ragusa, the Crimean Tartars – and even from Persia itself. There was also a constant stream of messengers, 'little ambassadors' (or 'nuncios') usually sent to prepare the way for a 'great ambassador', and ecclesiastics of various hues on essentially diplomatic errands. However, the diplomatic community in Constantinople was naturally rooted in its most stable element, that is to say, in those diplomats who were resident in the city.

There were, to begin with, a number of resident 'agents'. The Polish government – with which the Ottomans had been at war in 1620–21 and at the end of Roe's mission still maintained only 'an infirm peace'[20] – had an agent in Constantinople.[21] So, too, did Prince Bethlen Gabor, the Sultan's protestant vassal in Transylvania, whom the English ambassador was under instructions to stir up against Austria. An Austrian agent was also established in 1622,[22] and in 1625 an Italian was sent by Spain 'to live a spy, under the resident of the emperor'.[23] However, agents were the lowest form of diplomatic life and really had no degree of representative character at all – though their tasks were important. They gathered intelligence, prepared the way for visits by extraordinary embassies from home, and had limited dealings with Ottoman officials and other diplomats in the city. By virtue of their lowly status, however, agents appear not to have been able to attend meetings of the resident ambassadors and were therefore no more than satellites – 'inferiors', as Roe gently put it[24] – orbiting around, rather than being full members of, the diplomatic corps. As a deliberative body, this consisted exclusively of the resident *ambassadors* or 'ledgers' themselves.[25]

The members of the Constantinople diplomatic corps

There had been a Venetian representative – the 'baillie' – resident in Constantinople during the reign of the Byzantine emperors, and this post was only temporarily vacated by the fall of the city to the Ottomans in 1453. The bailo, as he was known subsequently to the English, was without question a full ambassador – and more.[26] But resident ambassadors did not begin to appear in numbers for roughly another century – led by the French in 1536, and not long afterwards followed (with lengthy interruptions) by the hated Austrians.[27] When Sir Thomas Roe arrived in 1621, there was no Austrian, but Dutch and English embassies had joined the French and were also well established. There had been an English embassy in Constantinople since 1583,[28] and a Dutch one since 1612, when Cornelis van Haga was appointed by the States General.

Haga, who loved the city, was still there when Roe arrived – and still there when he left. 'He has bought his house in fee,' Sir Thomas told one of his correspondents, 'trimmed it, adorned it, and planted it about, as if he meant to make it his mansion and tombe, and had', he added presciently, 'no fear of a removal'. (Haga remained Dutch ambassador at Constantinople until 1639.) Roe had a good working relationship with 'the states ledger', though as he saw more of him his reservations appear to have mounted. Writing to Sir Isaac Wake in Venice in 1626, he said that 'He has lived long in Turkey, and is so corrupted with their manners, that he is the shame of ambassadors ... and if necessity of business, wherein he has not much authority, did not hold us together, for my part I would not converse with him'.[29]

Roe had more respect for the Venetian representatives with whom he overlapped. 'Wise', 'discreet', 'wary', were the adjectives that often came to his lips when he mentioned them.[30] However, Roe despised the French ambassador, Philippe de Harlay, who had arrived in 1620 and was to remain in Constantinople for the greater part of the period until 1639.[31] He was, to the mind of the Englishman, far too stiff-necked on the issue of precedence (see below), impetuous, malicious, and inclined to brand as sour grapes subjects on which he could not secure the lead. He also possessed neither 'credit nor reputation in court nor city' for having got himself ruinously in debt.[32] That much of this debt was to members of the English colony did not increase his standing in Roe's eyes. In short, Roe told Sir Isaac Wake in 1626, 'he is not worth a good feather'.[33]

Of course, as with the diplomatic corps in all capitals, that in Constantinople had tensions that went beyond personalities. Some of these had their source in the rivalry between the trading colonies of the four states, which was sometimes intense. There were also differences between Roe and de Harlay over religion,[34] though these were offset to a great extent by their mutual hostility to the Habsburgs.[35] There remained, however, a serious procedural obstacle to the development of a corporate spirit within the diplomatic corps; this was the problem of precedence.

The problem of precedence

On the authority of the papal class list of 1504, the French claimed precedence over all of the other ambassadors in Constantinople – and the latter had previously conceded it. However, this was a situation that James I of England proved unwilling to tolerate, and Roe was instructed to demand at least equality. Predictably enough, his initial attempts to carry out this instruction merely sabotaged cooperative action by the diplomatic corps and direct communication between London and Paris failed to resolve the question.[36]

However, in 1624, forced by the urgency of a 'general grievance' to make *some* form of joint protest to the Porte, the diplomatic corps itself finally hit on a partial solution. First, a joint document would be employed which would refer for its authority to 'the 4 resident Christian ambassadors, without mention of any one in particular', thereby avoiding the issue of the order in which they should be presented. Secondly, only a relatively small space would be left for the ambassadors' signatures and seals between the last line of the text and the bottom of the page. This would make it impossible for the signatures (with their accompanying seals) to be inscribed in hierarchical columns. Contriving to be given first choice of where in this space to place his signature, Roe wrote it precisely in the middle. Since the left-hand side 'was the chiefest according to the Christian, and the right according to the Turkish, by reason of the difference in writing', this gave de Harlay a choice of second-best options to save his face.[37]

In any event, Roe had agreed to a joint, written protest because his name did not have to appear below de Harlay's and the latter had conceded, so he said, 'for the general good'. 'Since this time more courtesies have passed between us,' reported the English ambassador, somewhat complacently, 'and I find him very tractable and affable' – though de Harlay still had no money to pay his debts to the English merchants.[38]

This finesse over the form of joint, written protests certainly helped to prevent the quarrel over precedence from stifling the development of the diplomatic corps in Constantinople at this point. However, to what extent it was subsequently employed in Roe's period is not clear from his despatches. The chief reason why the diplomatic corps held together and probably strengthened its formal bonds despite the quarrel over precedence was that the advantages of unity were particularly compelling at this time. What were they?

The forces for unity

Fear

The four ambassadors had numerous meetings, though they seem to have been irregular. It has already been noted that the diplomatic body was small in number – just four ambassadors – and it is reasonable to assume that this made it easier to organize and easier to obtain decisions. Much more importantly, though, there was in Constantinople a particularly urgent need on the part of the ambassadors to stand together in self-defence.

When Roe arrived in Constantinople he was initially ignored and denied the 'usual courtesies' by the Porte; he also found the diplomatic corps demoralized.[39] Thus in a despatch to Secretary Calvert in 1621, he said: 'I have undertaken to begin a reformation; and because I would not run alone, and be left single, I have required articles of all the rest to stand with me, which they have promised.'[40]

The ambassadors also had more to worry about than discourtesies. For all their differences, they remained, after all, the representatives of Christian princes in a Muslim world, and even in quiet times hostility towards them was never far from the surface. '[W]e lived among enemies, where questions [squabbles] ought to be avoided', Roe reported himself saying to the French ambassador following a tussle over precedence in 1622.[41] Moreover, the first years of Roe's time in Constantinople were far from quiet. In fact, a janissary revolt, a sultan assassinated, and a feeble-minded successor, plunged the city into anarchy and led to a major rebellion in Anatolia. Until Mustafa I was deposed in favour of Murat IV in September 1623, the Ottoman Empire seemed on the verge of disintegration – and things did not get better overnight. In June 1622, Roe told Lord Doncaster that in Constantinople 'barbarism is philosophy, and mutiny justice', adding that 'though they [the janissaries] have offered us no injury, yet, when madness and fury rages, who is safe?'[42] And in the following year he voiced the conclusion that he had no doubt drawn much earlier: 'In these disordered times, when all nations suffer many injuries and oppressions, we have no refuge but to join our selves, which is a little bulwark'.[43]

Constantinople was also a capital in which diplomatic immunity was not even in principle respected. It is true that the ambassadors were regarded as leaders of resident 'nations' and in this capacity enjoyed privileges ('capitulations') from the hand of the sultan, notably protection.[44] Nevertheless, the security of their persons and their houses endured only so long as their princes remained in friendship with the sultan. In effect, the ambassadors were all hostages, and, as such, could be imprisoned indefinitely if this friendship should fail – as French and Imperial ambassadors had found to their cost quite recently.[45] Latent Muslim hostility, periodic anarchy on the streets, and their hostage status, all gave the ambassadors an interest in looking out for each other.

Defence of the capitulations

Another interest shared by the members of the diplomatic corps, and one that at this time was unique to Constantinople, was respect by the Ottoman authorities for the terms of their capitulations, especially where they concerned favourable trading arrangements. Such respect was often difficult to obtain in remote parts of the Empire but in disturbed times could be equally so in the capital itself. If an Ottoman official was allowed to get away with ignoring the terms of one state's capitulations a dangerous precedent would be established.

It was only shortly after Roe arrived in Constantinople that the French ambassador himself employed the cry of 'common interest' in order to secure help from his diplomatic colleagues in a case of this kind. The French had a grievance against the governor of Cairo and had already secured the support of the Dutch and Venetian ambassadors. In the event, Roe himself refused to add his own signature to the joint written protest produced by de Harlay because he insisted that his own name should go first. Excusing himself by claiming that the English had no commerce at Cairo, and 'unwilling any way', Roe reports, 'to break that unity which I myself had contracted', the English ambassador told his colleagues that he would 'not forsake them in any general cause'. As a result, he urged that they each make separate protests and thereby avoid the issue of precedence. How this was finally resolved Roe does not make clear but he claims to have soothed the French ambassador – who had threatened to reply in kind if in future the boot was on the other foot – with emollient words and by helping him out in some other matters.[46]

Soothing the Frenchman was important because it was not long before Roe did indeed need his support. In the middle of 1622, a tax which Roe believed contrary to the English capitulations was suddenly imposed on silk being shipped to Turkey in English vessels. He appealed for redress to the grand vizier but in vain. In a dispatch to Calvert that still palpably steams with indignation, Roe recounts his angry exchange with the grand vizier and how subsequently he enlisted the other ambassadors in his support, though not without 'much ado' and threatening to shame them by standing alone:

> the vizier took part against us, the veriest villain that ever lived; and used me with great contempt, threatened to hang my secretary, and drogermen [interpreters], if they spoke in my cause; whereupon I threw him my capitulations ... and unloaded my silk, resolved to stand it out. To this end, I procured all the ambassadors here to join; and we were on our way, with full resolution to go to court, and to procure his head, or to ask leave to remove our countrymen, and their estates, which are now in great danger.

Fortunately, Roe was able to report that 'God took my quarrel in hand'. On the way to the palace, the ambassadors heard that the grand vizier had also fallen foul of the janissaries, who were a far more serious threat than the diplomats to continuing intimacy between the head and the shoulders of this official. 'He is fled,' reported Roe with obvious satisfaction, 'and order given to kill him where he is first found'.[47] The English ambassador could have given many similar examples, though by late in 1623 he is found simply saying that 'we poor strangers suffer all manner of injuries, and all oppressions; no capitulations observed; double and new customs exacted to get money'.[48]

Shared services

The diplomatic corps in Constantinople was not only a society for mutual defence against the depredations of Ottoman officials. It was also one based on the obvious advantage of sharing important services, especially messengers and the acquisition and distribution of information.

The diplomatic corps in all capitals was always of great value to its members for the trading of information, both on local and international events. However, this was especially true of Constantinople because of its relative remoteness, particularly from the states of northern Europe. It was not long after his arrival that Roe was complaining to London of the absence of letters from England and his dependence on the other ambassadors for news of outside affairs, even – most humiliating of all – of events at home.[49] Throughout his time in the Ottoman Empire he had very few letters from the Secretary of State and complained about this with increasing stridency. It is true that he began to acquire information from the correspondence that he nurtured with English diplomatic colleagues elsewhere, especially in The Hague, Venice, and Savoy, and also had letters from other important persons in England itself, including the Archbishop of Canterbury.[50] The fact remains, however, that Roe was generally short of information – only 'fed with scraps and stale ends'[51] – and was correspondingly reliant on his colleagues. This was painfully evident in 1626, when he was confronted by an extraordinary ambassador from Bethlen Gabor who claimed 'that a conference at The Hague had decided that he, Sir Thomas, must assist his master to procure action by the pasha of Buda against the Emperor and "nourish" the Tartars against the king of Poland'. In the absence of any instruction on this point from London, the English ambassador had to rely on an assurance from the Venetian bailo that this was indeed true. This permitted Roe to advance cautiously on these fronts, and shortly afterwards he received a letter from the Secretary of State confirming that the king's intentions for him had been correctly represented.[52] In 1627 we find Roe still dwelling on his dependence on the Venetian.[53]

The other ambassadors may not have been as reliant on their colleagues for information on external events as was Roe but it would be surprising if they too did not value them as sources. Of course, Roe also pooled intelligence about Ottoman affairs, which he needed not only to fulfil his instructions from London but also to use as bait to elicit replies from his English diplomatic colleagues at other postings.

It was, however, little use obtaining local intelligence if it could not be got out, and communications with the outside world that were tolerably rapid, predictable, and secure were not easy to achieve in Constantinople, especially in winter.[54] Sometimes despatches did not even get out of the city: 'our letters of May', Roe observed drolly to Sir Dudley Carleton in 1623, 'were intercepted and sold in the city to wrap pepper'.[55] What this meant was great reliance on the Venetian postal service, as Roe soon found out.

Venice was relatively close to Constantinople, and had intimate relations with it going back to the Byzantine period. Moreover, though the republic itself was by this time past the peak of its prestige, it had a diplomatic service that was still regarded as the model for all Europe. In the second half of the 16th century the bailo was the unquestioned informal doyen of the nascent diplomatic corps.[56] It is hardly surprising, then, that Venice had the best communications with Constantinople and that the other ambassadors – especially the Dutch and the English – should have relied on them. In fact, the bailo acted as 'postmaster for the whole diplomatic body'.[57]

Roe is eloquent on his need for the Venetian post, and how this required him to ingratiate himself with the bailo.[58] This evidently paid off because their relations remained smooth throughout his time in Constantinople and his correspondence continued to be handled by the Venetian post. However, it is a mark of the absence of any serious alternative that the English ambassador continued to use it despite his belief – strongly shared in London – that the Venetians not only detained his post when it suited their purposes but also regularly opened it.[59]

A shared neighbourhood

It is clear from his despatches and private letters that Roe met his fellow ambassadors 'in council' quite often. This was facilitated by the fact that in Constantinople, as in other capitals, the diplomats tended to live in the same quarter. The concentration of diplomats in Pera, on the hill above Galata on the northern side of the Golden Horn, seems to have been a result of choice rather than compulsion. It was healthier and less congested than Constantinople, sufficiently separate from the heart of the city to make its 'Frankish', Christian atmosphere tolerable to its rulers – and yet close enough to them for the ready conduct of business.[60] But, no doubt by underlining their common culture as well as by virtue of physical proximity, the concentration of diplomats in Pera (and the families of many of their dragomans) also encouraged cooperation between the ambassadors.

Collective treatment by the Porte

It will be recalled that Mattingly is of the view that collective treatment by the pope of the Rome diplomatic corps was probably the main factor in encouraging the development of its corporate identity. Can a similar process be observed in Constantinople?

There is little evidence in Roe's *Negotiations* that the Porte treated the diplomatic corps as a collective body, and none that it was treated in this way on any ceremonial occasions. This is not surprising. First of all, the ambassadors were regarded by the Ottomans chiefly as protectors of the members of their 'nations' resident in the empire, analogous to the semi-autonomous religious communities (*millets*) established by Mehmet II after the conquest of Constantinople in 1453.[61] Since there were in fact religious differences between them, as well as legendary commercial rivalries, it is understandable that the Ottomans tended to think of the ambassador's reference group as his 'nation' rather than his professional 'colleagues'. Secondly, in direct contrast to the Pope in Rome, it was hardly in the interest of the Ottomans to treat the diplomats – all Christians – as a collective body and thereby encourage their solidarity; in fact, quite the opposite. With internal strife to contend with as well as a powerful enemy in Persia, the last thing that the Porte wanted was to do anything to encourage the unity of Christendom. Having said this, there is intriguing evidence in Roe's correspondence that on at least one occasion – when they were desperate – the Ottomans did just this.

Following the accession of Murat in September 1623, money had to be raised urgently because his coffers were empty and the janissaries 'sharply demanded' their pay – 'with threats of innovation'. Among other methods, his government sought to do this, wrote Roe in September 1623, by extorting contributions from 'every other order of men and officers, that are not of the sword. The vizier', he continued, 'sent solemnly to the four resident ambassadors to borrow 30,000 chequins, as the friends and allies of this Porte, to whom in confidence they dare open their secrets.' Roe added that there were experienced officials who thought this dishonourable and unlikely to be successful and, indeed, the ambassadors, pleading poverty themselves, refused.[62] The point is though that the Porte treated the diplomatic corps as an *order* of men, and no doubt obliged this order to consult together so that it might concert *its* response.

In sum, there was a small diplomatic body in Constantinople in the 1620s that deserved the name. Its members – the Venetians, French, English, and Dutch – were thrown together by common interests in resisting insult and violence, defending the capitulations, exchanging information, and preserving their communications with the outside world. Joint deliberations were also made easy by the fact that they lived in relatively close proximity to each other in Pera. Less important, though perhaps not entirely insignificant, on at least one occasion an attempt was made by the Porte to *tax* them as a collective body. It was for these reasons that, though the diplomatic corps was seriously threatened by a bitter argument over precedence between the English and French ambassadors, it eventually found a limited way out of this by its own exertions – after London-Paris diplomacy had failed.

Conclusion

The diplomatic corps appears first to have assumed significant form in Rome in the middle of the 15th century. Thereafter, it developed in other major centres of diplomacy, not least Constantinople and not least because this city was on Christendom's front-line. Here, and for this reason, the fact that the resident diplomats were not treated as a body in anything like the same degree as in Rome seems not to have diminished their desire to act like one but rather to have increased it. Today, Italy and Turkey continue to provide homes to important diplomatic corps, curiously enough because both states have two of them. Rome, of course, is now home to the government of the state of Italy as well as the Vatican city state. As a result, it has diplomats accredited to both, though only a small handful, including the United States, actually maintain separate embassies. As for Turkey, it has a *de jure* diplomatic corps in the capital, Ankara, and a *de facto* diplomatic corps represented by the Consuls-General in Istanbul. This great city remained home to the embassies to Turkey until Mustapha Kemal dragged them reluctantly to the windswept Anatolian plateau during the latter half of the 1920s. However, the Consuls-General who took their place in Istanbul, usually occupying the former embassy buildings, are still inclined to regard their 'chiefs' in Ankara merely as ambassadors to eastern Turkey, seeing themselves as 'ambassadors' to the western, and most important, part. Such is the tug of history – and money.

Notes

I wish to record my gratitude to the Nuffield Foundation for financial assistance to the research on which this chapter is based. Gerald E. Wickens, formerly of the Royal Botanical Gardens at Kew, and Aniko Kellner, a doctoral student at the Central European University in Budapest, were also of great help in correcting some factual errors. I am most grateful to them as well.

1 Sir Ernest Satow, *A Guide to Diplomatic Practice*, vol. I, 2nd edn (London: Longmans, Green, 1922), p. 3; Antoine Pecquet, *Discours sur L'Art de Négocier* (Paris: Nyon, 1737), p. 134.

2 In fact, not until after the French Revolution; see Robert A. Graham, S.J., *Vatican Diplomacy: A Study of Church and State on the International Plane* (Princeton, N.J.: Princeton University Press, 1959), p. 99.

3 Garrett Mattingly, *Renaissance Diplomacy* (Harmondsworth: Penguin Books, 1965), p. 100.

4 Mattingly, *Renaissance Diplomacy*, p. 100.

5 Envoys of ambassadorial rank, of which the papal master of ceremonies had a very precise notion, were entitled to 'a solemn reception at the gates of Rome by the households of the pope and the cardinals, audience in a public consistory, and a seat in the pope's chapel', B. Behrens, 'Origins of the Office of English Resident Ambassador in Rome', *English Historical Review*, vol. 49, no. 196 (Oct. 1934), p. 647.

6 Mattingly, *Renaissance Diplomacy*, pp. 99–100. For a good example, see *Memoirs of a Renaissance Pope: The Commentaries of Pius II. An Abridgment.*

Translated by Florence A. Gragg and edited by Leona C. Gabel (London: Allen & Unwin, 1960), pp. 347–9.

7　Mattingly, *Renaissance Diplomacy*, p. 100.
8　Mattingly, *Renaissance Diplomacy*, pp. 99–100; see also pp. 80–1 and 82–3.
9　*Memoirs of a Renaissance Pope*, p. 216; see also p. 182.
10　Emphasis added. Quoted in Cecilia M. Ady, *Pius II (Aeneas Silvius Piccolomini): The Humanist Pope* (London: Methuen, 1913), p. 255; see also *Memoirs of a Renaissance Pope*, pp. 245, 251, 347.
11　*Memoirs of a Renaissance Pope*, p. 237.
12　Mattingly, *Renaissance Diplomacy*, p. 100.
13　*The Negotiations of Sir Thomas Roe in His Embassy to the Ottoman Porte, from the Year 1621 to 1628* [hereafter '*The Negotiations*']. First published by the Society for the Encouragement of Learning in London in 1740, this collection runs to 838 pages and has recently been made available in a facsimile edition from UMI Books on Demand. The originals are held in The National Archives in London. On Roe himself, see Michael Strachan's excellent *Sir Thomas Roe, 1581–1644* (Salisbury: Michael Russell, 1989), which has two chapters on his Turkish embassy. I have modernized the spelling of all quotations from *The Negotiations*.
14　Of course, the arrival of the first resident ambassador (other than the Venetian *baillie*) in 1536 – a Frenchman – would have been a more appropriate starting point – than 1621. A full study of the origins of the Constantinople diplomatic corps would also require further investigation of the English sources before Roe (not to mention the original copies of Roe's own papers), together with study of the French, Venetian, Dutch, Austrian, and Ottoman archives – and quite possibly of the Polish ones as well. Nevertheless, there is barely a whiff of any 'diplomatic body' in *The Turkish Letters of Ogier Ghiselin de Busbecq*, trsl. by E. S. Forster (Clarendon Press: Oxford, 1927), an Austrian resident ambassador who arrived later in the 16th century.
15　P. Mansel, *Constantinople: City of the World's Desire, 1453–1924* (London: John Murray, 1995), p. 189.
16　See my 'Diplomatic integration with Europe before Selim III', in A. Nuri Yurdusev (ed.), *Ottoman Diplomacy: Conventional or unconventional?* (Basingstoke: Palgrave Macmillan, 2004), pp. 114–30.
17　Until roughly this time, prior to which their reception was likely to be mixed, the Venetians and the French had difficulty in finding people willing to go to Constantinople, L. S. Frey and M. L. Frey, *The History of Diplomatic Immunity* (Columbus, Ohio: Ohio State University Press, 1999), p. 139.
18　*The Negotiations*, p. 320. Mansel also notes that Constantinople attracted diplomats of high calibre, *Constantinople*, p. 199.
19　*The Negotiations*, p. 115; and D. Kolodziejczyk, 'Semiotics of behavior in early modern diplomacy: Polish embassies in Istanbul and Bahçesaray', *Journal of Early Modern History*, vol. 7, no. 3–4, Nov. 2003, pp. 255–6.
20　*The Negotiations*, p. 772.
21　From some time around the end of 1622 the Polish dragoman had also lived in Roe's own house, perhaps because the agent had by this time gone home, *The Negotiations*, p. 772.

22 *The Negotiations*, p. 91.
23 *The Negotiations*, p. 422.
24 *The Negotiations*, p. 356.
25 On this early modern terminology, see G. R. Berridge and Alan James, *A Dictionary of Diplomacy*, 2nd. ed (Basingstoke: Palgrave Macmillan, 2003).
26 H. F. Brown, *Studies in the History of Venice*, vol. II (London: John Murray, 1907), pp. 1–38; and Donald M. Nicol, *Byzantium and Venice: A study in diplomatic and cultural relations* (Cambridge: Cambridge University Press, 1988), pp. 289–1, 314, 352.
27 *The Turkish Letters of Ogier Ghiselin de Busbecq* (1927). Two Austrian resident ambassadors were also present in Constantinople in the second half of the 16th century: Charles Rym and David Ungnad (the latter definitely in 1573–8). There were also Polish and Genoese residents in the mid-16th century, P. Mansel, 'Art and diplomacy in Ottoman Constantinople', *History Today*, Aug. 1996.
28 S. A. Skilliter, *William Harborne and the Trade with Turkey 1578–1582* (Oxford: Oxford University Press, 1977); S. A. Skilliter, 'The organization of the first English embassy in Istanbul in 1583', *Asian Affairs*, 1979, vol. 10; and A. C. Wood, *A History of the Levant Company*, first publ. 1935 (London: Cass, 1964), ch. 5.
29 *The Negotiations*, p. 627.
30 *The Negotiations*, pp. 126, 609, 627, 639.
31 Jean-Michel Casa, *Le Palais de France à Istanbul: Un demi-millénaire d'alliance entre la Turquie et la France* (Istanbul: Yapi Kredi Yayinlari, 1995), p. 109.
32 *The Negotiations*, pp. 112, 113, 126, 610, 725.
33 *The Negotiations*, p. 627.
34 This was occasioned in particular by a struggle over the office of Patriarch and the role of the Jesuits in the city, Strachan, *Sir Thomas Roe*, pp. 170–5.
35 This led all four ambassadors to spend a great deal of time concerting their actions towards Bethlen Gabor, in order that he should remain a thorn in the Emperor's side. They also acted together most strenuously to oppose (in the event successfully) the arrival in Constantinople of a Spanish ambassador – the influence of whose gold at the Porte was feared more than his arguments.
36 *The Negotiations*, pp. 59, 148, 188, 244.
37 *The Negotiations*, p. 270. Strachan claims that this was Roe's motive, *Sir Thomas Roe*, p. 150. This is certainly plausible but the internal evidence of Roe's somewhat convoluted reasoning is not, I think, quite as conclusive as Strachan suggests.
38 *The Negotiations*, p. 270.
39 Mansel notes that Ottoman arrogance towards ambassadors was at its height in the 17th century, *Constantinople*, p. 193.
40 *The Negotiations*, p. 18.
41 *The Negotiations*, p. 113.
42 *The Negotiations*, pp. 54–5.
43 *The Negotiations*, p. 148.
44 Stanford J. Shaw, *History of the Ottoman Empire and Modern Turkey*, vol. 1 (Cambridge: Cambridge University Press, 1976), pp. 163–4.
45 Mansel, *Constantinople*, pp. 192–3.

46   *The Negotiations*, pp. 112–13.
47   *The Negotiations*, pp. 61–2.
48   *The Negotiations*, p. 188.
49   *The Negotiations*, p. 22.
50   Many of these are reproduced in *The Negotiations*.
51   *The Negotiations*, p. 355.
52   *The Negotiations*, pp. 522–3, 528.
53   *The Negotiations*, p. 663.
54   The King's Messenger service of the English government did not begin to provide a proper service to any diplomatic post until it was reorganized in 1772, M. A. Thomson, *The Secretaries of State, 1681–1782* (London: Cass, 1968), p. 142; and V. Wheeler-Holohan, *The History of the King's Messengers* (London: Grayson, 1935), chs. 3–5. On diplomatic communications in this period generally, see John B. Allen, *Post and Courier Service in the Diplomacy of Early Modern Europe* (The Hague: Nijhoff, 1972).
55   *The Negotiations*, p. 157.
56   His law court, established by a treaty of 1454 to exercise jurisdiction over the Venetian community in the city, was the civil court for *all* foreigners. In the 1590s, even the English ambassador submitted to his jurisdiction, Brown, *Studies in the History of Venice*, pp. 4–5.
57   Brown, *Studies in the History of Venice*, p. 32; Allen, *Post and Courier Service in the Diplomacy of Early Modern Europe*, pp. 26, 38, 66, 86.
58   *The Negotiations*, p. 20.
59   This was admitted by the Venetian ambassador in London, who pleaded excessive zeal on the part of the post office, *The Negotiations*, pp. 113, 160–1, 178. Perhaps because of English protests these abuses diminished. In 1627, in commenting on the delay of some letters from Venice, Roe remarked that he had 'no cause to mistrust the bailo, whose friendship is my only comfort here', *The Negotiations*, p. 695.
60   Nicol, *Byzantium and Venice*, p. 190; D. Goffman, *Britons in the Ottoman Empire, 1642–1660* (Seattle and London: University of Washington Press, 1998), pp. 34–5; Mansel, *Constantinople*, p. 194; and Stanley Mayes, *An Organ for the Sultan* (London: Putnam, 1956), p. 157.
61   Shaw, *History of the Ottoman Empire and Modern Turkey*, pp. 58–9; Niels Steensgaard, 'Consuls and nations in the Levant from 1570 to 1650', *The Scandinavian Economic History Review*, vol. XV nos. 1 & 2, 1967; and H. Inalcik, 'Imtiyazat', *The Encyclopaedia of Islam*, new ed., vol. III (Leiden: Brill; London: Luzac, 1971), pp. 1183–4.
62   The Negotiations, p. 180.

2
The Diplomatic Corps as a Symbol of Diplomatic Culture

Sasson Sofer

Since its emergence in the middle of the 15th century, the diplomatic corps is referred to in an anecdotal way in the life stories of ambassadors, and its ceremonial functions are enumerated dryly in diplomatic protocols.[1] This negligence is not justified. The diplomatic corps is a primary symbol of diplomatic culture. Its rites and ceremonies confirm the existence of an international society which acts according to agreed upon laws and norms. Indeed, the potential repertoire of the corps has not yet been exhausted, and its internal discourse is poorly researched. The diplomatic corps is, in a way, the phantom of international politics – enduring in its existence, but random in its membership. This is a social group that constantly changes.

Early modern European history did not provide diplomats with the best environment to act in a joint manner.[2] Precedence and court intrigues almost eliminated such a possibility. The requirements of court life were, at times, quite brutal. In ceremonies and entries which aimed to dazzle and impress was a strong element of competition. This obsessive preoccupation with precedence reflected the struggle of great powers for a higher place in the hierarchy of the European balance of power.[3] The apparent paradox is that the diplomatic corps was comprised of the traditional aristocracies of Europe. Diplomats who shared similarities of education and outlook were fighting for international seniority instead of acting in unison on substantial matters.

The Règlement of Vienna introduced simple solutions and rationality to the problem of precedence that had plagued European diplomacy for centuries. Aristocratic manners were perfected as conventions, and agreed upon as rules. Seniority was now decided according to the date of notification of arrival at the capital. In case of disagreement among members of the diplomatic body as to precedence, the rules were to be decided by the host country.[4]

What remains of the ceremonial elements seems to be both essential and sensible. Ceremonial niceties lost their importance, unless used as an act of protest or international insult. Protocol provided and continues to provide a framework for diplomats to concentrate on substantial issues. It also enabled the diplomatic body to emerge as a distinct group that could, if required, act with some professional collegiality.

Diplomats are bound together in the diplomatic body – the community of diplomats assembled at any seat of government in a certain period of history.[5] Surprisingly, the diplomatic corps is not mentioned at all in the Vienna Convention of 1961. There is no doubt as to its existence in customary diplomatic law, but its role was not considered to be of sufficient importance.[6]

Hovering above the diplomatic corps, as first among equals, is the doyen (dean). As a rule he or she is granted limited power.[7] The dean is the recognized intermediary between the corps and the government to which its members are accredited. The dean is not an independent actor, as he should obtain the approval of his colleagues before acting on their behalf, usually on matters of prerogatives and privileges. He may extend his influence somehow in the way he conveys information to other diplomats, and in the manner he insures the cohesion of the diplomatic corps.

Most of the attention in the diplomatic literature is given to formal aspects, particularly to matters of etiquette. Neglected is the internal dialogue among diplomats, the informal part of their interaction, which is seldom recorded nor reported. The delicate manoeuvres of the corps surface, if at all, when either success or failure becomes apparent. This duality of the formal and the informal, universal values and particularistic necessities, are permanent part of the structure and action of every diplomatic body.

The internal exchanges among a diplomatic corps could be defined as the diplomacy of indirect approach – gathering information and influencing in matters not necessarily related to the diplomat's principal duties as an accredited envoy to his country of mission. Diplomats must find the right balance between their activity within the diplomatic corps, and the main task of investing most of their efforts in the government, institutions and the public.[8]

In receptions, balls and soirées there is an overlap between the private and public spheres. In such events the diplomat carries on his traditional role as a courtier and intuitive operator. The opportunity of gaining important information or a new understanding of some aspect of the host government depends on the diplomat's resourcefulness and talents. Callières writes succinctly that 'there is between ministers a commerce of mutual intelligence; one must give, in order to receive'.[9] Not a few diplomats consider informal diplomatic gatherings as a waste of time. John Galbraith observed, with more than a glimpse of arrogance, that he 'never learned anything at a cocktail party or dinner that I didn't already know'.[10]

It is in such informal activity that the diplomats' spouses are of importance. By the end of the 19th century the 'ambassador's family' gained a new meaning.[11] Spouses of diplomats enjoy the same privileges and honours.[12] But more than the ceremonial part, the informal activity of spouses could be pivotal to the success of diplomatic envoys. Spouses' role is neither sufficiently explored nor duly appreciated. The burden of career partners is a new addition to the complexity of diplomatic assignment.

The repertoire of collective action

As an institution not dependent on any formal constitutional act, nor on whether it holds formal meetings and proceedings, the diplomatic corps is open to voluntary initiatives and to a flexibility beyond diplomatic routine and protocol. Recent writings bring to our attention its role as a multilateral broker, guiding new regimes into membership in the international society, and serving as a outpost of the international community in providing a collective judgement on a particular crisis.[13] It is a voluntary trusteeship given to the corps for a short period of time. By aspiring to a constant dialogue and mutual adjustment of interests, the corps reflects the essential norms of the diplomatic culture.

The repertoire of the diplomatic corps is larger in scope than is usually assumed. Diplomats act according to their governments' orders, and the opportunities of a particular international order. The activity of the corps, however, does not always reflect the international orientations prevalent at a certain moment of history. The diplomatic corps makes it possible to interact with the envoys of states, even rival states, or those in a state of war, in a way not possible in the formal diplomatic relationships.[14]

To a large extent the corps' room for manoeuvre is determined by the nature of the host country and its political system. The diplomatic corps plays a more prominent role in autocratic or failed states, where information is censored and diplomats are regarded a threat. In such cases the corps acts, at times, as the whistle blower of international politics. It brings to the attention of governments, or reveals to the world public abuses of human rights, and the coming of impending events such as civil wars and *coups d'état*. The diplomatic corps may also counterbalance the standpoint or the propaganda of the host country.

The probability that the diplomatic corps will perform as a unitary actor is high when its privileges are threatened or curtailed. If so, the corps acts like a grand coalition during a war – when victory is achieved the coalition loses its *raison d'être* and its forces disperse.

A collective action which is also effective is infrequent in diplomatic history, particularly when great powers are involved. Satow remarks that 'at Washington such joint *démarches* of the diplomatic body have been generally declined by the Department of State'.[15] During the Cold War era, however, the diplomatic corps emerged as a useful diplomatic broker, and as a normal organ of 'good offices'. Washington has found, for instance, that the diplomatic corps of Beijing was the only possible venue for establishing a dialogue with North Korea.[16]

A joint action by the diplomatic corps, particularly a démarche, is becoming quite rare, mainly because the corps' room for manoeuvre is dependent on the degree of unity among a large number of states. Unilateralism and the decline of great power responsibility reduce significantly the potential for an effective démarche. Apart from the interpretation of such acts as an interference in the domestic affairs of the host country, a démarche raises the question of the collective responsibility of the corps for a diplomatic failure.

The diplomatic corps as the custodian of international society

The particular qualities of a diplomatic corps, in terms of personalities and talents, are highly subjective. Diplomats assemble in a capital in a random way. The corps membership is controlled by no state.[17] Vita Sackville-West, a person not particularly enamoured with diplomatic life, remarked cynically that the diplomatic corps is a collection of people thrown together 'through a purely fortuitous circumstance, with nothing in common except the place we happen to find ourselves in'.[18] The growing number of diplomats complicated further the cohesion and function of the diplomatic corps.[19]

But in a fragmented world, and against the ever-changing structures of world order, the diplomatic corps proved to be an equal, unitary and distinct social group. Immunities and privileges set it apart from ordinary citizens, and despite being of different nationalities, diplomats are supposed to keep day by day to the permanent and universal standards of international society. The diplomatic corps is a coherent group with shared professional roles and obligations.[20]

In Rome, a city of priests, Mattingly writes, ambassadors developed a sense of solidarity and a growing *esprit de corps*.[21] Antoine Pecquet, it seems, was the first to draw attention to the diplomatic body as a sort of independent community: 'they live closely together and treat each other politely and with honesty even when their sovereign masters are at war'.[22]

The unity of the diplomatic corps until the beginning of the 20th century was based on its aristocratic origins. A unity of virtues based on the same understanding of the practical benefits of diplomacy and professional solidarity replaced aristocratic fraternity. There is, indeed, a certain exaggeration in portraying the corps as a brotherhood. At the centre of their relationship stands the commitment, not to each other, but to the diplomatic norms of international society. Diplomats constantly attempt to find the right balance between the interests of their country and their activity within the diplomatic corps, particularly when diplomatic norms clash with policy. It is a contrast between national identity and corporate identity.

The observance of common professional norms, no doubt, tends to enhance a closer sense of affinity among diplomats, the feeling of being members in a distinct group with its own traditions and standards.[23] Solidarity among diplomats, however, should not be exaggerated. Diplomatic routine calls upon the diplomat to remain a lone wolf, guarding first and foremost his country's interests. Callières puts it nicely: 'It is the saying of an ancient philosopher, that the friendship which is between men, is only a commerce wherein everyone seeks his interest'.[24] The duality of closeness and estrangement is inherent in diplomacy, as it is always surrounded by suspicion and divided loyalties.[25]

Our understanding of diplomatic culture has not advanced much since Hedley Bull's thoughts on the subject. The literature on diplomacy conveys three different meanings of diplomatic culture. In the first, the corps is defined as a distinct social group; the second refers to common patterns of thought and shared meanings where the corps is portrayed as a transnational epistemic community, a meta-community and a form of identity formation;[26] the third describes the collegiality embedded in the manners and inter-subjective relationship among professional diplomats. Hedley Bull's definition falls in between these three notions. He first refers to 'the common stock of ideas and values possessed by the official representatives of state', and then to norms of the international society that comprise the international political culture.[27] Most of the writers on diplomacy are, indeed, aware of the difference between the universal standards of the diplomatic culture and discernible national cultures.[28]

James Der Derian portrays accurately the predicament of the diplomat in pointing to the duality of solidarity and estrangement.[29] In order to fully understand the diplomatic corps, we must take into consideration the divided loyalties of the diplomat: his solidarity with colleagues in the corps against the interests of his country which does not always correspond to his diplomatic conviction. Notwithstanding its portrayal as a hegemonic narrative, diplomacy remains cosmopolitan in outlook, yet carries a sense of ethical and social exclusiveness. Diplomacy withstood the challenges directed against it for the simple fact that it offers the most reasonable way of conducting relations in a pluralistic world order.

The foremost premise regarding the corps effectiveness is that it operates according to the pluralist ideas of international society. Diplomats are the custodians of the idea of international society, and are the guardians of international ethics.[30] The diplomat is unique among state's practitioners in the inherent connection between his ethics and professional competence. Indeed, most diplomats adhere to principles that are at the core of international ethics – prudence, sound judgement, and responsibility.

Tending to the interests of one's country does not negate the moral obligation to guard the norms of international society. The diplomatic corps maintains the formal and legal equality of states. Being the embodiment of diplomatic culture, it is perhaps the diplomat's best venue to function expertly.[31] Pluralistic and multinational by its nature, the diplomatic corps is an idealized icon of international society at any period of history; perhaps also of the imaginary and peaceful international society that could have been.

Notes

1 R. Cohen, 'Reflections on the New Global Diplomacy: Statecraft from 2500 BC to 2000 AD', in J. Melissen (ed.), *Innovation in Diplomatic Practice* (London: Macmillan, 1999), p. 8. Cohen suggests that a diplomatic corps existed already in the ancient Middle East.

2 G. Mattingly, *Renaissance Diplomacy* (Harmondsworth: Penguin, 1965), pp. 99–101; G. R. Berridge, *Diplomacy*, 2nd edn (London: Palgrave, 2002),

pp. 16–17. In the past, governments regarded the diplomatic corps as a mixed blessing. Autocratic states still find it convenient or necessary to confine foreign missions to a designated quarter.

3 M. S. Anderson, *The Rise of Modern Diplomacy, 1450–1919* (London: Longman, 1993), pp. 17–20, 63–8, 120–2; K. Hamilton and R. Langhorne, *The Practice of Diplomacy* (London: Routledge, 1995), pp. 64–8.

4 E. Satow, *A Guide to Diplomatic Practice*, 4th ed. (London: Longmans, Green and Co., 1957), pp, 171, 225–6; J. R. Wood and J. Serres, *Diplomatic Ceremonial and Protocol* (New York: Columbia University Press, 1970), pp. 25, 94. Plenipotentiaries at a conference would sign treaties in alphabetical order. The French ambassador in some Francophone African countries, and the Apostolic nuncio in certain Catholic states, serve as deans.

5 Satow, *A Guide to Diplomatic Practice*, pp. 2–3. The expression 'diplomatic corps' appeared in the first time in Vienna about the middle of the 18th century; E. Clark, *Corps Diplomatique* (London: Allen Lane, 1973), p. 18; Wood and Serres, *Diplomatic Ceremonial and Protocol*, pp. 29, 32, 35.

6 L. Dembinski, *The Modern Law of Diplomacy* (Dordrecht: Martinus Nijhoff Publishers, 1988), pp. 109–10.

7 Satow, *A Guide to Diplomatic Practice*, pp. 145, 254; Wood and Serres, *Diplomatic Ceremonial and Protocol*, pp. 30–1, 41–2, 127.

8 At times, a diplomat finds it useful to initiate social and professional ties with a colleague in the hope that they might find themselves in the future accredited to the same capital; Berridge, *Diplomacy*, pp. 16–17. Governments have found out how useful a diplomatic corps could be for spreading important information.

9 François de Callières, *The Art of Diplomacy*, M. Keens-Soper and K. W. Schweizer (eds) (Leicester: Leicester University Press, 1983), p. 76. See also p. 116, 'a good table is the easiest and best way of getting intelligence'.

10 J. K. Galbraith, *A Life in Our Times* (Boston: Houghton Mifflin, 1981), pp. 99–100; K. Hickman, *Daughters of Britannia* (London: Flamingo, 2000), p. 53. The Earl of Stair, British ambassador to Paris in 1715, was noted for the splendour of his hospitality, and for his custom to withdraw to his room and return incognito to find out the secrets of the day.

11 C. Enloe, *Bananas, Beaches and Bases* (Berkeley: University of California Press, 1990), pp. 93–123; Hickman, *Daughters of Britannia*, p. 63.

12 On the role of wives see, Satow, *A Guide to Diplomatic Practice*, pp. 255, 257; Wood and Serres, *Diplomatic Ceremonial and Protocol*, pp. 30, 35, 42–3.

13 G. R. Berridge and N. Gallo, 'The Role of the Diplomatic Corps: The US-North Korea Talks in Beijing, 1988–94', in Melissen, *Innovation in Diplomatic Practice*, pp. 214–26; see also chapters by Paul Sharp and Geoffrey Wiseman in this volume.

14 Many of the informal talks between Israeli and Arab diplomats emerged within the framework of the diplomatic corps.

15 Satow, *A Guide to Diplomatic Practice*, p. 254; see also pp. 111, 189; Wood and Serres, *Diplomatic Ceremonial and Protocol*, p. 83. Ceremonial discontinuity is used not once as an intentional insult or protest; Berridge, *Diplomacy*, p. 109. Berridge writes that the diplomatic corps perhaps reached its most glorious moment in the successful defence of the legation quarter in Peking during the Boxer uprising in 1900.

16 Berridge and Gallo, 'The Role of the Diplomatic Corps', pp. 214–30.
17 On the 'diplomatic list' see, Satow, *A Guide to Diplomatic Practice*, p. 254; Wood and Serres, *Diplomatic Ceremonial and Protocol*, pp. 32, 35; Dembinski, *The modern Law of Diplomacy*, p. 112.
18 Quoted in Hickman, *Daughters of Britannia*, p. 272.
19 Berridge, *Diplomacy*, p. 129; see also, A. Black, 'The Changing Culture of Diplomatic Spouses: Some Fieldnotes from Brussels', *Diplomacy and Statecraft*, 6 (1995), pp. 196–222.
20 Anderson, *The Rise of Modern Diplomacy*, p. 121; Wood and Serres, *Diplomatic Ceremonial and Protocol*, pp. 30, 94. Ceremonially, the unity of the diplomatic corps should at all times be respected.
21 Mattingly, *Renaissance Diplomacy*, p. 100.
22 G. R. Berridge, M. Keens-Soper and T. G. Otte, *Diplomatic Theory from Machiavelli to Kissinger* (New York: Palgrave, 2001), p. 119; Clark, *Corps Diplomatique*, p. 18. Diplomats find in other diplomats an open mindedness, and the same pattern of thought.
23 See also, A. Eban, *Autobiography* (New York: Random House, 1977), p. 591.
24 Callières. *The Art of Diplomacy*, p. 110; see also Clark, *Corps Diplomatique*, p. 20. In private diplomats can be sharp and ungenerous about foreign colleagues, a compensation perhaps for having to be charming face to face day after day.
25 See also, S. Sofer, *The Diplomatic Encounter: Conventions and Rituals Reappraised*, Center for the Study of Diplomacy, University of Leicester, 2001.
26 C. Jönsson and Martin Hall, *Essence of Diplomacy* (London: Palgrave Macmillan, 2005), pp. 40–1; Geoffrey Wiseman, 'Pax Americana: Bumping into Diplomatic Culture', *International Studies Perspectives*, 6 (2005), pp. 409–30.
27 H. Bull, *The Anarchical Society* (London: Macmillan, 1977), p. 316.
28 R. Cohen, *Negotiating Across Cultures: International Communication in an Interdependent World* (Washington, DC: United States Institute of Peace, 2003); P. Sharp, 'The Idea of Diplomatic Culture and Its Sources', Annual Convention of the International Studies Association, Montreal, March 2004.
29 J. Der Derian, *On Diplomacy* (Oxford: Basil Blackwell, 1987), pp. 30–43; see also, S. Sofer, 'The Diplomat as a Stranger', *Diplomacy and Statecraft*, 8 (1997), pp. 177–86.
30 S. Sofer, 'Guardians of the Practitioners' Virtue: Diplomats at the Warrior's Den', *Diplomacy and Statecraft*, 16 (2005), pp. 1–12.
31 Berridge, Keens-Soper and Otte, *Diplomatic Theory from Machiavelli to Kissinger*, p. 119; Hamilton and Langhorne, *The Practice of Diplomacy*, p. 67.

Part II

The Diplomatic Corps as a Settled Affair

3
The Washington Diplomatic Corps: The Place, the Professionals, and their Performance

Alan K. Henrikson

'What is the genius of this place?', the American diplomat, Ambassador Edmund A. Gullion, used to ask, conceptually, when heading an inspection team that was evaluating the work of a US embassy – its premises, its staff, its operations, and, above all, its mission. His criterion of assessment, more qualitative than quantitative, derived from his insight that every diplomatic situation is unique. The diplomat, he liked to say, is 'the man of the occasion'.[1] All diplomatic posts – the embassies of foreign countries in the United States as well – have their own potentialities and their own limitations, special opportunities for those who occupy them to make a difference and also, sometimes, distinctive disadvantages and obstructions they may have to overcome.

The 'open doors' as well as the 'closed doors' that confront an ambassador and his staff at Washington DC may be peculiar to them, owing mainly to their country's relationship with the United States. The political setting and the wider environment of the American capital, however, also affect the *entire* body of diplomats serving there. These are the members of the diplomatic corps or *corps diplomatique* (CD).[2] An assessment of the whole Washington CD, therefore, must take into account the total political ecology of the place.[3] A diplomatic corps in a particular location cannot be judged only theoretically or comparatively, by reference to normative or historical standards alone. It must be studied *in situ*, in relation to the actual situation into which its members find themselves and perform their assigned tasks. As their very jobs are defined somewhat by the context in which they work, its 'performance', too, should be assessed, along with what diplomats themselves bring, in the way of skill and ambition, to their posts, individually and collectively.

The US capital – formally, 'Washington, District of Columbia' – is an unusual location for foreign diplomats, in part because they themselves make up a significant part of it and have shaped its character over time. They are elements of its society, as well of 'international society' – or, in the view of critics, a 'diplomatic set'. Diplomats in Washington do, to a degree, blend in locally. A recent representative of Egypt, Ambassador Ahmed Maher El Sayed, observed, as other foreign diplomats also have done, 'This is one of the few cities where the ambassador is considered important. You are solicited by charities'. To respond is to engage and even help to create American civil society. 'You meet new people, you become part of a community, and you help a cause.'[4]

The Washington Community, with its resident diplomats temporarily included, is unusually complex. Because of differences in income, education, and race, as well as country of origin, the outlooks of its inhabitants vary greatly. Some Washingtonians are narrowly municipal in focus. For them the city is 'The District'. Other Washingtonians, including of course its diplomats, are broadly international in their perspectives. For them it is 'The World Capital' – perhaps more precisely, 'the political capital of the world'. Some Washingtonians are, in a curious way, provincial and cosmopolitan. Theirs is 'a small, cozy town, global in scope' – in the fine phrase of Alice Roosevelt Longworth, the redoubtable daughter of Theodore Roosevelt and dowager duchess of Old Washington.[5]

The City of Washington – the prototype of the 'American'-type, or artificial, capital – was created almost out of nothing, but with very large things in mind.[6] The country that built it symbolically asserted, as the very term 'District of Columbia' suggests, a kind of headship in the New World, even Western Hemisphere predominance. It also had ideological aspirations. '*NOVUS ORDO SECLORUM*' – a New Order of the Ages – the Great Seal of the United States proclaims. Washington, DC, has become, owing to the North American continent's size and population growth, military victory in two world wars, and the West's triumph in the Cold War, the world's most powerful national capital. The United States is enjoying what has been called its 'unipolar moment' in history.[7] As the focus of the world's political attention, the US capital is second to none, rivalled not by any other national capital but only by New York, which is the headquarters site of the United Nations (UN) and the primary centre of multilateral diplomacy.[8]

Although still a 'small town' city, Washington is host to, arguably, the largest diplomatic community in the world. The foreign diplomats accredited and resident there – 4,038 'principals' of embassies, and all the embassies' entire personnel numbering 28,393 – are the continuing (if constantly rotating) core of it.[9] Some 182 nations now have embassies in Washington.[10] In addition, there is the Apostolic Nunciatura of the Holy See (Vatican City), the Delegation of the Commission of the European Union, and various other representative offices, including those of countries such as Cuba and Iran that in the past have had but do not currently enjoy diplomatic relations with the United States. They do, however, have 'interests sections' – Cuba's, with the embassy of Switzerland, and Iran's, with the embassy of Pakistan. Libya – the Great Socialist People's Libyan Arab Jamahiriya under Colonel Muammar al-Gaddafi – also has been under US sanctions, but, in May 2006 Secretary of State Condoleezza Rice announced the restoration of full diplomatic relations between that country and the United States. The Palestine Liberation Organization (PLO), too, has a mission in Washington. It is skilfully maintained by Afif Safieh, who previously served as the Palestinian envoy to the United Kingdom and the Vatican. 'My assignment is a tough one', he acknowledges, 'in the sense that I have all the duties of an ambassador and more, and I represent a people under occupation, yet I don't have the privileges.'[11]

Is this, the 'body' of diplomats posted at the seat of the US federal government, also the world's best – the most effective, the most innovative, the most exemplary of all the international community's diplomatic bodies? I shall argue that it is, but that it has unrealized potential, particularly as a 'force' in support of international law, consultation, and cooperation, if not formal organization. The Washington diplomatic corps has within itself, in its opportune situation, a capacity to grow into an almost institutionalized bond of international 'connection', better *joining* the United States of America to the world. It may even be able to engender, not just engineer, a greater awareness among Americans of what might be called the '*international* interest' of the USA, a nation, that, under its 18th century Constitution, has tended to act unilaterally and with reference to the 'national interest' alone.[12]

This admittedly bold idea – essentially, that foreign diplomats could further 'internationalize' American domestic politics without 'interfering' in them – raises obvious questions. One concerns the realities of power. Given the global predominance of the United States at present, could outside pressure, of whatever character, be sufficient to sway the country in its foreign policies and international behaviour? Another concerns the influence of diplomacy itself. Is 'diplomatic culture', however intellectually advanced and well-articulated, capable, intrinsically, of altering the attitudes of other countries, especially one as large, diverse, and physically separate as the United States.[13] Still another, of most immediate concern in this study of the Washington diplomatic corps, concerns the actual 'corporate' character of diplomacy as an institution. Is the Washington diplomatic corps truly *organized* enough – internally cohesive enough, ideologically like-minded enough, and politically unified enough – to exercise maximum 'international' influence upon the United States? As an entity, *is the Washington diplomatic corps greater than, or less than, the sum of its parts?*

Are Washington's diplomats actually a group? Or do they operate largely independently, either on their own motion or in accordance with their individual governments' instructions? Do they typically compete, as rivals – or do they generally cooperate as colleagues? If they do join together, how often do they do so, regarding which issues, and in what combinations? Thus is there, in general, harmony or discord among them? If harmony is the norm, how does such *esprit de corps* arise, through the orchestrating influence of leaders – nominally, the dean and also vice-dean – of the diplomatic corps, or from the many ambassadorial players' own sense of comity and shared interest, and on occasion even common purpose? Or does it come from outside 'direction', possibly that of the US government's Chief of Protocol? To shift from the musical to an anatomical analogy: Does the 'body' of diplomats at Washington have a head, arms, and legs, as well as *esprit*, or is it a disjointed and perhaps dispirited thing, a non-functioning entity – with formal 'organic' unity but, as a real political factor, *quantité négligéable?*

My impression is that the diplomatic corps in Washington is distinctly *less* than the sum of its parts, but that it is so in some very interesting ways. Certain of its 'parts', particularly the regionally associated countries within it, have more influence than they otherwise would, as individual states, as members of *subgroups* within the corps. Being members of the overall Washington CD – which serves as a kind of legitimating umbrella – they have a 'sub-corporate' status, and a cover for their separate identities and projects.

The picture, although there can be kaleidoscopic combinations and permutations, is one of fairly well-defined pluralism. There is the 'Latin American diplomatic corps' and also an 'African diplomatic corps', as those regional ambassadorial groupings commonly are known. The 'Central American ambassadors' sometimes caucus. Then there is the well-coordinated and influential grouping of the 27 member states of the European Union (EU). The countries of the vast Asia-Pacific region, being more spread out, more diverse, and less cohesive, do not function at all as a unit. Even the Asia-Pacific countries, however, have less expansive self-identifying groups such as the 'Pacific island states' and, of course, the membership of the Association of Southeast Asian Nations (ASEAN), whose ambassadors consult among themselves in Washington.

It may even be hypothesized that the *lesser* – that is, the smaller – these various 'corps' are in geographical scope, the *greater* their sense of self-identification and resulting group influence. Belonging to formal organizations, such as the EU or ASEAN, or the Organization of American States (OAS), League of Arab States (LAS), or new African Union (AU), does, provide reinforcement. The added-up influence of the various, mostly regional subgroups of the Washington diplomatic corps possibly exceeds that of the Washington CD as a whole. Their agendas, however, are different, so that such a direct comparison is not entirely meaningful, as would be any attempt at measurement. The smaller regional groupings tend to focus on matters of substantive policy, such as trade, whereas the diplomatic corps in its entirety engages the United States mainly in the context of state occasions, and of course with regard to matters of diplomatic privilege and immunity – for which the Vienna Convention on Diplomatic Relations provides the framework.[14] Apart from that, the diplomatic corps does 'very little as a group'.[15]

Matters of 'social ceremonial' and 'housekeeping' that are the ordinary substance of relations between the Department of State – its Office of the Chief of Protocol and its Office of Foreign Missions – and the membership of the Washington diplomatic corps do have their importance. Exchanges over these matters weave the fabric of relations between 'international society' and American civil society. What most often attracts press and popular attention are, however, the unpaid parking tickets and the sometimes more serious offences, including trafficking and the abuse of domestic workers, and, in a separate category, espionage, which is handled differently.[16]

Instances have also occurred of foreign diplomats themselves suffering offences, including racial and other discrimination. Diplomats from the newly decolonized countries of Africa in the early 1960s were especially vulnerable. Secretary of State Dean Rusk, testifying before Congress in favour of what became the Civil Rights Act of 1964, found this pattern of behaviour unacceptable for *American* reasons as well as for international ones. 'It is not my view that we should resolve these problems here at home merely in order to look good abroad', he declared. 'We must try to eliminate discrimination due to race, color, religion, not to make others think better of us but because it is incompatible with the great ideals to which our democratic society is dedicated.'[17]

Civility can be reinforced by protocol as well as by legislation. Protocol is the body of law, custom, and practice that governs actual diplomatic conduct, including that of the interface between the host government and emissaries of the sending state. Although protocol, broadly defined, is not a 'politicized' sphere, it can become so. For existing countries and also nations-without-states in search of US recognition, the initial establishment or, in some cases, restoration of relations with the United States, matters of protocol can assume high importance. What is at stake is the very membership of international society. Such aspiring entities – an example being the Palestine National Authority – are mostly individually contested cases, which may not be of great concern to the CD as a whole or even to the pertinent regional or other sub groupings. Diplomatic relations are negotiated bilaterally, even though the Vienna Convention on Diplomatic Relations provides an overall multilateral framework for the formulation and establishment of them 'by mutual consent' (Article 2). As itself the 'first new nation', born in revolution, the United States of America has a special sensitivity, albeit sometimes negative, to the arrival of new polities on the world stage. Most of these do find representation, in some role or guise, in Washington, DC, however.

What are the factors, apart from its large and still-increasing size, that define the Washington diplomatic community and make it what it is? One conditioning factor, as noted, is *where* the diplomats are – that is, the physical-geographical, the social-economic, and, especially, the constitutional-political setting of the United States of America. A second determinant is *who* the diplomats are – their backgrounds, their training, their skills, their personal identities, and, perhaps even, their characteristics as a group. A third factor, the most dynamic of all, is *what* the diplomats are engaged in – what their objectives and instructions are, the strategies they are trying to follow, the tactics they are choosing, and the actual steps, today often transgressive, they are taking, separately and even as a corps. The Washington CD is a living thing and, because of the changes within it and all around it, an evolving thing. It is informed by its place, by its people, and by the record of its performance.

The place

The diplomatic 'post' of Washington DC is, in a strict sense, not a site. It is a subjective place, an assignment. 'Washington' as a base of diplomatic activity is an amalgam – a set of individualized 'posts,' clustered together. To be sure, these can, for convenience, be viewed as one post, although Geoffrey Berridge's conception of the diplomatic corps as all the missions 'in the same capital' is more accurate.[18] Representation by most of the world's sovereign nations and also by a number of treaty-based international organizations at the common 'post' is what identifies Washington, and, to a degree, makes it what it is as a centre of diplomatic life.

If common residence at a location, as here suggested, fundamentally 'makes' a diplomatic corps, then the nature of the place itself is essential to its character. The presence of diplomats is part of a historical, social, and political landscape. Washington DC was a new capital, deliberately set apart from existing cities, notably the relative metropolis of Philadelphia where American Independence had been declared and the US Constitution devised. The result of a North-South sectional bargain, the decision to build a capital *de novo* was done to assure more 'impartial' national governance – under the thumb of no urban elite, and in theory responsive to all the states and the American people as a whole.

The situation gave foreign governments an opportunity to exert unmeasured influence. Initially, the federal establishment, including the Department of State with which the few foreign diplomats in Washington dealt, was pitifully small. In 1802 the headquarters of the State Department, plus the Patent Office, included just ten persons. In this setting, foreign diplomats felt little restraint. 'Being thrown together in Washington's wilderness seemed merely to multiply the opportunities for acting out, in their social relations, the conflicts of national interest among them. A prolonged and bitter social warfare between the British and French legations at Washington accompanied the hostilities between the sovereigns they represented, culminating in a near-fight between the British and French ministers at a White House dinner which the President prevented by intervening with his saber at the ready', as the historian James Sterling Young has written of Washington in the time of Thomas Jefferson. 'Foreign envoys insinuated themselves into the politics of their host community in ways that would today be intolerable, but which were then considered no impropriety against a new nation not even meriting the recognition of being dealt with by envoys of full ambassadorial rank.'[19] At the time, of course, only the great powers sent full ambassadors to each other.

From a military perspective, the city, some 200 miles from the Atlantic Ocean but situated on the navigable part of the Potomac River, was indefensible; and during the War of 1812 British troops attacked and occupied it, burning most of its public buildings. Washington just barely survived that conflict, and, as the United States expanded westward and settled the country's interior, it became more and more eccentric. Then, as at later junctures in US history, proposals were made to relocate the 'nation's capital' to more central, presumably safer, and arguably more authentic and representative locations – such as Cincinnati, Ohio, or St. Louis, Missouri, or ultimately even Denver, Colorado.[20] It remains geographically and also culturally anomalous. Washington, as President John F. Kennedy said wryly, in support of what became the Kennedy Center for the Performing Arts, is 'a city of Northern charm and Southern efficiency'.[21] It still retains, for many Americans, a backward-looking, deferential 'European' bias, whereas the growth of the country has suggested a more forward-looking, more open, more positive 'Asia-Pacific' orientation, as well as a familiar, quasi-domestic 'Pan American' vocation and view.[22]

The natural coastal and 'Atlanticist' bias of Washington DC has to a considerable extent been structurally offset by the American federal system – centred on 'the Federal City'.[23] The US constitutional framework has equilibrated the relationships between the parts of the United States in its internal workings much better than it has the country's external involvement. Here is where the Washington diplomatic corps with its 'larger' view comes in – or *could* enter in – as a moderating and globalizing factor. The balance between the Presidency and the Congress with regard to international activity is the most crucial relationship – for, in foreign and defence policy and also in international economic matters, authority, though constitutionally distributed between them, has to be shared. In the foreign affairs area, as the constitutional scholar Edward S. Corwin commented famously, the Constitution is 'an invitation to struggle'.[24]

Most foreign diplomats arriving in the US capital are accustomed to systems in which there is a single authority and one voice – and a relatively clear 'government' position on things. In Washington, a sole focal point of policymaking regarding issues of vital concern to their countries may not exist. Diplomats have as a result often been confused, even stymied in their search for a locus of decision, the *genius loci*. 'You don't have a system of government', exclaimed Sir Nicholas Henderson, Britain's ambassador at the time of the Falklands/Malvinas crisis of 1982. 'In France or Germany, if you want to persuade the Government of a particular point of view, or find out their view on something, it's quite clear where the power resides. It resides with the Government. Here there's a whole maze of different corridors of power and influence. There's the Administration. There's the Congress. There are the staffers. There's the press. There are the institutions. There's the judiciary. The lawyers in this town. You know, it's difficult not to believe that the Mayflower was full of lawyers.' Admitting, perhaps, his own occasional wanderings and quandaries, he noted: 'A familiar sight in Washington is to see some bemused diplomat pacing the corridors of the Capitol, trying to find out where the decisions are being taken. And when he's found that out, he may find it isn't on the Hill after all. It's somewhere else.'[25]

The basic structural polarities of Washington DC are concretized in its very layout, deriving from Major Pierre Charles Enfant's initial plan. Pennsylvania Avenue, with the Capitol at one end and the White House at the other, is the main axis of rivalry. Other centres of real influence are the Pentagon across the Potomac River in Virginia and also the new private enterprises, including major contractors to the military, located around the Capital Beltway (Interstate 495). The power map of the Washington area is almost graphic, and diplomats have to know it – as well as what lies *beyond* 'the Beltway.' The Washington world now includes the lobbying firms on 'K' Street. Not only companies but also some foreign governments now engage these to advance their interests, spread their messages, and burnish their images.[26]

The more formally 'international' character of the city is established by the presence there of major international economic institutions: the Bretton Woods bodies – the International Monetary Fund and the World Bank – and the Inter-American Development Bank. A more general international organization, the OAS, is ensconced in the Pan American Union Building, dating from the Union's founding in 1890. The Pan American Health Organization (PAHO) and a Regional Office of the International Committee of the Red Cross (ICRC) also are located in Washington. In addition, there is an increasing number of non-governmental and private voluntary organizations that are engaged in international policy discussion and even 'diplomatic' practice in foreign fields. Similarly involved, though less operationally, are many of Washington's 'think-tanks', or policy-oriented research institutes. Even some state and local governments with offices or agents in Washington are concerned with international matters, beyond just trade promotion and investment attraction.

'In Washington, there are a 1,000 points of decision-making', said Walter Cutler, a former American ambassador. 'There is a diffusion of decision-making power and because of this ambassadors here are stretched so thin because they have to touch so many bases. They have to cover Washington, both the executive and the legislative branches.

And they have to go out to the Dulles corridor, to Silicon Valley and many, many other places that have an impact on policy and on the economy. Diplomats have to be aware of the views and influence of dozens of interest groups that have a real impact.'[27]

The very multiplicity of centres of authority, power, interest, and expertise in Washington somewhat levels the playing-field for diplomats. It equalizes, to a degree, the chances that ambassadors have whether from countries large or small. 'In European capitals, things are much more formal', says Ambassador Jón Baldvin Hannibalsson of Iceland. 'Here it is quite open. People often come up to you, and they don't even ask where you are from. They ask: "What do you have to say. What are your arguments?" There is more equality of opportunity here than in more formal systems.'[28] The very fluidity of movement and flow of argument in Washington can, however, be distracting to diplomats, leaving them uncertain as to where their priorities lie.

To *position* themselves well within the 'system' of Washington DC, foreign governments and their diplomats have vied to buy or build grand edifices – in some cases, virtually 'European'-style residential palaces – usually at prime locations in the city. The traditional axis of diplomatic life is Embassy Row – along Massachusetts Avenue and its cross streets between Thomas Circle downtown and Ward Circle farther out, with the majority of embassies being between Scott Circle and Wisconsin Avenue.[29] The first to be built there was the impressive British Embassy designed, in the Queen Anne style of brown brick, by the architect Sir Edwin Lutyens. 'We are no longer an imperial power and we are not a superpower', said a recent British ambassador, Sir Christopher Meyer; 'but Britain is a great power and requires a great house in Washington that reflects its status.'[30] Russia, also concerned about preserving its great power (if not superpower) position, has erected a large new embassy high above Washington on Wisconsin Avenue. The Canadian government, having realized that most of its problems with the United States are legislative and stem from Congress, has succeeded in locating its new embassy building – a more modern but hardly less imposing structure – on Pennsylvania Avenue, close to the Capitol. Other governments, too, have used their real estate, bought or built, to gain positional advantage, if not through sheer location then through architectural distinction. The new 'House of Sweden', located on the Potomac River, is a crystalline showcase of Swedish modernity. Although Washington DC is a New World capital, it thus is filled with Old World *palazzi*, however futuristic their design, décor, and other artwork including sculpture. These structures and associated symbols 'represent' on American soil the national styles as well as the proud sovereignty of the sending states.

The position of Washington DC itself has been enhanced by its foreign embassies, as well as by the global institutions – the IMF and World Bank – as well as the OAS and other 'inter-American' bodies that were established there during and after the Second World War. The American capital city was a new 'Rome' to which all roads – not just those of the New World – seemed to lead.[31] Most countries, if they had not already done so, then exchanged ambassadors (rather than ministers) with the United States, and opened embassies (rather than legations) in the US capital.[32] This included many countries, both large and small, that formerly had been colonies, dominions, or otherwise under European control. Participation in diplomacy at Washington heightened their importance as well.

'Given the U.S.'s stature in the world, almost everything an ambassador does here is important', reflected a later ambassador of Egypt, Nabil Fahmy. 'Diplomacy in Washington is interesting and challenging, partly because of the U.S.'s role in the world.'[33] The issues discussed there have come to include major questions of 'international' policy as well as bilateral relationships. 'Washington is the capital of the world for public policy', Iceland's Ambassador Hannibalsson comments. 'Virtually all important public policy issues pass through Washington in one form or another. The discussions and debates you have in this city are very wide ranging and cover every conceivable topic. For example, with all the conferences that are held here you can learn as much about what is going on in Russia in Washington as in Moscow.'[34] Washington, despite its residual 'small town' characteristics, was, for its diplomats and also because of them, truly 'global in scope'.

The professionals

A diplomatic corps is not just the emplacement but also an embodiment of a group of diplomats. As Geoffrey Berridge notes, 'The diplomatic body is embodied most obviously in its dean', a single individual.[35] How controlling is this central figure? Is he (or potentially, she) a figurehead, largely a ceremonial leader – or a genuine political force, and diplomatically a unifying one? Is it appropriate even to expect the dean, or vice-dean, whose position is determined by years of service in Washington as ambassador rather than according to some other criterion – such as national identity, size of country, professional competence, or personal charm – to be a dominant figure, capable of making the entire diplomatic corps operate as one body, and to do so muscularly, for important purposes?[36]

At the outset of the United States, the matter was simple, for the *'corps diplomatique'* in America consisted of one person: the French emissary to the Continental Congress. The continuity of the French connection with America was emphasized by a much-later doyen of the diplomatic corps, Jules Jusserand, Ambassador of France to the United States from 1902 to 1924. Jusserand was, as he himself observed in 1916: 'The dean now, not only of the diplomatic corps in Washington, but of all my predecessors from the early days, when, on a raised platform in Independence Hall, my diplomatic ancestor, Gérard de Rayneval, presented to Congress the first credentials brought here from abroad (and Gérard was then, he alone, the whole diplomatic body)'.[37]

The British too – once the War of 1812 was past, the difficult Civil War period negotiated, and the Great Rapprochement of the turn of the century achieved – have at times taken an almost proprietary view of diplomatic relations with the United States.[38] The British ambassador during part of the time that the great French emissary, Jusserand, served in Washington, was Sir Cecil Spring-Rice. His ambassadorship (1912–18) which included the First World War years and Woodrow Wilson's presidency was based in part on the close friendship he had formed, during earlier visits in London and Washington, with President Theodore Roosevelt – 'Theodore Rex'. Owing to the latter's vibrant personality and worldly interests, diplomacy, like almost everything else in Washington, had begun to revolve around the Presidency.[39] For Jusserand, Spring Rice, and the German ambassador of Roosevelt's time, Baron Hermann Speck von Sternberg, the diplomatic game there was an almost European one of 'court' politics.[40] It was one of the antecedents of the 'imperial presidency'.[41]

In the years since the Second World War, during a time when the diplomatic service of Britain became more professionalized, British ambassadors have tried to play very much the same game, of seeking striving to maintain what has come to be known as, in Winston Churchill's phrase, the 'special relationship'.[42] What the former British prime minister had in mind was not only a fraternal association of English-speaking peoples – or an anglophone form of 'international society' – but also an intimate relationship between the British and American governments, at the highest level. A particular frank expression of this Churchillian imperative was the instruction, received and recounted with delight by its recipient, Ambassador Sir Christopher

Meyer, when he was preparing to take up his post in Washington in 1997: '"We want you to get up the arse of the White House and stay there." So spoke the Prime Minister's chief of staff, Jonathan Powell, in the splendour of one of Downing Street's reception rooms.'[43] Meyer became celebrated, at Downing Street and in Whitehall even somewhat envied, for largely succeeding in his mission – his easy familiarity with President Bill Clinton and, after him, President George W. Bush.

What the above diplomatic-historical vignettes do show is that some members of the Washington diplomatic corps are more 'equal' than others, as Casimir Yost of Georgetown University's Institute for the Study of Diplomacy expresses the point. He acknowledges the unfairness of it: 'That's just how it works. Some ambassadors have more natural prominence than others. For example, ambassadors from Israel, the U.K., France, and Germany tend to be more prominent than others.'[44] The ambassadors of certain other countries, too, have achieved prominence and influence. From the other 'old great powers' of Europe, there is post-communist Russia; and from the rising 'new great powers' of Asia, there is, most notably, the People's Republic of China. Their representatives usually can command the attention they need. Some other ambassadors, too, may be able to reach those whom they wish to reach, when they wish to, in the US government. For the diplomatic representatives of most other countries, however, life in the 'nation's capital' is a constant struggle for access.

It is a challenge for them, too, to find something to gain access *with*. One way is to be relevant – that is, to have useful, interesting, and tradable information, even insightful gossip, to share. 'Access is the lifeblood of diplomacy in Washington and relevance is the oxygen', comments a Canadian ambassador, Derek Burney.[45] The representative of another northern middle power, Sweden, elaborates upon this point. 'In Washington, if you are a Russian or British ambassador you are automatically taken seriously', said Swedish Ambassador Jan Eliasson whose country held the European Union Presidency (in the first half of 2001). 'But if you are a Swedish ambassador you have to be well briefed and well prepared. You have to have something to contribute. That's why I'm reading so much. That's why I'm well prepared when I go to meetings. And if I can be a pretty good ambassador in the EU context, it adds to their interest in me.' Part of Eliasson's own readiness came from his full exploitation of Washington's many research centres. 'Think tanks are my secret love', he confessed. 'They mean all sorts of things to me. I'm increasingly informal. I want to think aloud, break new ground. I think the greatest difference in Washington between now and the 1970s is the vitality of the think tanks.'[46]

Service in Washington, because of its competitiveness as well as the complexity of most of the issues that have to be addressed, puts a premium on ability and on achievement. 'More than one hundred eighty nations have embassies there and virtually all are represented by the best envoys that they have', writes John Shaw. 'Career diplomats, former prime ministers, foreign ministers, and finance ministers are dispatched to Washington'. There are not many 'former used-car sales-men or strip-mall developers' among them (as there sometimes are, by implication, among US ambassadorial appointees to other countries' capitals). 'The city has an unusually deep pool of diplomatic talent and political clout.'[47]

Interestingly, more than a few of Washington's ambassadors have not been professionally trained diplomats at all but, rather, are, as Gail Scott has pointed out, from spheres of life other than politics. 'In fact, many of them are scientists, doctors, lawyers or teachers, chosen by their newly independent nations because they weren't affiliated with the Communist Party or another former regime and are there-fore "clean."' Her examples include Slovakia's ambassador, Branislav Lichardus, and his wife, Dr. Eva Kellerova, who were 'their country's preeminent medical research scientists'. Another example is Ukraine's Ambassador Yuri Shcherbak, 'not only a physician but a well-known novelist'. Following his exposé of the Chernobyl disaster, he became his country's first minister of environmental protection.[48]

Of course, other embassies too, especially the ones of the wealthier and larger countries, have specialist officers on their rosters. In addi-tion to their political sections, they have offices dealing with trade and investment matters, science and technology, cultural affairs, and press and communication. In Washington, the officers dealing with military affairs and defence cooperation are especially important. There is even a grouping of defence attachés, which selects its own 'dean'.[49] There is also an Agricultural Counselors Forum, a voluntary group formed to improve communication within the diplomatic corps concerning agricultural and 'food systems' issues.[50]

The composition of the Washington diplomatic corps is being augmented in another important respect: the increasing number of women in it – including, now, more than 20 heads of mission. During Austria's EU presidency (in the first half of 2006), its ambassador, Dr. Eva Nowotny, coordinated European Union diplomacy at

Washington.[51] This was after President Clinton had appointed Dr. Madeleine Albright to the position of Secretary of State, and President Bush had chosen Dr. Condoleezza Rice for that role. The actions of those presidents set a precedent, and presumably entered into the considerations of some governments in selecting envoys for Washington. Secretary Albright, when earlier serving as US permanent representative at the UN, and Secretary Rice, in office in Washington, met separately with their female counterparts and other female professionals in recognition of their 'arrival'. In her memoir, *Madam Secretary*, Madeleine Albright recalled: 'Shortly after I was sworn in as Secretary of State, Henry Kissinger introduced me to an audience by formally welcoming me into the "fraternity" of those who had held that position. Replying, I said, "Henry, I hate to tell you, but it's not a fraternity anymore."'[52]

Last, but not least in importance, among the changes in the composition and the character of the Washington diplomatic corps is that it is noticeably becoming more 'youthful'.[53] Washington is not necessarily, anymore, the place where diplomats go, 'at the peak of their career', before they retire. Part of the explanation of the youthfulness of the Washington diplomatic corps is that many of the countries represented are small ones. 'The fact that I come from a small country allowed me to become an ambassador at my age', said an ambassador from Luxembourg, Arlette Conzemius Paccoud, at age 42.[54] Many of the newer small countries, especially, are likely to have young ambassadors because, as in the case of the successor states resulting from the break-up of Yugoslavia and also the Soviet Union, they had to form their diplomatic services quickly, with an intake of new recruits. Most were given rapid, if not always the most up-to-date and useful, training.[55] Many heads of mission from developing countries of Africa, Latin America, and Asia also have been appointed relatively 'young'. Their energy level is high.

Their performance

What is it, exactly, that Washington's diplomats *do*? This question, often asked by observers from outside the profession (and sometimes even members of it), has a particularly significant bearing when applied to the CD in the capital of the United States. Resident diplomats there are conscious of departing from old forms of conduct, without having yet deliberately developed a new professional 'code' of behaviour, beyond the procedural rules found in manuals of protocol.[56] They are aware of the fact, however, that their individual and group behaviour in Washington is innovative, and likely to spread, partly *via* diplomatic reciprocation. The interactive and replicatory processes of globalization can carry the changes that are occurring in diplomacy at Washington across the world. We are seeing the development of an 'American politics as world politics' model.[57]

Traditionally, diplomacy even at the New World capital of Washington has been viewed as a kind of 'dance'. The title of her book *Diplomatic Dance* (1999) alone, wrote Gail Scott, 'intrigues and prompts ambassadors to smile, laugh and even admit their latest move on the diplomatic dance floor. Diplomacy, the political art of negotiating between countries, has always involved intricate steps.'[58] Much of Washington embassy life is a polite, rule-governed, almost rhythmic activity of national day buffets, annual benefit balls, and, on a more public level, attendance at Joint Sessions of Congress and quadrennial presidential inaugurals. The regularity of this orderly sequence is punctuated by state visits, funerals, and, more unpredictably, international and even local crises. A noteworthy local crisis involving members of the diplomatic corps was the 1977 seizure by a group of Hanafi Muslims of the District Building, B'nai Brith headquarters, and the Islamic Center in Washington. That the resulting toll in lives was not higher, reported *Time* magazine, was 'most of all' due to 'the courageous intervention of three Muslim ambassadors, Egypt's Ashraf Ghorbal, Pakistan's Sahabzada Yaqub-Khan and Iran's Ardeshir Zahedi'[59] The serenity of international life in Washington was much more profoundly disrupted years later, when on 11 September 2001, the terrorist group Al Qaeda directed a passenger plane into the Pentagon building, and apparently sought to crash one into the White House as well.

John Shaw, writing earlier in that year, already had perceived more chaotic elements in the diplomatic scene, and sensed a greater dynamism and even structural upheaval within it. To him, Washington diplomacy was not a 'dance' but a 'scramble'. 'Participants and observers agree', he then reported, 'that Washington diplomacy is a free-wheeling, informal, highly complex scramble to shape the American debate on international affairs and to influence U.S. policies that often have global consequences. In Washington, timeless traditions and long established rules that are scrupulously adhered to in other capitals are often turned on their heads or reformulated in ways that make them unrecognizable.'[60]

Among these changes was a breakdown in the very distinction between 'domestic' and 'foreign'. The labels could even be reversed. What had been looked upon in the United States as matters of domestic policy – agricultural subsidies, military procurement, civil-rights legislation, anti-terrorism measures, etc. – could be viewed by other countries as challenges, even threats. The country that has experienced the pressure most directly, owing to its proximity, is Canada. So interdependent have these two North American countries become that Canada is more affected by US domestic policies than by explicit US 'foreign policy' toward Canada.

One of the first to understand the full logic of this situation was Allan Gotlieb when he served as Canadian ambassador in Washington from 1981 to 1989. If 'American foreign policy is largely an aggregation of domestic economic thrusts', he later explained, the result is that 'Canadian foreign policy is the obverse side of American domestic policy affecting Canada'. This implied that Canadians could not rely on their 'principal interlocutors' in the US federal government (including the Canada Desk of the State Department) to protect their interests or to speak up for them. Canadians had to 'recognize, realistically, that a great deal of work has to be done ourselves'.[61] In order to do so, they had to act more like Americans.

Canadian diplomacy came to involve open advocacy – if with a Canadian 'difference'. Colin Robertson, who had served as Canada's Consul-General in Los Angeles before being assigned to the embassy as minister in charge of setting up a 'Washington Advocacy Secretariat', described his own new code of conduct as follows: 'preserve Canadian politeness but practice American forthrightness. Take risks. Don't let anything pass. Be in your face. In short, play the game the way Americans play it.'[62] Such 'Americanization' of diplomacy required not just adaptation but also self-transformation. In order to succeed in, and at the same time to remain 'above', the American domestic game, diplomats had to become players in it. John Shaw wrote of the new diplomatic practice: 'It has been said that if diplomats acted in other capitals as they do in Washington they would be declared *persona non grata*. But if they don't follow these practices here they would be rebuked for not doing their jobs.'[63]

Their main 'transgression' was their increasing involvement in matters that were, in the language of the Charter of the United Nations (Article 2, paragraph 7), 'essentially with the domestic jurisdiction' of a state. The Vienna Convention on Diplomatic Relations was explicit about diplomats' 'duty not to interfere in the internal affairs of that State' (Article 41, paragraph 1). Although there are no international guidelines for what constitutes inadmissible interference in internal affairs, in the US context this has meant, historically, impermissible touching of the 'third rail' of *electoral* politics.[64] The Vienna Convention also restricts diplomats in their dealings with host governments to approved channels: 'All official business with the receiving State entrusted to the mission by the sending State shall be conducted with or through the Ministry for Foreign Affairs of the receiving State or such other ministry as may be agreed' (Article 41, paragraph 2).[65] To confine their dealings with the US government only to the Department of State or even other 'agreed' department(s) has become increasingly unrealistic. 'Most diplomats in Washington', Shaw has estimated, 'need to deal, at a minimum with the White House, the National Security Council, the departments of Agriculture, Commerce, Defense, Justice, State, Treasury and Transportation and the U.S. Trade Office.' Then there is Congress. 'The complexity of the executive branch is replicated on Capitol Hill where a bewildering number of committees and subcommittees have important jurisdictions and influence.'[66] These, too, often have to be dealt with.

'This is a political job', acknowledged Ambassador Raymond Chrétien, Canada's representative in Washington from 1994 to 2000. 'I have been an ambassador four times [previously in Zaire, Mexico, and Belgium] and never before have I been put in a post where I felt the need to be as public and political as I have been here. I like it. It is not usually done in other places in the world.'[67] A career professional who happened to be the nephew of Canada's then Prime Minister Jean Chrétien, the ambassador used his new-found 'public and political' persona not merely to promote immediate Canadian interests but also to advance his country's higher 'international' purposes, in a way that suggests the Washington CD's larger potential.

Beyond his 'business' role, Ambassador Chrétien in major speeches around the country used Canada's relationship with the United States to remind its *people* to 'fight the forces of global disengagement'. Speaking in 1997 to the Carnegie Endowment for International Peace, for instance, he provocatively told his audience: 'I will speak through you today to President Clinton and the new Congress.' He specifically called for repeal of the Helms-Burton Act, which was aimed at isolating the Castro regime, because 'it has angered your friends and will not be productive'. He furthermore indirectly advised Congress to pay its long overdue bill to the United Nations – to stop holding the organization 'hostage'. He similarly urged the United States to continue its 'usual generosity' in the face of humanitarian crises abroad. 'While it is true you cannot be the world's sole policeman or physician', argued Chrétien, 'you cannot be a disinterested bystander either. Genocide, famine or aggression literally anywhere in the world must be an alarm bell for American action'.[68]

In Washington, as well as on the international stage, diplomatic action generally is most effective when undertaken in groups, and when 'allies', or political partners, are engaged within *domestic* society – such as the Black Caucus in Congress. A notable example of such diplomatic-political collaboration was the passage in 2000 by the US Congress of the African Growth and Opportunity Act (AGOA). A major trade-and-investment measure, AGOA was in part the result of a two-year effort by the 48 ambassadors from the nations, large and small, of sub-Saharan Africa. When the AGOA bill encountered opposition from protectionist interests and also from some critics who feared its being exploited by US corporations, members of the 'African diplomatic corps' weighed in as a body.[69] 'We believe, as Ambassadors of sovereign nations, we are acting both collectively and independently in the best interests of our continent and countries', the group's press release stated.[70] The AGOA effort affirmed, as Uganda's ambassador Edith Ssempala said, that smaller nations can have greater weight if they form coalitions.[71]

At the forefront of the AGOA effort was the chair of Africa Diplomatic Corps – also the dean of the entire diplomatic corps in Washington, where he had served since 1988 – Roble Olhaye, Ambassador of Djibouti to the United States, 'dually accredited' as his country's Permanent Representative to the United Nations.[72] It is historically not uncommon for smaller countries to have the deanship in Washington. In some cases, their governments have left them there implicitly for that purpose. Nicaragua's Guillermo Sevilla-Sacasa 'had been Nicaragua's ambassador to the United States since 1943 – when Gromyko was our ambassador in Washington', remarked his successor in 1979, Ambassador Anatoly Dobrynin of the Soviet Union.[73]

Dobrynin, who 'ambled through the streets of Washington like a Russian bear', was, not merely because of the large and powerful country he represented, the dominant ambassador of his time.[74] Jovial and yet judicious, he enjoyed 'confidential channel' or, to use Henry Kissinger's term, 'backchannel' access to the White House when, as during the presidency of Richard Nixon, 'détente' with the USSR was US policy. Nonetheless, he had difficulty later, after the Soviet invasion of Afghanistan and the replacement in the presidency of Jimmy Carter by Ronald Reagan, when he had to represent the diplomatic corps. 'I was immediately faced with two problems', he recalled.

> First, I simply did not have the time to attend the numerous receptions at all of Washington's embassies, of which there were about 150 at the time. Each staged at least one reception annually to

celebrate its national holiday, and there were other occasions demanding the attendance of the dean of the diplomatic corps – plus official ceremonies at the White House when heads of state arrived. That led to the second problem. Some of these countries had unfriendly relations with the Soviet Union or no diplomatic relations at all. That did not formally affect my status as dean of the diplomatic corps, but I sometimes felt out of my element at the ceremonies. Worst of all, President Reagan in his welcoming speeches could almost never forbear from criticizing the Soviet Union, its policies, its ideology. It became something of a ritual with him. But there was absolutely no point in making the Soviet ambassador listen to it again and again.

The Office of the Chief of Protocol helped him out. 'The professional diplomats in the State Department were fully aware of the sensitivity of the situation', remembers Dobrynin, 'so every time Washington was visited by heads of states unfriendly to the Soviet Union, or the State Department knew that Reagan would lash out at the Soviet Union in his welcoming speech, the Swedish ambassador, Wilhelm Wachmeister, who was next to me in seniority, would attend in my place. We cooperated very well in this way.'[75]

Despite the occasional 'bear baiting' by the President Reagan himself, Ambassador Dobrynin acquitted himself well. At a dinner at the White House given by President and Mrs. Reagan for chiefs of diplomatic missions, Dobrynin, speaking as dean, combined humour with an appreciation of the occasion's significance. 'To my memory, this is the first time that the President hosts such a special dinner for the diplomatic corps at the White House – if I am not mistaken, from [the time of] President Eisenhower', he said. 'There is a widespread and not exactly correct legend, as you may know, Mr. President, that diplomats are pin-striped party-goers whose days – and even nights – are mostly spent on consuming caviar under the clinking sounds of crystal glasses. But the real story is that diplomats lead a difficult and laborious life. They feed on a mixed salad of often unreliable pieces of news, so-called "leaks" – as well as "not nutritious rumors" – before finding "an edible or final truth" to report.'[76]

He then went on to make important points about professional diplomacy, the security of the diplomats within international society, and their common higher purpose despite their cultural and political differences. 'In a way, to all of my colleagues here, ambassadors present here tonight, this is a kind, if you would like, of summit meeting, which we so cherish in our professional activities.' He quoted with gratitude a statement the President earlier had made that 'an attack on any diplomat is a crime against mankind'. That is 'also the policy of our governments', Dobrynin said. 'The Washington Diplomatic Corps represents all the continents of the globe, different races and different cultures. We brought here our own ideals and philosophies. We came here to maintain and, if possible, to improve relations between the United States and our countries, to explain as much as possible, the basic and current policies of our governments to the United States leaders and the American people, and to try to understand politics and policies of this country. We all believe that there is one goal we share, and that is to preserve peace at the most important thing in the troubled world today. Diplomacy should play a leading role in achieving this noble goal, and we know that your Secretary of State, Mr. [Alexander] Haig, fully shares this view.'[77]

The only nearly comparable figure as dean of the Washington diplomatic corps since Dobrynin has been Saudi Arabia's ambassador, Prince Bandar bin Sultan, who was the kingdom's representative in the United States for 22 years, until the middle of 2005.[78] He had 'direct access to presidents and cabinet members', noted Robin Wright of the *Washington Post*.[79] After the attacks on the Pentagon and World Trade Center on 11 September 2001, and the tensions that then developed in the US-Saudi relationship, Prince Bandar became much less visible.[80] He never, in fact, exercised much leadership in the diplomatic corps, in which he did not seem much interested.

Except for formal occasions – presidential inaugurations or joint sessions of Congress – the diplomatic corps as a whole seldom meets. Broad 'transnational' collaboration such as that of the African ambassadors' AGOA campaign also is rare. 'Intercontinental' encounters such as the 'special meeting' of the Permanent Council of the OAS and the representatives of the African countries to the United States that took place at the Pan American Union building in December 2002 are as uncommon as they are somewhat formalistic.[81] Real collaboration among *all* the members of the Washington diplomatic corps – acting as a body – does not exist.

'We don't see much of our colleagues except at receptions', said George Saliba, ambassador from Malta. The ambassadors are all 'working on their own. There are no teams. Everybody is so busy and they are working by themselves.'[82] Ambassador Saliba is not wrong. Yet he is not right. Groups do exist. At one time, the socialist countries' ambassadors – the 'friends', as Ambassador Dobrynin refers to them

– met monthly in the Soviet embassy to 'freely trade diplomatic information and Washington gossip'.[83] Other groups, mostly geographically based ones, meet as well. The members of the League of Arab
States and the African Union are examples. 'The Arab ambassadors
have a formal meeting every month and also I have to attend the
formal meetings of the African ambassadors', said Ambassador El
Sayed of Egypt. 'You acquire friends from the smaller groups.'[84] The
ambassadors of all the member countries of the European Union, as
well as the head of the Delegation of European Commission in
Washington, meet regularly to concert approaches, not only in the
area of trade policy where the Commission is the competent negotiating authority. To be sure, diplomats of the larger European powers
sometimes have chafed under such EU 'concertation' – unless their
country happened to be the one holding its six-month presidency.
Britain's Sir Christopher Meyer, mentioning that his French colleague,
François Bujon de l'Estang, was 'forever firing off letters of protest'
to the Commission's Delegate, Dr. Günther Burghardt, confessed that,
in contrast: 'My technique was to ignore Burghardt altogether.'[85]
Sweden's ambassador Jan Eliasson dutifully attended the monthly
EU meetings. However, he reportedly was 'not reluctant to duck
out if he felt the sessions were not productive', feeling it made
more sense 'to meet in smaller groups and do substantive diplomatic
work' – in particular, in league with the other Nordic and Baltic
ambassadors.[86]

An assessment

In the last analysis, as Ambassador Eliasson declared of Washington,
'This is a bilateral city'.[87] He himself went on to become president of
the General Assembly of the United Nations in New York – a 'multilateral' city. There, however, the diplomatic community, relative to the
entirety of the place, is much less prominent, however sizeable and
important internationally. 'Washington is more fun', he admitted.
'Bilateral diplomacy is more solid; multilateral diplomacy is more fluid
and diverse', he said, contrasting his Washington post with his UN
position, where he found himself in the midst of the maelstrom over
UN reform.[88]

The Washington diplomatic process remains much more a 'scramble'
than a 'dance'. A recurrent observation among its participants is the
'competitiveness' of it all. 'Washington is a city awash with information
and competing agendas', the director of the Egyptian Press and

Information Office, Karim Haggag, has said. 'The audiences we target – the executive branch, the Congress, the media, think tanks, advocacy groups – are deluged with information and we have to compete with others to be heard.'[89] The basic cause of the competition is not so much rivalry within the diplomatic corps as it is contextual – the demands of the place itself, and the limits of the attention-space of the officials and others whom the diplomats wish to reach. The 'scrambling' – sometimes ambassadors and members of their staffs have to contact and even visit five or six offices around the city when dealing with just one issue – invigorates and toughens them. 'Of course, it's very competitive here', said Edith Ssempala of Uganda. 'But I don't mind the competitiveness. What I do mind is the competition for my time. There are so many issues to deal with. And for small nations, the biggest challenges are in resources.' For the smaller, and less wealthy, countries particularly, concentration becomes necessary. 'You have to focus, to target. And to be truly effective here, it's important to travel, to get outside of Washington. And this is such a big country.'[90]

The 'place' of Washington diplomacy thus is no longer just the District of Columbia itself – or, of course, just Embassy Row – or even the Beltway. The sphere of Washington ambassadorial activity has to extend throughout the country and, for some of the corps' members, even into neighbouring Canada and Mexico, the states of Central America and the Caribbean, and even countries in South America. Their purview also extends beyond the administrative network of the consulates and honorary consulates which many maintain and must supervise. They often have direct contact of their own as well with corporate headquarters and production centres where their governments, companies, and citizens may have interests. They frequently are in touch as well with prominent expatriates and diasporic communities.

They also are engaging in new activities, beyond formal representation, particularly in the areas of lobbying, public relations, and advocacy. 'Public diplomacy' many of their governments now term it, adopting an American neologism that some professional diplomats, especially older ones, consider 'oxymoronic'.[91] Speaking out, and otherwise connecting with the American public, are now considered imperative. 'The United States is a country of advocacy', as Ambassador Fahmy of Egypt said. 'To be successful here, you have to engage with all the people, not just with the government. In no other place that I'm aware of does domestic politics meet with foreign policy at such an intense level.'[92]

Diplomats who serve in Washington undergo a unique form of socialization – an 'Americanization' of diplomacy. Ambassadors, today younger in age as well as in style, who have had one or more tours of duty as diplomats in Washington not infrequently today go on to serve in other positions, even other bilateral ambassadorships, afterward.[93] The processes they engaged in while posted at the American capital are becoming, through their example and agency, a new pattern of world diplomacy. Its distinguishing characteristics are openness, informality, flexibility, directness, goal-orientedness, and assertiveness – even transgressiveness. Its purpose is not such much 'representation' as it is 'projection'.[94] In projecting their countries into the United States, through their own presence and activity and also through the World Wide Web and other means of communication their embassies use, Washington's ambassadors are part of the larger process of globalization. Even while operating formally with the framework of the Vienna Convention on Diplomatic Relations, they are breaking its bounds.

How should the Washington diplomatic corps, finally, be assessed within the world of diplomacy thus being transformed? As a body, it is, plainly, *less* than the sum of its parts. The corps itself – '*corps diplomatique*' membership – is not the primary identification of diplomats in the 'bilateral' city that Washington, District of Columbia, unmistakably is. Nor is it, even in its institutionalized role at state functions or on social occasions, significant as a factor, a determinant of what happens. Its leaders – the deans – have not exerted real influence, even though some deans have been highly respected.[95] They sometimes either have been too 'strong' for the job, because of the countries they are from or because of their personalities, or they have been too 'weak', largely because they have been in Washington a long time and are detached from their own countries' national agendas. Their very 'neutrality', or disinterestedness in this respect, somewhat neutralizes them, except when, infrequently, they speak on behalf of the corps to the Department of State about technical or other matters of common concern to the corps. The 'coordinator' of the corps – a kind of hidden hand – is often in fact the head of the State Department's Office of the Chief of Protocol. The Chief of Protocol, usually a political appointee of some distinction having a close connection to the White House, the ceremonial affairs of which he (or she) also oversees, can subtly influence the corps and even help to give shape to it. Donald Burnham Ensenat, the current holder of the position, says very naturally, 'My personal relationship with the president is always an unstated asset in this job.'[96]

The primary reason for the lack of initiative and hence the ineffectiveness of the Washington diplomatic corps, as an entity, is that it has never had, and does not now have, a common, corporate agenda – such as the permanent representatives to the United Nations sometimes have had in, for example, collectively addressing the challenge of UN reform. More particularly, its members do not have a shared *political* agenda. The lack of solidarity of the corps in this respect is not mainly due to broad historical, cultural, ideological, or other divisions – 'East' vs. 'West', 'North' vs. 'South', the 'old' Europe vs. 'new' Europe, and so on. The cause is more practical, more basic: most of the issues that Washington's diplomats have to deal with are highly specific ones, requiring detailed knowledge, close attention, and focused effort – as well as youthful energy. They are involved in 'complexity management'.[97]

The 'targets' they are aiming at are many and moving. As Canada's Allan Gotlieb has emphasized, ambassadors in Washington must work with a wide range of actors 'that are constantly shifting, aligning and realigning in ways that can affect or damage the interests of the country he represents'. Therefore a specific strategy needs to be developed for each issue.[98] Much smaller countries, with limited budgets and fewer personnel, may have to concentrate their efforts. For instance, the Serbian embassy, according to its press counsellor Jelena Cukić Matić, decided to target in its communications strategy those journalists who had an interest in her country and the Balkans.[99]

A great power such as the United Kingdom that is deeply invested in the United States cannot so easily be selective. 'In my time as ambassador', Sir Christopher Meyer recalls, 'much energy was wasted in London in debate about the areas on which Britain's representatives in the US should concentrate: notably, should it be the business sector or should it be the politicians? Dumb question. As with the ambassador in Washington, so with the Consuls-General in the great American cities: you had to do everything, to cover all the bases. It was all a single piece of elaborate machinery and you had to be familiar with each of its moving parts.'[100]

Engaging these parts requires networking. 'Network diplomacy' has been contrasted with 'club diplomacy', and it has been put forward as the new and superior model for practicing the craft.[101] Something is lost, however, with the disappearance – or the non-functioning – of the 'club', which is how the diplomatic corps traditionally has been regarded. Could it have new life, as a corporate force, locally applied, of the international community? Individual countries, especially the larger allies of the United States, have been able to exert major influence at Washington. Ambassador Meyer regretted in hindsight that the 'leverage' the British embassy thought the United Kingdom had in 2002 during the period when the US government was preparing for war in Iraq was not used. 'We may have been the junior partner in the enterprise; but the ace up our sleeve was that America did not want to go it alone?'[102] What if the entire diplomatic corps in Washington, not just ambassadors of countries with strong, even special 'bilateral' relationships with the United States, had demanded greater consultation and deliberation before the essentially 'unilateral' American military move of 20 March 2003? 'Multilateral' consideration did not have to be left to the Security Council or other organs of the United Nations in New York. The body of diplomats posted at the US national capital of Washington DC too – where the 'international' decision for war actually was taken – could act. When in Rome, act like Romans. The *genius loci* of those at the place, and the place itself, did not perform.

Notes

1   Gullion served, during the presidency of John F. Kennedy, as US ambassador to the Congo. He later was dean of The Fletcher School of Law and Diplomacy (1964–1978).

2   Sir Ernest Satow, in *Satow's Guide to Diplomatic Practice*, ed. Lord Gore-Booth and Desmond Pakenham (5th ed.; New York: Longman, 1979), defines the 'diplomatic body' (corps diplomatique) as comprising 'the heads and the diplomatic staff of all the missions accredited to a government' (p. 161). Not all diplomats *accredited* to a government of a country actually reside and continuously work in the country's capital city, however. Geoffrey Berridge defines the 'diplomatic corps', not only legally but also somewhat sociologically and geographically, as 'the community of diplomats representing different states' who are 'resident in the same capital'. G. R. Berridge, *Diplomacy: Theory and Practice* (3rd ed.; Houndmills, Basingstoke: Palgrave Macmillan, 2005), p. 112.

3   Harold and Margaret Sprout, *An Ecological Paradigm for the Study of International Politics* (Princeton NJ: Center of International Studies, Woodrow Wilson School of Public and International Affairs, 1968). On the significance of diplomatic sites and their selection, see Alan K. Henrikson, 'The Geography of Diplomacy', in *The Geography of War and Peace: From Death Camps to Diplomacy*, ed. Colin Flint (New York: Oxford University Press, 2005), pp. 369–94.

4   Quoted in Gail Scott, *Diplomatic Dance: The New Embassy Life in America* (Golden CO: Fulcrum Publishing, 1999), p. 118.

5   Michael Teague, *Mrs. L: Conversations with Alice Roosevelt Longworth* (Garden City NY: Doubleday, 1981), p. 198. Cf. the journalist Russell Baker's observation: 'The rhythm of life is small-town and middle-class, which makes the town comfortable. What makes it easy is the cos-

mopolitan worldliness of the people.' Russell Baker, 'It's Middletown-on-the-Potomac', *Washington: A Reader*, ed. Bill Adler (New York: Meredith Press, 1967), pp. 195–204, quotation on p. 200.

6   Alan K. Henrikson, 'A Small, Cozy Town, Global in Scope': Washington, D.C., *EKISTICS*/ΟΙΚΙΣΤΙΚΗ: *The Science and Study of Human Settlements*, vol. 50, no. 299, March/April 1983, pp. 123–45, 149.

7   Charles Krauthammer, 'The Unipolar Moment', *Foreign Affairs: America and the World*, vol. 70, no. 1, winter 1990–1991, pp. 23–33.

8   Some foreign diplomats accredited to the United States, mostly from smaller countries, also are their countries' UN representatives, and they move back and forth between Washington and New York. A size-comparison of the 'diplomatic worlds' of the two cities is actually quite a complicated matter. Washington contains more persons with actual 'diplomatic' status in missions than does New York (4,036 vs. 3,195). In addition, there are 348 'diplomatic' principals in missions to the OAS, and three persons of 'diplomatic'-principal status at the OAS Secretariat. New York, however, has the large UN Secretariat staff (25,950 persons, 91 of them having 'diplomatic'-principal status) and also a sizeable and important consular community. The total personnel of the missions to the UN number 16,143. Thus the grand total of international personnel in New York would be larger, more than 40,000 – against over 30,000 for Washington. These up-to-date figures were helpfully provided by Patricia A. Jackson, a Protocol Officer in the Office of Protocol of the US Department of State, on 26 April 2007. The author would like to thank her, and also Lawrence Dunham, the now-retired Assistant Chief of Protocol, for his analytical counsel and invaluable perspective on this subject. See also Geoffrey Wiseman's chapter in this volume for a treatment of the UN diplomatic corps.

9   The diplomatic 'community' is somewhat broader than the Diplomatic List. It includes not only the professionals and some other staff members of national embassies but also many of the personnel of the international organizations in Washington – as well as many of the officials of the Department of State, some of them themselves career diplomats (Foreign Service Officers), as well as other US government officials who regularly interact with resident foreign diplomats and also foreign-government officials who pass through the city.

10   US Department of State, *Diplomatic List*, winter 2006, www.state.gov/s/cpr/rls/dpl/winter.

11   Larry Luxner, 'Hamas Victory Complicates Mission of Palestinian Diplomat', *The Washington Diplomat*, March 2006.

12   This is an argument advanced, with particular reference to US-European relations, in Alan K. Henrikson, 'A Structural Approach to Transatlantic Unity – A Shift to a New Center of Gravity?', *Slovak Foreign Policy Affairs: Review for International Politics, Security and Integration*, vol. 5, no. 1, spring 2004, pp. 11–23.

13   On the concept of 'diplomatic culture', see Geoffrey Wiseman, 'Pax Americana: Bumping into Diplomatic Culture', *International Studies Perspectives*, vol. 8, no. 4, November 2005, pp. 409–30. He emphasizes 'five norms of that culture: the use of force only as last resort, transparency, continuous dialogue, multilateralism, and civility' (p. 420).

14   Vienna Convention on Diplomatic Relations, 1961, done at Vienna on 18 April 1991, entered into force on 24 April 1964. United Nations, *Treaty Series*, vol. 500, pp. 95ff. For an analysis, see Eileen Denza, *Diplomatic Law: Commentary on the Vienna Convention on Diplomatic Relations* (2nd ed.; Oxford: Clarendon Press, 1998).

15   An observation by a former US State Department official, in telephone conversation with author, 24 April 2007.

16   John Shaw, 'Privilege of Diplomatic Immunity Facing Challenges From All Sides', *The Washington Diplomat*, March 2002. In 'serious' cases, if a prosecutor advises that, except for diplomatic immunity, charges would be pursued, the State Department requests from the sending government a waiver of immunity. If a waiver is refused, the offender's visa is withdrawn, and the offender is expelled. In cases of espionage, a holder of diplomatic immunity may not be arrested as a spy, but is subject to being sent home as *persona non grata*.

17   Renée Romano, 'No Diplomatic Immunity: African Diplomats, the State Department, and Civil Rights, 1961–1964', *The Journal of American History*, vol. 87, no. 2, September 2000, pp. 546–79, quotation on p. 546.

18   Berridge, *Diplomacy*, p. 112.

19   James Sterling Young, *The Washington Community, 1800–1828* (New York: Harcourt Brace Jovanovich, 1966), pp. 31, 219. In 1892 all the European great powers, except for Austria-Hungary, 'raised their legations in Washington to embassies'. Austria-Hungary made its envoy an ambassador in 1902. Ernest R. May, *Imperial Democracy: The Emergence of America as a Great Power* (New York: Harcourt, Brace and World, 1961), p. 5.

20   Henrikson, 'A Small, Cozy Town, Global in Scope': Washington, DC, pp. 133–4, 137. 'In a land of "purple mountain majesty above the fruited plain"', wrote the Oregonian journalist (later US Senator) Richard L. Neuberger following the Second World War, 'the capital is built in a pumped-out swamp.' Neuberger also objected to the racial discrimination he had witnessed in Washington – to 'the Americans who fought in battle against the bigotry of Hitler', completely unacceptable. Richard L. Neuberger, 'Should We Move the Capital to the Rockies?', *The New York Times Magazine*, 6 October 1946.

21   'Remarks to the Trustees and Advisory Committee of the National Cultural Center', 14 November 1961, *Public Papers of the Presidents of the United States: John F. Kennedy, 1961* (Washington DC: United States Government Printing Office, 1961), pp. 719–20.

22   Gretchen Murphy, *Hemispheric Imaginings: The Monroe Doctrine and Narratives of US Empire* (Durham NC: Duke University Press, 2005).

23   Frederick Gutheim, *The Federal City: Plans & Realities*, with the Exhibition by Wilcomb E. Washburn (Washington DC: Smithsonian Institution Press, in cooperation with the National Capital Planning Commission, 1981).

24   Edward S. Corwin, *The President: Office and Powers 1787–1957* (New York: New York University Press, 1957), p. 171. For comprehensive analyses of the problem, see Louis Henkin, *Foreign Affairs and the Constitution* (New York: W. W. Norton, 1975), and Michael J. Glennon, *Constitutional Diplomacy* (Princeton NJ: Princeton University Press, 1990).

25   Lynn Rosellini, 'British Ambassador: Days in Crisis', *The New York Times*, 21 April 1982.
26   See the *Washington Post* series, by Robert G. Kaiser with others, 'Citizen K Street – The Life and Career of Gerald S. J. Cassidy: How Lobbying Became Washington's Biggest Business', blog.washingtonpost.com/citizen-k-street. Also instructive are Simon Romero, 'Republican Strategist Is Taking Heat for Taking Mexico as Client', *The New York Times*, 28 December 2005, and John Shaw, 'Embassies Face Daunting Task of Getting Heard in Washington', *The Washington Diplomat*, April 2007.
27   John Shaw, 'The Peculiar World of Washington Diplomacy: Complexity of System, Pressure on Diplomats Create Intense Mix', *The Washington Diplomat*, February 2001. Twice the US ambassador to Saudi Arabia, Walter Cutler was then president of the non-profit Meridian House International, which works closely with the diplomatic community.
28   Shaw, 'The Peculiar World of Washington Diplomacy'.
29   The present Embassy Row dates from the 1930s. For a virtual 'Embassy Row Tour', see www.embassy.org/embassy_row. An earlier Embassy Row, around the year 1900, ran along 16th Street northward from the White House and Lafayette Park.
30   Sir Christopher Meyer, *DC Confidential: The Controversial Memoirs of Britain's Ambassador to the U.S. at the Time of 9/11 and the Run-up to the Iraq War* (London: Phoenix, 2005), ch. 9 'The Great House', quotation on p. 69.
31   Alan K. Henrikson, 'America's Changing Place in the World', in *Centre and Periphery: Spatial Variation in Politics*, ed. Jean Gottmann (Beverly Hills CA: SAGE Publications, 1980), p. 86.
32   Exceptions were the Baltic states of Estonia, Latvia, and Lithuania, whose takeover and incorporation early in the Second World War by the Soviet Union were not recognized by the United States. Latvia's and Lithuania's prewar legations in Washington continued to function, as did Estonia's Consulate General in New York.
33   Shaw, 'The Peculiar World of Washington Diplomacy'.
34   Shaw, 'The Peculiar World of Washington Diplomacy'.
35   Geoffrey Berridge, Notes on the Origins of the Diplomatic Corps: Constantinople in the 1620s, *Discussion Papers in Diplomacy* [Netherlands Institute of International Relations 'Clingendael'], no. 92, May 2004, p. 1. He continues: 'This person is generally the longest-serving member of the highest class of diplomat accredited to the country in question. He or she acts as mouthpiece to the government of the receiving state on matters of professional concern as well as the representative of the diplomatic corps on certain ceremonial occasions. The diplomatic body has its own meetings, which are presided over by the dean, who is often supported by a vice-dean.'
36   Eileen Denza, noting that the Vienna Convention on Diplomatic Relations does not define the role of the doyen of the corps diplomatique, states, somewhat restrictively: 'The doyen acts as spokesman on the basis of informal consultation with colleagues and is not expected to become involved in political questions.' Denza, *Diplomatic Law*, p. 98.

37   J. J. Jusserand, 'Dedication', in his *With Americans of Past and Present* (New York: C. Scribner, 1916).

38   Charles S. Campbell, Jr., *Anglo-American Understanding* (Baltimore: The Johns Hopkins Press, 1957); Bradford Perkins, *The Great Rapprochement: England and the United States, 1895–1914* (New York: Atheneum, 1968).

39   Howard K. Beale, *Theodore Roosevelt and the Rise of America to World Power* (New York: Collier Books, 1962); Edmund Morris, *Theodore Rex* (New York: Random House, 2001).

40   Nelson Manfred Blake, 'Ambassadors at the Court of Theodore Roosevelt', *Mississippi Valley Historical Review*, vol. 42, no. 2, September 1995, pp. 179–206.

41   Arthur M. Schlesinger, Jr., *The Imperial Presidency* (Boston: Houghton Mifflin, 1973).

42   Wm. Roger Louis and Hedley Bull (eds), *The 'Special Relationship': Anglo-American Relations since 1945* (New York: Oxford University Press, 1986).

43   Christopher Meyer, *DC Confidential: The Controversial Memoirs of Britain's Ambassador to the U.S. at the Time of 9/11 and the Run-up to the Iraq War* (London: Phoenix, 2005), p. 1. It is noteworthy that Meyer banned the Embassy staff's use of the 'special relationship' phrase: 'I wanted our diplomats to take nothing for granted' (p. 56).

44   John Shaw, 'Wide Range of Qualities Distinguish Effective Ambassadors in Washington', *The Washington Diplomat*, April 2006.

45   D. H. Burney, 'Canada-U.S. Relations: Are We Getting It Right?', remarks before The Ranchmen's Club, Calgary, Alberta, 17 November 2005.

46   John Shaw, *The Ambassador: Inside the Life of a Working Diplomat* (Sterling VA: Capital Books, 2006), pp. 56–7, 96.

47   Shaw, *The Ambassador*, p. 44. The correspondent John Shaw, a regular contributor to *The Washington Diplomat*, is a long-time observer of the diplomatic community.

48   Scott, *Diplomatic Dance*, p. xix. Gail Scott is a former Washington DC television anchorwoman and Embassy Row reporter.

49   Craig Mauro, 'Dutch Diplomat Chosen to Be Dean of Defense Attachés in the United States', *The Washington Diplomat*, November 2005.

50   Agricultural Counselors Forum, www.agribusinesscouncil.org/ag.forum.htm.

51   'Ambassador Eva Nowotny Speaks on Austria's Changing Diplomatic Tradition', The Fletcher School of Law and Diplomacy, Tufts University, Medford MA, 22 February 2007, fletcher.tufts.edu/news/2007/02/nowotny.shtml.

52   Madeleine Albright, *Madam Secretary* (New York: Miramax Books, 2003), p. 340.

53   Sanjay Talwani, 'Young Diplomats in D.C. Tackle Big-Time Roles', *The Washington Diplomat*, January 2007.

54   Scott, *Diplomatic Dance*, 206.

55   This was facilitated by the existence, since 1972, of an informal network of diplomatic academies and institutes of international relations, The International Forum on Diplomatic Training (IFDT), textus.diplomacy.edu. See A. H. M. Kirk-Greene, Ralph Feltham, and Ernst Sucharipa, 'International Forum on Diplomatic Training', and Alan Henrikson,

'A Growing Appreciation', in *250 Jahre: Von der Orientalischen zur Diplomatischen Akademie in Wien*, ed. Oliver Rathkolb (Innsbruck: StudienVerlag, 2004), pp. 283–308. Ambassador Jorge Heine of Chile observes that 'many young diplomats from young countries today are being socialized into a certain way of practicing diplomacy precisely at the time when it is becoming obsolete'. Heine, On the Manner of Practising the New Diplomacy, *Working Paper: Reshaping Diplomacy* [The Centre for International Governance Innovation, Waterloo, Ontario], no. 11, October 2006, p. 11.

56   For example, *Protocol for the Modern Diplomat*, prepared by the Transition Center, Foreign Service Institute, US Department of State, Washington DC, 2005, www.state.gov/documents/organization/15742.pdf.

57   This is suggested in Alan K. Henrikson, 'Diplomacy's Possible Futures', *The Hague Journal of Diplomacy*, vol. 1, no. 1 (2006), pp. 3–27, especially pp. 20–6.

58   Scott, *Diplomatic Dance*, p. xvi.

59   'The 38 Hours: Trial by Terror', *Time*, vol. 109, no. 12, 21 March 1977, pp. 14–20.

60   Shaw, 'The Peculiar World of Washington Diplomacy'.

61   Allan E. Gotlieb, 'Canada-US Relations: Some Thoughts about Public Diplomacy', address to The Empire Club of Canada, 10 November 1983, *The Empire Club of Canada Speeches 1983–1984* (Toronto: The Empire Club Foundation, 1984), pp. 101–15. See also Allan Gotlieb, *'I'll Be with You in a Minute, Mr. Ambassador': The Education of a Canadian Diplomat in Washington* (Toronto: University of Toronto Press, 1991), and *The Washington Diaries, 1981–1989* (New York: Random House, 2006).

62   Colin Robertson, *Working with America After 9/11*, January 2005, www.geo.international.gc.ca/can-am/washington/secretariat/p200501-en.asp.

63   Shaw, 'The Peculiar World of Washington Diplomacy'.

64   Denza, *Diplomatic Law*, pp. 375–8. The most famous case was Sir Lionel Sackville-West's 'politically' expressing an apparent preference for the re-election of President Grover Cleveland in 1888 – which prompted his being declared *persona non grata*. Charles S. Campbell, Jr., 'The Dismissal of Lord Sackville', *The Mississippi Historical Review*, vol. 44, no. 4, March 1958, pp. 635–48. Sackville-West was the father-in-law of the authority on diplomacy, Sir Harold Nicolson. This is not the example, however, that Nicolson gives of an ambassador or other envoy becoming 'intolerably obnoxious', and thus ceasing to be 'persona grata', in *Diplomacy* (3rd ed.; New York: Oxford University Press, 1964), pp. 133–4.

65   As Denza comments, the last phrase of Article 41.2 indicates that under 'modern practice' it is 'becoming more usual for direct contact with other government departments to be permitted'. Denza, *Diplomatic Law*, p. 378.

66   Shaw, 'The Peculiar World of Washington Diplomacy'.

67   Scott, *Diplomatic Dance*, p. 28.

68   Scott, *Diplomatic Dance*, pp. 27–8. Ambassador Chrétien, with strong backing from his prime ministerial uncle, sought American support for a

10,000-person multinational force, which Canada offered to lead with the help also of other middle powers, to protect the thousands of Rwandan refugees stranded in camps in Zaire. When some of the refugees started to return to Rwanda, the Canadian initiative lost needed US and international support.

69   African country ambassadors accredited to the United States established an 'umbrella organization' of 'the community of African Ambassadors', called Africa Diplomatic Corps (ADC). The 'vision' of ADC, stated South Africa's Ambassador Barbara Joyce Mosima Masakela, as chair of its Image and Communication Committee, was 'to position the African continent in the USA with the objective to further leverage its contribution to the development of Africa'. 'Africa Diplomatic Corps Launches Africa Week Celebration – May 22–25, 2006 in Washington, DC', allafrica. com/stories/printable/200605180802.html.

70   Africa Diplomatic Corps, 'African Ambassadors Highly Sceptical About the Motives of the Opponents of Africa Bill (African Growth and Opportunity Act)', press release, 29 June 1999.

71   Shaw, 'The Peculiar World of Washington Diplomacy'.

72   US Department of State, *Diplomatic List*.

73   Anatoly Dobrynin, *In Confidence: Moscow's Ambassador to America's Six Cold War Presidents (1962–1986)* (New York: Times Books, Random House, 1995), pp. 493–4. Dobrynin noted of his predecessor (a 'cheerful man', 'friendly to everybody', 'not overburdened with routine business'): 'Sevilla-Sacasa attended all events at Washington's embassies demanded by protocol, until the revolution in Nicaragua deprived him of his ambassadorial post. The same revolution, which was of course anathema to the Reagan administration, made me dean of the diplomatic corps, since I was second only to Sevilla-Sacasa in my length of service in Washington' (p. 494).

74   Hugh Sidey, 'Barometer of Superpowers', *Time*, vol. 127, no. 11, 17 March 1986, p. 41.

75   Dobrynin, *In Confidence*, 494. Gail Scott, in *Diplomatic Dance*, writes (p. 82): 'Count Wilhelm Wachmeister, a favorite tennis partner of President George [H.W.] Bush, served Sweden for 15 years in Washington and was dean of the Washington diplomatic corps from 1986 to 1989. He and his wife, Countess Ulla Wachmeister, chose to stay here after his retirement and are still revered by Washington's old guard as the ultimate diplomatic couple.'

76   'Remarks at a White House Dinner Honoring the Chiefs of Diplomatic Missions', 18 February 1982, *Public Papers of the Presidents of the United States: Ronald Reagan, 1982 – January 1 to July 2, 1982* (Washington DC: Government Printing Office, 1983), pp. 190–2. Actually this was the second of two dinners the Reagans gave, as the entire diplomatic corps and spouses could not be accommodated at one sitting. Ambassador Dobrynin, at the time in Moscow, had not been able to attend the first dinner.

77   'Remarks at a White House Dinner Honoring the Chiefs of Diplomatic Missions'. In a brief conversation with President Reagan afforded by the occasion, Ambassador Dobrynin 'told him frankly that our relations

were, if anything, at their lowest point since the end of World War II'. It later gave him an admitted if mixed pleasure, however, to read in Reagan's *An American Life* the President's written impressions of the evening: 'Everything we've heard is true. They are a most likable couple. In fact, so much so you wonder how they can stick with the Soviet system.' Dobrynin, *In Confidence*, p. 504. Reagan recalls in his memoir that on the day before the dinner he 'had been given a briefing on the astonishing Soviet arms buildup, which left me amazed at its scale, cost, and breadth and the danger it posed to our country'. Ronald Reagan, *An American Life* (New York: Simon and Schuster, 1990), p. 551.

78 Steven R. Weisman, 'Saudi Arabia's Longtime Ambassador to the U.S. Is Resigning', *The New York Times*, 21 July 2005.

79 Robin Wright, 'Saudi Ambassador to U.S. Steps Down After 22 Years', *Washington Post*, 21 July 2005.

80 Helen Cooper and Jim Rutenberg, 'As Saudi Steps Surprise U.S., A Prince Is Sounding Off-Key', *The New York Times*, 29 April 2007.

81 Speech by Ambassador Denis Antoine, chairman of the Permanent Council of the Organization of American States, Washington DC, 11 December 2002, www.oas.org/speeches/speech.asp?sCodigo=02=0495. Antoine, Grenada's permanent representative to the OAS and also its ambassador to the United States, functions as 'Dean of the Ambassadors of the Western Hemisphere and Coordinator of CARICOM Ambassadors in Washington, DC'. www.grenadaembassyusa.org/Ambassador.html.

82 Shaw, 'The Peculiar World of Washington Diplomacy'.

83 Dobrynin, *In Confidence*, p. 547. Dobrynin emphasizes that *policy*, as distinct from diplomacy, was coordinated in Moscow.

84 Scott, *Diplomatic Dance*, p. 118.

85 Meyer, *DC Confidential*, p. 117.

86 Shaw, *The Ambassador*, p. 129.

87 Shaw, *The Ambassador*, p. 47.

88 Nora Bustany, 'Skills Honed in Washington Pay Off for Swede at the U.N.', *The Washington Post*, 21 April 2006.

89 Shaw, 'Embassies Face Daunting Task of Getting Heard in Washington'.

90 Shaw, 'The Peculiar World of Washington Diplomacy'.

91 To Anatoly Dobrynin, habituated to confidential diplomacy, it was 'a virtual oxymoron'. Dobrynin, *In Confidence*, p. 535. On the origin of the term, coined by Edmund Gullion in the early 1960s, see the website of The Edward R. Murrow Center of Public Diplomacy at The Fletcher School of Law and Diplomacy, fletcher.tufts.edu/murrow. For the evolution of the concept, see Jan Melissen (ed.), *The New Public Diplomacy: Soft Power in International Relations* (Houndmills, Basingstoke: Palgrave Macmillan, 2005), and Alan K. Henrikson, What Can Public Diplomacy Achieve?, *Discussion Papers in Diplomacy* [Netherlands Institute of International Relations 'Clingendael'], no. 104, September 2006.

92 Shaw, 'The Peculiar World of Washington Diplomacy'.

93 An example is Wolfgang Ischinger, who served as ambassador of the Federal Republic of Germany in Washington from 2001 to 2006. He went on to London to serve at the Court of St. James's. See also Larry Luxner,

'Many of Washington's Ex-Ambassadors Continue in High-Profile Careers', *The Washington Diplomat*, May 2005.

94   Heine, On the Manner of Practising the New Diplomacy, pp. 12, 18.

95   Sweden's Count Wachmeister surely would be one of these.

96   John Shaw, 'Protocol Chief Relishes Making Diplomacy Direct and Personal', *The Washington Diplomat*, January 2006. For a complete list of the Chiefs of Protocol from the year 1928, see www.state.gov/r/pa/ho/po/12110.htm.

97   Heine, 'On the Manner of Practising the New Diplomacy', p. 5.

98   Shaw, 'Wide Range of Qualities Distinguish Effective Ambassadors in Washington'.

99   Shaw, 'Embassies Face Daunting Task of Getting Heard in Washington'.

100   Meyer, *DC Confidential*, p. 62.

101   Heine, 'On the Manner of Practising the New Diplomacy'.

102   Meyer, *DC Confidential*, pp. 281–2.

4
The London Diplomatic Corps

Peter Lyon

London is a metropolis, a major city, and has been recognized as such since the early 18th century and in some circles from much earlier. Nathan Bailey, an English lexicographer (just before Samuel Johnson) wrote in his *An Universal Etymological English Dictionary,* first published in 1721, that 'London... the Metropolis of Great Britain founded before the City of Rome, walled by Constantine the Great, [is] no ways inferior to the greatest in Europe for Riches and Greatness.' London and hyperbole quite often go together, although diplomacy and carefully contrived understatement are not uncommon.

Very little seems to have been written about the London diplomatic corps or about the office or title of doyen either in London or elsewhere. But it has long been customary for the senior serving diplomat from the date of their accreditation to the Court of Elizabeth II to act as principal representative and spokesperson for the London-based diplomatic corps. Precedence generally is determined by time since the head of mission was accredited in London. In 2006 there is a slight adaptation of this system in that it is Kuwait's Ambassador – the number two in point of seniority – accredited since 1993 who is doyen rather than the Ambassador of the United Arab Emirates, accredited since November 1991, ostensibly because the latter is very often away from London on official business for his government.

In December 2005 the longest serving senior Commonwealth diplomat in London is the High Commissioner for Guyana – in mission, since July 1993. But it is not common to refer to the senior Commonwealth diplomat in London as doyen, perhaps because of the stronger influence of the Commonwealth Secretariat based in London since 1965. The contemporary Commonwealth is functionally a very London-centric association despite its multilateral, even globalizing, rhetoric.

Antecedents

The London Diplomatic Corps may be said to have a long pedigree dating back over four centuries. By the 16th century resident embassies were common throughout Europe. The presence of a number of ambassadors, each purportedly representing the dignity and interests of his sovereign led to contentious issues of precedence among the proto-diplomatic corps. Much diplomatic protocol practiced today derives from solutions pioneered then. In the 17th century the preoccupations of diplomacy began to change emphasis – from representing personal sovereigns to championing state interest; to direct and coordinate this service. In 1626 Cardinal Richelieu set up in France the first modern foreign ministry. This precedent was copied increasingly in the 19th century as sovereignty passed from royal courts to cabinets. The pattern of European diplomacy began to be adopted and adapted by other powers – such as Japan and Thailand, Brazil, the United States and the new countries of South America. By the end of the 19th century the European diplomatic services (especially those of France and Britain) were paradigms for the rest of the world.

Advances in transportation and communications in the 19th and 20th centuries changed the conduct of diplomacy. Ambassadors communicated more frequently and intensely with political leaders in capital cities. Politicians took an increasingly active and detailed role in diplomatic negotiations. Heads of State had participated in major diplomatic conferences (such as the Congress of Vienna of 1814–15 or the Congress of Berlin 1878). But in the late 20th century summitry, other international conferences and the spawning of international organizations brought further standardization and rules for diplomatic processes.

In recent decades, diplomatic tasks have broadened considerably to include economic, cultural, disarmament, technological and other negotiations, usually conducted by or with the support of negotiators who are specialists in particular fields. Diplomats themselves generally have become more specialized in training and expertizes; though some countries, especially small ones, by choice or necessity continue to favour generalists in staffing their small missions.

The notion that there is in being a London diplomatic corps has a long pedigree as readers of Ernest Satow's classic *A Guide to Diplomatic Practice*, first published in 1917, are made aware. Today the London Diplomatic List published annually, by The Stationary Office (TSO), http://www.tsoshop.co.uk is a valuable guide to London's diplomatic world. It contains an alphabetical list of all the representatives of foreign states and Commonwealth countries in London at a particular time, with the names and designations of the persons recorded as composing their Diplomatic Staff. In addition to listing the accredited personnel of the foreign embassies and Commonwealth High Commissions in London, the 'list' provides also their addresses and office telephone numbers and may outline some of their main sectional divisions. In the first and lengthiest, section information is given in alphabetical order of country (over 180 entries). There follows a list of representatives in order of their precedence, a table of each country's National Days, a directory of International Organizations based in Britain, a list of career Consuls-General and Consuls and of Honorary Consuls, and a list also of other representatives offices and of other international organizations located in Britain.

Some knowledge of the geography of London and of the world is indispensable in an appreciation of the London Diplomatic Corps. With so many embassies, high commissions, diplomats' residences and other offices, almost every country included in the diplomatic list is likely to have several other missions as near neighbours. In terms of postal addresses a considerable number of embassies and high commissions in London are to be found in the fashionable W1 and SW1 districts. Requisite office accommodation and appropriate living quarters in London are of great importance for staff and their well being but also from the point of view of the images of their country which they project.

Genius Loci?

Connoisseurs of the topography, transport systems and buildings of London, especially of Embassies and High Commissions, are aware of some of the incongruities of neighbourhood and of location. But it should be noted that London for all its overall size, is a compact city with almost all of the diplomatic missions located within an area which is north of the river Thames, no further east than 'the square mile' of the City, not west of Belgravia, Pimlico and Hammersmith nor north of Regent's Park.

During the decades of British imperial showmanship, there was from 1858 to 1947 an India office within Whitehall and today this history is still aptly commemorated in the India Office library. Today also the offices of the High Commission for India (in a building designed by the famous imperial architect Herbert Baker) are located in Aldwych near to Australia House, the BBC's Overseas Service, the London School of Economics (LSE) and Political Science and the International Institute for Strategic Studies, whereas the High Commission 'for the Islamic Republic of Pakistan' is in Lowndes Square, SW1, near to Knightsbridge and Sloan Street. Pakistan's current head of mission Dr Maleeha Lodhi has a doctorate in politics from the LSE and has also twice served as Pakistan's ambassador in Washington, DC.

Australia, like Canada in having a federal form of government, maintains a sizeable mission amongst the Commonwealth and 'middle powers' accredited in London. Australia House and other Australian-related offices are located very near to India House, the LSE, the BBC Overseas Service. These two senior erstwhile Dominions have much reduced their distinct and physically separate state and provincial offices in recent years. Quebec House very near to the Commonwealth Secretariat in Pall Mall, remains active and courts a high profile even though generally Quebec plays more actively in Paris than in London.

Whatever the size and character of the London Diplomatic Corps today it would be a naïve mistake to assume that it will stay unchanged in the future. By the mid-1980s it seemed to many commentators that with classic decolonization and the consequent spawning of many newly independent states, almost over, there would not be much more than some post-imperial tidying up involving remnants such as Gibraltar, the Falklands and a few more cases (though, ironically, the largest departmental staff in the Foreign and Commonwealth Office (FCO) today is that of the Overseas Territories department). But the collapse of Yugoslavia and then of the Soviet Union meant more successor states and, in London terms, the search for new missions and residencies – and served reminders that the world's political map of sovereignties seldom remains exactly the same for long.

Saudi Arabia's embassy, now one of the biggest in London in size of personnel, is situated in Charles Street in the heart of Mayfair. Another sizeable and nearby Embassy is that of Japan in Piccadilly a few hundred yards from Piccadilly Circus. But by some way the most populous Embassy in London in this age of the *Pax Americana*, is the Embassy of the USA, sprawling over the whole of the western side of Grosvenor Square, with Canada's High Commission building, Macdonald House, directly opposite in the building that once was the American embassy. Canada maintains the Commonwealth's biggest High Commission in London, with about 50 diplomats. As well as the diplomatic and other business conducted from Macdonald House it has a sizeable building, Canada House, on the west side of Trafalgar Square. Formerly Canada's main mission in London, it is now used primarily for Consular and Passport and Cultural purposes.

Zimbabwe, outside the Commonwealth since the 2003 Commonwealth Heads of Government Meeting in Nigeria, has an embassy at the west end of the Strand very near to Charing Cross station, Trafalgar Square and to South Africa's High Commission – all places saturated by recent British history. Nigeria, is the most populous country in Africa. In Commonwealth and demographic terms it is larger than any Commonwealth countries other than India, Bangladesh and Pakistan. It has its High Commission building in Northumberland Avenue, a notoriously crowded street for traffic or parking, opposite the Royal Commonwealth Society's building, the Commonwealth Club, which was another of Herbert Baker's designs. The Commonwealth is eminently a practitioner and user of 'soft power' and thus eminently a diplomatic, rather than a military, organization. Most but not all member states maintain resident missions in London and, thus, London is *par excellence* a centre for practising 'soft diplomacy', a centre for 'think-tanks', learned societies and research and publications concerning diplomacy and international affairs generally.

Think-Tanks

Chatham House in St James Square, present home of the Royal Institute of International Affairs (RIIA and formerly home of W. E. Gladstone) *inter alia* is sometimes nowadays described as a client or dependent of the FCO; whereas devotees of RIIA might claim that they sometimes provide research findings and longer-term perspective on critical issues than is supplied by the FCO. Two other think-tanks may be seen as serious valuable contributors to intellectual discussion of international affairs in London. First and foremost in terms of its age and impact, is the International Institute for Strategic Studies (IISS). Founded in 1958, it is now located just south of the east end of the Strand near Temple underground station. It is thus only a few yards from King's College's prestigious War Studies department and the London School of Economics and Political Science. Second is the Royal United Services Institute (RUSI) located in Whitehall virtually opposite the Horse Guard's parade. RUSI has added to and widened its activities and linkages with other think-tanks in recent years.

Some analysts might add the Commonwealth Club (home of the Royal Commonwealth Society (RCS) since the late 1920s – earlier known as the Royal Empire Society and before that as the Royal

Colonial Society, from the 1860s). But the RCS had to sell its excellent library to Cambridge University over a decade ago, and is identified these days more as a Club than a Learned Society despite the expertise it can mobilize on Commonwealth matters. The RCS is located in Northumberland Avenue (as has been remarked) right opposite Nigeria House. And one should add the Royal Overseas League founded in 1901, now located in Park Street quite near to St James Palace. A full contemporary assessment of think-tanks or societies of interest to diplomats in London would have to include the Westminster Foundation.

Marshall of the London-based Diplomatic Corps

Her Majesty's Marshal of the Diplomatic Corps is a senior member of the Royal Household of the Sovereign of the United Kingdom, and is quintessentially the Queen's principal link with the diplomatic community in London. The office was created in 1920 to replace the former Master of the Ceremonies, an office dating from about 1620. The Marshal organizes the regular presentation of credentials ceremonies for Ambassadors and High Commissioners, and supervises attendances of diplomats at state events. The office which is normally for a ten year term is usually held by a retired senior military man, though the current Marshal is a diplomat, Sir Anthony Figgis, in office as Marshal since 2001, albeit having unusually been Vice-Marshal some time beforehand, from 1991–96. As well as Her Majesty's Vice-Marshal of the Diplomatic Corps, there is at present also Her Majesty's First Assistant Marshal and Her Majesty's Assistant Marshals. And all around London are traces of royalty, the British Crown and family: Buckingham Palace and Windsor Castle, the royal parks, with virtually daily reports of their doings in the self-styled quality newspapers. Rumour has it that at investitures and farewell audiences the Queen is liable to give more time to incoming or outgoing Commonwealth diplomats, not least because she knows about and probably has visited their countries, and she takes very seriously her title as Head of the Commonwealth, a title accepted and appropriate in many senses since she became Britain's reigning monarch in 1952. The London Diplomatic Corps occasionally and politely genuflects to Britain's monarch (less so to the Royal family but unmistakably this corps is an up-to-date modernist and pragmatic set of sub-assemblages.

Paris today is the centre and setting for the Francophone world as, though to a lesser extent, Madrid is capital of the Hispanic and Lisbon of the Lusophone world. And each of these linguistic – cultural capitals nowadays finds some diplomatic – cum post-imperial organizational expression with bureaucracies in their capitals – la Francophonie, the Hispanic and Lusophone 'worlds'. London, according to most Britons, is the principal cultural centre of the English-speaking world despite the undeniable fact that the United States of America, is the much more populous and powerful expression of an English-speaking identity (albeit, a country where Hispanic identity is an increasing and obtrusive linguistic issue, especially throughout the southern border states), and it retains a magnetic 'pull' in this sense which Americans, especially, may tend to underestimate.

International organizations

The London Diplomatic List customarily includes a directory of International Organizations of bodies with a base in London. Such international organizations, and their staff, do not enjoy privileges and immunities as defined in the Diplomatic Privileges Act 1964, but by virtue of separate legislation to which reference is made in each entry of the Directory which make up the Diplomatic List. There are usually about 30 such international organizations. The two principal diplomatic organizations are the Commonwealth Secretariat (ComSec) and the International Maritime Organisation (IMO). There are about 11 European organizations with offices in London and these include the European Commission and the European Parliament.

The International Maritime Organization (formerly the Inter Governmental Maritime Consultative Organization (IMCO)) was established as a specialized agency of the UN by a convention drafted in 1948 at a UN maritime conference in Geneva. The Convention became effective on 17 March 1958 when it had been ratified by 21 countries, including seven with at least 1 million gross tons of shipping each. The IMCO started operations in 1959 and changed its name to the IMO in 1982. It publishes regularly 'IMO News'. The size and character of IMO today reflects the great expansion of maritime matters since the late 1950s – for the Law of the Sea, concerns about the marine environment, exclusive economic zones, fishing regimes or deep sea mining and oil extraction, for example. Located on the Albert Embankment, IMO is a multilingual but not much publicized body. Its principal operative languages are those of the UN family i.e., Arabic, Chinese, English, French, Russian and Spanish.

Three other representative offices and organizations are located in the United Kingdom and listed in the current edition of the London

Diplomatic List. They are the League of Arab States and the 'Palestinian General Delegation', both situated in London. The third delights in the neo-Orwellian title of the 'Independent International Commission on Decommissioning' and is located in Belfast, with the well-known Canadian, General John de Chastelain as Chairman. To these three offices the Diplomatic list attaches the delphic words 'some of the persons listed may have certain privileges and immunities'.

London today, can deservedly be called a multicultural city. Among its many cultures is also diplomatic culture with all the diversities, similarities and adaptabilities this protean and little known – still less, written about – 'culture' entails.

5
The Emergence and Practices of the Oslo Diplomatic Corps

Halvard Leira and Iver B. Neumann

A diplomatic corps is similar to all other collectives in that its identity is relational – i.e., constituted by difference from an Other.[1] It differs from most other collectives in that this Other *must* be of a special kind, representing an internationally recognized state. Without a court or a Ministry of Foreign Affairs, there can be no diplomatic corps. However, these institutions are no longer the defining Other. With the gradual democratization of political life, starting in the 18th century, but gaining in importance chiefly in the 20th century, another group replaced the ministries of foreign affairs as the most important Other for the diplomatic corps; the host societies. In this chapter we provide a longitudinal study of the diplomatic corps in Kristiania/Oslo,[2] through the prism of the triangular identity-relationship between the corps, the Norwegian Ministry of Foreign Affairs and Norwegian society.

There are a couple of particular features that make the Norwegian case particularly relevant for comparative purposes. Firstly, the Norwegian state was one of the few newly independent European states between the Napoleonic wars and the First World War, and as such the establishment of its diplomatic corps is one of a very few cases from a transitional period in the history of diplomacy.[3] Secondly, the corps can be studied not only in its regular practices in Oslo; most of it also followed the Norwegian government into exile in Britain during the Second World War. Finally, and following from the above points, even though there was substantial continuity, the case of the diplomatic corps in Oslo offers the opportunity to study two separate constitutions of a corps; in 1905 and 1945. In the rest of the chapter, we thus pay special attention to these two constitutions, and the interactions between the corps, the Norwegian Ministry of Foreign Affairs and Norwegian society in the years just after 1905 and 1945.

The emergence of a corps

Norway sought full independence in 1905, largely because of a desire to control foreign relations.[4] The country was a parliamentary democracy with universal male suffrage, and with scarcely any domestic nobility and little tradition for thinking about foreign affairs, the foreign policy discourse was permeated by liberal ideas about trade and neutrality. Diplomacy was seen as something inherently distrustful, whereas consuls were seen as useful.[5] The establishment of a diplomatic corps in Kristiania took place in the middle of the democratic transition where both host societies and diplomatic services gradually became more democratic, in a country where the society was fiercely national-democratic, and where privileges of all kinds were suspect. The problem facing the Norwegian Ministry of Foreign Affairs was thus the reconciliation of a suspicious society with a diplomatic corps still heavily influenced by nobility, while establishing its own status as a competent actor in international affairs.

The Norwegian parliament declared independence on 7 June 1905, but Norway was not recognized as an independent state until the Swedish king accepted the dissolution of the union on 26 October. The first foreign diplomat, the former Russian Consul-General, was accredited to the Norwegian court on 30 October, and was shortly followed by representatives of Great Britain, France, Germany, Denmark, Sweden and the United States. These great powers and neighbours were followed by Uruguay in 1906 and Cuba in 1909, and a handful of other countries that side-accredited their ministers in other capitals to Kristiania as well. Kristiania was clearly not counted among the most important diplomatic stations. The relative nearness to the main European capitals nonetheless made it more attractive than many overseas posts. When the British and French ministers were relocated to Mexico and Central America respectively in 1910, the diplomatic corps in Kristiania saw these as obvious demotions.[6]

The resident diplomatic corps remained modest in size until after the Second World War. In 1909, the seven legations were manned by 14 diplomats, of whom six were accompanied by a wife. The number of children was not registered, but the total diplomatic corps including families can hardly have exceeded 35 people.[7] Although the number of states accredited to Kristiania/Oslo grew following the increase in number of states and international organizations in general, there were still as few as 17 foreign legations in Kristiania in the early 1920s. The first female minister was Alexandra Kollontaj, who was in Norway from

1922, and became the first female minister in the world when Norway officially recognized the Soviet Union in 1924.

Novices in the Ministry of Foreign Affairs

Foreign nationals had been present in Norway as consuls since the late 17th century, but in relatively low numbers. They got their exequatur from the king in Copenhagen until 1814, and from 1818 from Norwegian authorities. The Norwegian understanding of international customs and regulations that detail the privileges of diplomats and consuls was nevertheless very limited. The very first entry in the dossier about the diplomatic corps for example deals with what the ministers should be provided when arriving in Oslo. The list included the accoutrements of diplomatic life; duty free lists, circulation cards, diplomatic lists, admission cards to parliament, rules for audience and parliamentary records, the latter according to 'international custom'. A taste of Norway was also included; all ministers received tickets to the Holmenkollen ski festival, skiing being a defining trait of Norwegian national identity.[8] Following the custom of other capitals, the minister of foreign affairs also arranged weekly receptions for the diplomatic corps, a practice that was continued until 1947, only interrupted by the world wars. Correspondence between the Ministry of Foreign Affairs and the diplomatic corps was conducted in French, but incoming letters from the British, American, German, Austrian, Danish and Swedish legations were in the respective languages of those states, and they were answered in Norwegian.

Routine interaction was established relatively easily, but there was some discord. It comes as no surprise that the Swedish representatives were reporting home with a mixture of glee and frustration about the '*manque de politesse*' of the Norwegian Ministry of Foreign Affairs.[9] 'Direct contact between the Norwegian government and foreign diplomats is, as we all know, a relatively new thing, and it is indisputable that every once in a while incidents occur that demonstrate said government's inexperience.'[10]

Frustrations were mutual. The administrative head of the Ministry of Foreign Affairs, Arne Scheel, wrote a long PM (*pro memoria*)[11] in 1908 where he argued that the Ministry's standing *vis-à-vis* the diplomatic corps had to be enhanced, so as to create

> a certain respect for it in the *corps diplomatique*, which is conducive for the professional relationship between the ministry and the

foreign diplomats. [...] One had to expect some suspicion from the foreign representatives, since the ministry's employees were new to diplomacy. It was easy to assume that they were ignorant parvenus, and treat them accordingly. [...] The Norwegian ministry of foreign affairs could be said to rank with the ministry in a smaller, partly civilised overseas state.[12]

Scheel's estimation of how the diplomatic corps perceived the ministry seems accurate, as indicated in a note from the Swedish minister Falkenberg about Scheel:

He has failed to make a favourable impression on the residing heads of mission, and a couple of them have rejected his aspirations for personal decorations. [...] He has, for reasons unknown, been granted a leave of absence to go abroad to a diplomatic station, which led my Russian colleague to congratulate him on this opportunity to experience foreign relations first hand; an opportunity that Mr. Kroupensky believed would serve both him and other Norwegian diplomats well. Mr. Scheel for obvious reasons resented this insinuation, and ended by saying: 'Notre diplomatie est aussi capable et aussi expérimentée que beaucoup d'autres'. 'Non, Monsieur Scheel', Mr. Kroupensky retorted 'Non, elle ne saurait l'étre, car elle n'a quatre ans'.[13]

The scepticism on behalf of the diplomatic corps is not surprising if the administrative head of the ministry actively sought decorations for himself. Kroupensky's comment on the other hand indicates that the diplomatic corps indeed saw the ministry as consisting mostly of 'ignorant parvenus'. Falkenberg would in a like vein some years later wearily comment on the 'violations of the extraterritorial principle that both the Ministry of Foreign Affairs and local authorities seem to be unable to abandon'.[14] Nevertheless, routines were established relatively quickly. Two factors made for smoother sailing. First, the same man was in charge of the contact with the foreign diplomats from 1905 to 1934. Second, as the ministers were rotated out of Kristiania/Oslo, the living memories of the first feeble years also disappeared from the diplomatic corps.

Unruly diplomats

The Norwegian disregard for diplomats, coupled with national fervour in the years after 1905, meant that there were soon complaints about the diplomatic corps from the Norwegian public. The many complaints of the period offer the best glimpse of the interaction between Norwegian society, the Ministry of Foreign Affairs and the diplomatic corps. The complaints bring to the fore patterns of interaction and organization that are invisible in routine matters, and clearly show where the line was drawn with regards to acceptable behaviour and diplomatic immunity and where assimilation was attempted.

The common denominator is the conflict between Norwegian ideas about appropriate behaviour and diplomatic immunity, for bipeds as well as quadrupeds. For example, in the spring of 1909, complaints about the American minister Peirce's dog's attacks on other dogs as well as people were received by the Ministry of Foreign Affairs,[15] and the minister of foreign affairs reacted by sending a personal note to the American minister and trying to solve the issue informally. The Ministry and the minister thus tried to show some tact, but the lack of decisive action backfired when the bulldog was killed in 1911 by the owner of another dog following a dogfight. The press had a field day, discussing the 'dog murder' for more than a week. The complainant from 1909 saluted the act in one of the leading papers, writing that 'When Norwegian law and the Norwegian police are unable to protect me and my property from assaults from the wild beast of a foreign diplomat, there is no other solution than self-defence.'[16] When the Ministry of Foreign Affairs failed to act upon issues that the press and the larger society considered trespassing by the foreign diplomats, it reaped a storm.

We can nevertheless observe 'learning' on behalf of the Ministry of Foreign Affairs, as in the case of what the major Kristiania broadsheet dubbed 'An international showdown in the harbour' in the summer of 1914, where a junior US diplomat and a Norwegian official had a spat over anchoring rights.[17] The incident was seen as a challenge to Norwegian sovereignty and, in the tense climate of the summer of 1914, it was noted by papers in Denmark, Sweden, Germany, Britain and the US.[18] The more radical of the Norwegian papers demanded that the diplomat be recalled by American authorities, and the official complained to the Ministry of Foreign Affairs and considered pressing charges. The Ministry of Foreign Affairs instead arranged for a gentlemen's agreement between the two parties, which was duly publicized. The US legation apologized. The Ministry of Foreign Affairs had learnt the art of diplomatic practice.

The mode of transport that caused most waves, however, was not the boat. Diplomats have lined up to break traffic regulations ever since

Daimler and Benz put a combustion-engine in a car, and the members of the diplomatic corps of Kristiania/Oslo were no exception to this rule. A separate dossier for traffic incidents was created in 1915, and there are hundreds of specific cases in it before the Second World War.[19] The complaints and charges cover irregular driving, speeding, hazardous overtaking and a plethora of parking violations. If need be, the standard response from the Ministry of Foreign Affairs was a verbal note. To the extent that the legations even bothered to reply, they sent some reassuring comments and promised to notify the driver. Considering the modest size of the diplomatic corps throughout the period, the high number of complaints could plausibly be caused by the police and society in general paying special attention to cars with diplomatic plates. This might again be a reflection of who the regular offenders were, or that there were relatively few cars in Norway at the time.[20]

Some of the diplomats resided permanently at the expensive hotels of Kristiania, but the larger legations soon acquired their own offices and houses, tightly bunched in the equally expensive and fashionable west end of the city. Junior diplomats usually rented apartments, and complaints regarding such arrangements, particularly tardiness or complete absence of payments of rent, are second only to the driving infractions. Few legations took any responsibility for their diplomats, particularly those who had left the country, and the Ministry of Foreign Affairs left it to the landlords to raise charges against the perpetrators in their home country. There is, however, one single example from this period of the Ministry of Foreign Affairs laying down the law when a diplomat failed to pay his dues. The delinquent is once again to be found in the US legation; the chancellor of the legation, Edgar M. Campion, who, starting in 1922, repeatedly neglected to pay his bills and imported large quantities of alcohol regardless of prohibition and other regulations.[21] In November 1924, following repeated transgressions, the secretary-general asked for a PM from his subordinates 'so that the minister of foreign affairs can talk to [minister] Swenson about the issue and ask for C.'s removal from the US legation'.[22] Asking for the rappel of a foreign diplomat is obviously a serious matter, in diplomatic terms second only to declaring him *persona non grata* and expelling him. After yet more complaints, the Ministry of Foreign Affairs were finally prepared to ask for Campion's removal in 1926, but an informal call on the minister revealed that by then he himself had asked to be relieved of his duties.[23]

L'affaire Campion demonstrates that the Ministry of Foreign Affairs was willing to let the diplomatic corps get away with extensive violations of the accepted behavioural code. The pattern of interaction is also obvious, and different from the early years when the ministers only wanted to discuss matters with the minister of foreign affairs. The chief of protocol handled the regular interaction and formal requests, while diplomats could be summoned to the secretary-general or even the minister in case of more serious problems. Even if such conferences were formal and sombre, the approach to the problem at hand was typically informal. The conferences were conducted face-to-face, usually without any other persons present, and without written records. Official notes were only sent if informal procedures failed.

Such interaction is not only in line with diplomatic courtesy; it helped, and still helps, save the diplomat's face at home. A diplomat does not have to send reports home about informal conferences, whereas formal notes will be archived at the station and possibly be attached to the personal file of the diplomat. The oft-noted establishment of a 'new' diplomacy following the First World War thus did not undermine the diplomatic sense of community. By giving Campion a chance to resign with his reputation at home intact, the Ministry of Foreign Affairs confirmed a practice that could also benefit Norwegian diplomats abroad.

During the prohibition years the illegal selling of alcohol was a serious matter. The diplomatic corps was entitled to import alcohol for its own consumption, and could buy additional quanta with local wine sellers.[24] Only legations could buy liquor, and only by providing special slips. In spite of this, the minister of foreign affairs made a 'gentlemen's agreement' with the British minister, allowing the British consuls to import liquor. This was clearly in breach of Norwegian regulations, and a clear example of how some foreign representatives were more equal than others, in spite of the formal equality among the members of the diplomatic corps.

The press eagerly spread rumours about illegal sales of liquor by the foreign legations. When a leading abolitionist in January 1925 suggested that several legations in Oslo engaged in bootlegging, the reaction from the diplomatic corps was swift. The doyen complained to the Ministry of Foreign Affairs, and the secretary-general promptly told the press that 'Apart from one particular occasion, we know of no instance where foreign diplomats have abused the diplomatic privilege of free imports'.[25] This was at best only partly true, as several cases had been glossed over, as when a Swedish secretary of legation was removed and demoted by the Swedish minister, and 'the issue thus was solved without correspondence'. This comment is telling, even more so because it is the only archival reference to the incident whatsoever. The comment demonstrates how the Ministry of Foreign Affairs and the diplomatic corps had come to be on close terms. The Ministry of Foreign Affairs made serious efforts to shield the diplomatic corps, even if diplomats had broken Norwegian law, and to protect them against unwanted attention and loss of face, if the diplomats in return put their house in order.

The major scandal of the period involved the German courier, baron von Rautenfels, during the First World War.[26] He and two associates had hid 600–700 kg of bombs and explosives in an apartment in Kristiania, explosives that had been brought to the country in suitcases sealed with 'Auswärtiges Amt, Berlin', addressed to the German legation. The explosives were intended for ships departing Norway. The incident caused an enormous uproar. German authorities protested against the arrest, and demanded that the courier be released. The Ministry of Foreign Affairs knew that this would be the final outcome, but the courier was kept behind bars for a few days, primarily as it would seem to placate the police and the press. In this case, the right to self-defence outweighed diplomatic immunity and the inviolability of diplomatic luggage. In this, the Norwegian Ministry of Foreign Affairs was most likely in line with most of its foreign counterparts.

Norwegian society clearly saw the diplomatic corps as strangers in the early years, and the often virulent attacks on diplomats in the papers indicate that at least some members of society would prefer to isolate the diplomatic corps from the larger society. The Ministry of Foreign Affairs, on the other hand, as soon as they had learnt the basics, treated the diplomats with politeness bordering on servility. Extraterritorial rights were respected as long as the diplomats refrained from importing bombs or ridiculous amounts of alcohol, and did not drive while intoxicated. The general impression is that on most occasions the Ministry of Foreign Affairs bent over backwards in an effort to accommodate the diplomatic corps. This is perhaps what one would expect from the Ministry of Foreign Affairs of a small country that first and foremost wanted to be recognized as a sovereign state. A more benevolent reading would be that the relations between the Ministry of Foreign Affairs and the diplomatic corps were marked by increasing mutual respect, understanding and community spirit. The Ministry of Foreign Affairs was not only concerned about the fit between the diplomatic corps and Norwegian society, its diplomats desperately wanted to be recognized as competent actors themselves. Increasingly, they came to see themselves as members of a larger international community of diplomats and Ministries of Foreign Affairs. The fit between the larger diplomatic community and the Norwegian diplomats was thus also at stake. In the mediation between a diplomatic corps still infused with the ideals of nobility and a democratic society, the Ministry of Foreign Affairs made sure that the diplomatic corps did not have to change too much. By protecting the diplomats in Kristiania/ Oslo from too much 'hassle', general diplomatic privileges were upheld, privileges that Norwegian diplomats also enjoyed. If the challenge posed to national values by the conduct of diplomats was strong then these values might prevail over international norms, but in the day-to-day business the international context for diplomatic interaction prevailed.

Friends and allies

On 9 April 1940, German troops invaded Norway, and after a two-month campaign the King and the Government fled the country for London. A diplomatic corps is supposed to be where the Ministry of Foreign Affairs is, and as the Ministry of Foreign Affairs evacuated Oslo and was split up, so was the diplomatic corps. Quite a few members of the diplomatic corps joined the Government in fleeing Oslo, and the representatives of countries at war with Germany followed the government all the way to London, after leaving representatives of neutral countries in charge of their affairs in Norway. The neutral representatives returned to Oslo, while the Swedish secretary of legation acted as a liaison between Norwegian and Swedish authorities, crossing the border on skis on more than one occasion. As long as there were expectations of a Quisling regime in Norway, the diplomats from neutral countries were allowed to stay, but in early July an end was put to these expectations.[27] The diplomats and their families were given two weeks to pack up and leave, while minimal consular representation was accepted.

While the diplomatic corps in Oslo was dismantled, the rebuilding of one in London commenced, to a larger extent than before centred on the King. In the early years, most allied powers and neutrals accredited one of their diplomats already in London to the Norwegian court in London, but as the tide of war turned and Norway gained respect as an ally, the status was increased. In 1942, the major allied powers decided to upgrade their representation with the smaller allies, like the Netherlands and Norway. Thus, Anthony J. Drexel Biddle, Jr. of the US was the first ambassador to Norway and according to rank automatically became doyen.[28] Other governments in exile followed the same procedure, and the Norwegian government had ministers accredited to the Belgian, Dutch and Polish governments in London. The belief was that exile should interfere as little as possible with representational logic, even if the actual practices were necessarily somewhat improvized.

Meanwhile, back in Oslo, what was left of the administrative structures of the Ministry of Foreign Affairs kept up contacts with the rapidly diminishing consular corps, where at least some of the representatives conducted some clandestine diplomacy as well. In the first year of the war, the Swedish consulate acted as an informal central of contact between Norwegians abroad and in Norway. The number of foreign consuls declined from ten in 1940 to six in 1941, four in 1943 and just three (Denmark, Sweden and Italy) in 1944–45.[29] Social interaction was kept up among the consuls, and between the consuls and the German authorities and the Norwegian puppet regime, much to the chagrin of the Norwegian representatives in exile.

Mutual understanding

As the Second World War wound down, the Ministry of Foreign Affairs realized that it, and Norway, could ill afford a repeat of the first stumbling years after 1905. This was made even clearer by the reports of chaotic scenes that met the first diplomats to return to Brussels from exile in 1944. The Ministry of Foreign Affairs wanted to do better in Oslo, and decided to recreate a protocol department, 'with an older minister as chief of protocol'.[30] It proved wise to be well prepared, as the first foreign diplomats (three Americans and a Briton) were in Oslo on 19 May, less than two weeks after the final surrender of German troops in Norway.[31] A large contingent of diplomats followed the Government on its return in late May, for example 19 American diplomats and clerks and the US ambassador's wife.[32] As soon as the Ministry of Foreign Affairs had made sure that the situation in Oslo was stable and secure, the rest of the diplomatic corps was invited to follow suit.

The draft diplomatic lists from the summer of 1945 detail nine legations and embassies in Oslo, a number that increased steadily as diplomatic interaction picked up after the war.[33] In early 1946, 30 countries were represented in Oslo, of which 22 at least in principle were physically present. The numbers continued to grow, and in 1960 there were 36 diplomatic stations in Oslo.[34] As the number of stations grew, so did the diplomatic corps. There were 103 diplomats in the diplomatic list of 1946, most of them with wives. The largest station was the American embassy, which employed 121 men and women in 1946. The British embassy was a distant second, with 32 employees.[35] In early 1957 there were 455 people in the diplomatic list, and the total number of foreigners, including junior employees, servants and family, exceeded 1,200.[36]

Small-talk and gossip

In spite of the increase in number of diplomats, and the concurrent increase in possibilities for blunders, the protocol department seems to have handled the procedural subtleties a lot better than their counterparts in 1905. From 1945 to 1960, there are only two registered complaints by the diplomatic corps. This might imply that complaints were presented orally, but from what we can see in other archives, the attitude seems to have been one of satisfaction. There will, nevertheless, always be some malcontents. The British ambassador Wright for example reported in 1951 that the wife of his Danish colleague had 'a caustic tongue and cannot refrain from comparing Oslo to its disadvantage with The Hague, her husband's last post – which has earned her the title of "the Danish Ambassador's Dutch wife"'.[37]

Upon becoming doyen in 1950, US ambassador Bay took steps to make interaction more standardized. On the basis of comments on an original draft, he presented what amounts to the first 'Protocol Recommended for Observance by the Diplomatic Corps in Oslo' in 1953.[38] The Soviet dean tried to instigate common diplomatic corps activities and presented revised rules of protocol in 1961, but had little luck: 'The response from the Corps has been largely unenthusiastic, in some cases antagonistic',[39] was the comment from the US embassy in an Aerogram bearing the heading 'The Diplomatic Corps under the Red Dean'. The Cold War affected the diplomatic corps, but there were some attempts at general activities: 'For a number of years there has existed in Oslo a most irregular and informal luncheon arrangement for diplomats below the rank of Chief of Mission, called "Diplomats Uninhibited". [...] the consensus of NATO diplomats is that the organization, while otherwise of little or no use, is clearly welcomed by Bloc diplomats who have far less opportunity to meet their colleagues than do Westerners'.[40]

There were also a few regular venues where all members of the diplomatic corps could meet. Both the king and the minister of foreign

affairs gave annual dinners for the diplomatic corps, but regular receptions for heads of mission in the ministry were abandoned in 1947, as the
diplomatic corps grew too big and the international political climate
became tenser. Other dinners and receptions were as common as in every
other capital, and the diplomats certainly met enough to be able to report
home. Such reports offer some of the best snapshots of the inner life of
the diplomatic corps, and also of the interactions between the diplomatic
corps and the Ministry of Foreign Affairs, as seen through the eyes of the
diplomats. The British ambassador Collier, for example, could scarcely
hide his satisfaction when reporting how the Yugoslav minister 'presented his credentials as minister on 14 April, 1947, and shortly afterwards shocked the Oslo press (and those of his diplomatic colleagues who
heard about it) by issuing a virulent attack upon Great Britain and the
United States, for which he was privately rebuked by the Norwegian
Ministry for Foreign Affairs'.[41] Collier's successor, Wright, must also have
been satisfied with his description of his Czechoslovak counterpart, who
'looks what he doubtless is – a negative timeserver without character and
without convictions'.[42] Representatives of neutral countries were also
weighed, the Mexican minister in 1947 was:

> the most picturesque figure in the Diplomatic Corps and a godsend
> to the press photographers of Oslo. He has an enormous white
> beard, a solemn expression, something of a Regency flourish and an
> astonishing appetite. He is a man of long and awesome silences,
> which he breaks to utter unpredictable remarks in any one of three
> languages, none of which he fully commands.[43]

Even allied representatives were scrutinized, and the French representatives fared worst. The ambassador and his wife were in 1947 'in
spite of their social distinction (or perhaps because of it), [...] not
popular in Norwegian society, which finds them too "stand-offish"'.
When we learn that the ambassador brought 'three "chefs" and three
maitresses des Hotel and 17 servants', it comes as no surprise that he
had a hard time fitting into Norwegian society even though 'the lunch
was very tasty'.[44] The subsequent French ambassador fared even worse,
in 1951 Wright commented that he: 'seems amiable and intelligent but
his appearance is rather unimpressive and I do not think that he belies
it'. The reports are, however, generally positive when dealing with the
leading Norwegian personalities.

Ties to the US were also strong, and grew in importance as the Cold
War grew colder. The US practice of picking ambassadors to Oslo with

familial ties to Norway further intensified the relations. Ambassador Bay, who arrived in 1946, was for example a nephew of an earlier Norwegian cabinet minister, and would prove to be enormously popular.[45] In different press-clippings from the late 1940s, we learn that he and his wife gave talks and lectures about Norway while they were in the US on holidays, and that they invited orphaned children to Christmas parties in their home. The couple also adopted three Norwegian children, and the Crown Prince of Norway was godfather to them. Bay also adopted the characteristically Norwegian activities. The main Labour newspaper described how he could be found 'in his sailing-boat in June, fishing salmon in August and skiing in the mountains in winter'[46] When Bay left in 1953, he was given a royal send-off. As in the British reports, the American ones are brim-full of items about conversations with leading Norwegians, and also some contacts of a more undisclosed nature. Sources in the Ministry of Foreign Affairs are in such instances referred to as 'our source' and 'our informant'.[47]

Annoyances

Diplomats from allied countries got away with more than diplomats from neutral countries. With regards to diplomats from communist countries, the Ministry of Foreign Affairs had to balance reactions, so as to not provoke retaliations. The complaints follow the same pattern as before; the problems were dogs, currency transactions, smuggling, reckless driving and diplomats who overstepped the boundaries of acceptable behaviour. The number of complaints was nevertheless not as high as in the previous period. One major difference from the prewar years lies in the willingness of the Ministry of Foreign Affairs to act on behalf of Norwegians who felt cheated. This change is mirrored by an increased willingness among the Ministries of Foreign Affairs of the world to either force their diplomats to pay up, or cover their bills through the Ministry of Foreign Affairs budget.

The dog-problems seem to have diminished after the Second World War, although the Turkish minister's dog bit passers-by in 1952.[48] The combination of diplomats and combustion engines, however, continued to be an explosive one, although there was a sharp drop in charges of wrongful parking in the immediate after-war years, probably due to the creation of special diplomatic corps parking zones.[49] We are, however, unable to trace these developments, as the newer dossiers on parking are, incidentally, among the very few to have been shredded.

Bootlegging had been a recurring problem regarding the diplomatic corps during the prohibition years, and as there were import restrictions on a whole host of goods following the Second World War, the scope for items to be smuggled was larger. Drawing on previous experience, the Ministry of Foreign Affairs arranged for a simplified procedure for tax-free orders from the diplomatic corps as early as July 1945. The spirit of the times was still one of control, and the Ministry did pay attention. In an internal exchange of notes from the autumn of 1945 we find the following: 'I believe that the Czechs drink too much cognac! Have a look at their orders, and let me know what you think'. Reply: 'it is conceivable that the legation finds it more <u>practical</u> to order more at the time. I don't think that we should react, <u>yet</u>'.[50] It was duly noted that the Czechoslovak legation received 128,000 cigarettes and 1,450 cigars between December 1946 and July 1947. Since the legation included two diplomats and six non-diplomats, this equals 75 cigarettes and a cigar per person per day. Over the course of a month and a half during the summer of 1947, the legation also ordered 160 bottles of liquor and 64 bottles of wine. The situation was 'described informally for the head of the legation. Since the ministry has been informed that there will shortly be a change of personnel at the legation, I found it neither necessary nor desirable to take any further action'.[51] The Ministry of Foreign Affairs followed its *modus operandi*; stayed back and allowed matters to resolve themselves, rather than taking any specific action. The most curious case of smuggling concerns the Cuban minister's unmusical imports in 1951. The British ambassador reported:

> It has just been announced that Señor Xiques is to be transferred to the Far East but his replacement has not yet arrived. His departure is connected with the discovery that during his eighteen months in Norway he has imported under diplomatic privilege and then sold twelve grand pianos.[52]

There were several rather embarrassing drunk-driving incidents among the diplomats in the 1950s.[53] The Belgian minister was caught in 1950, and again in 1952 and 1953, but although summoned to the ministry, faced no further consequences. It is tempting to see this as a result of Belgium being an allied state, particularly when we compare his situation to the one of the Cuban minister. When the Belgian was caught while driving drunk in 1956, the leading liberal paper demanded his immediate recall. When the minister was brought to the emergency ward two weeks later, dead drunk and with a cut over the nose, the secretary-general of the Ministry of Foreign Affairs reacted:

> I told him that he had to understand that under the circumstances he could not continue as minister to Norway, and I asked him to arrange a transfer as soon as possible. He promised to do so, adding that he would visit Copenhagen and Stockholm, where he is also accredited, and that he would not return to Oslo after that.

Once again the incident found a solution that allowed the diplomat to save face, and saved the Ministry of Foreign Affairs from the unpleasantness of declaring him *persona non grata*.

The first secretary of the Turkish legation was less lucky. He was involved in three separate incidents during the autumn and winter 1952–53, including drunken driving, rowdiness, battery and threats against the police, before the Turkish minister was asked to arrange for his recall. He managed to be involved in yet another car crash before he left the following autumn. Even here the Ministry of Foreign Affairs avoided involving the Ministry of Foreign Affairs of the visiting diplomat directly, but arranged matters bilaterally with the Turkish legation. Some legations would also enforce internal discipline, as when the Czechoslovak commercial attaché left on 'vacation' shortly after being caught driving drunk.

Norwegian society seems to have had a more relaxed attitude towards the diplomatic corps in the years after 1945 than in the years after 1905. The attacks in the press were fewer and less virulent, and even if most Norwegians had little understanding of diplomacy as such, they seem to have realized the importance of having good diplomatic relations with other states. The further democratization of diplomacy that followed the Second World War must also have contributed to this changing attitude, as the gulf between the values of the diplomatic corps and the values of Norwegian society seemed less wide. The Ministry of Foreign Affairs continued its balancing act, but took a firmer stand on behalf of Norwegian interests. We might well interpret this as an indication of the secure position the Ministry of Foreign Affairs now had in international society.

As for the diplomatic corps, a degree of assimilation clearly influenced both how the diplomats were seen in society, how they were treated by the Ministry of Foreign Affairs and the informal hierarchies of the diplomatic corps. Representatives of the major allies had considerable leeway, and seem sometimes almost to have 'gone native'.

Representatives of lesser allies and culturally close countries were also generally seen in a positive light, while communist diplomats were given formal treatment by the Ministry of Foreign Affairs and there were no attempts at assimilation. Even though not isolated by Norwegian society, the communist diplomats themselves had only limited interaction with Norwegians, and the possibility of assimilation never seems to have presented itself.

During the Cold War, the diplomatic corps in Oslo continued to grow, partly through an increase in the number of employees, partly through an increase of legations in Oslo. The end of the Cold War provided a particularly quick spurt of growth. Interactions were institutionalized, with the central relationship being the one between the head of the protocol department and the doyen. In addition to the yearly dinners and receptions for the diplomatic corps, an annual (later bi-annual) excursion was arranged for the entire diplomatic corps. It lasted for two to three days, and included meetings between the Ministry of Foreign Affairs and the diplomatic corps discussing current topics in Norwegian foreign policy. The routine is also obvious in one secretary-general's summary of what a speech at a farewell dinner for a departing ambassador sounded like:

> We will miss the ambassador. The ambassador has made loads of friends in Norway. The ambassador has shown great hospitality. The ambassador has made a valuable contribution in strengthening the ties between our countries. Then I decorate the ambassador with the Grand Cross of the order of St. Olav.[54]

The number of mishaps and incidents continued to decline. There were the odd collisions and cases of drunken driving, some excessive imports of alcohol and breaches of the gun-law. Matters only came to a head on very rare occasions. The general attitude of the Ministry of Foreign Affairs was still that embassies were allowed to withdraw diplomats rather than suffer the embarrassment of expulsion.

Based on cursory interviews, the diplomatic corps of Oslo today seems to be of most importance for higher-level diplomats from smaller embassies with no particular ties to Norway, and of use as a social network and as a vehicle for exchange of information. The diplomats from larger embassies, often with closer ties to Norway, handle their information-gathering bilaterally with the Ministry of Foreign Affairs, and are, due to the size of their ex-patriot communities, less in need of the social safety-net that the corps provides.

Conclusion

The dearth of juicy stories from the last recent decades is not only due to missing source materials. Generally, the activities of the diplomatic corps are not a theme in Norwegian public discourse, in stark contrast to the situation in the decades after 1905.[55] First, the composition of the diplomatic corps has changed significantly. Increasing demo-cratization and bureaucratization of diplomacy as such, as well as the codification of acceptable behaviour, have led the average diplomat to become a lot more similar to the average Norwegian, and a lot less likely to cause any incidents. Secondly, Norwegian society has also undergone major changes in the wake of globalization. As Norwegians increasingly travel abroad and become conversant with other coun-tries and cultures, the diplomats become less exotic. The influx of immigrants, refugees and asylum seekers further diluted their special character. There were obviously immigrants and refugees in Kristiania in the years around 1905 as well, but there were fewer of them, they were less visible in dress and skin-colour, and, above all, they were less visible in the part of town where the leaders of public discourse gen-erally resided, the west end. Seen from the perspective of a bourgeois west-ender around 1905, the diplomats must have been the most obvious 'strangers'. A century later, the observable differences between the diplomatic corps and a much more heterogeneous and less hierar-chical society are smaller. Differences in identity, economy and social standing between the average diplomat and the average Norwegian are a lot smaller, and the spectre of normalcy for the average Nor-wegian is a lot wider. Thus, the felt necessity of assimilation has all but disappeared. As the diplomats ceased to be the most visible 'strangers' in Norwegian society, the attempts at assimilation were directed elsewhere. Finally, what with terrorism, sex, violence, murder, sports and the other preoccupations of consumer journalism, the media care a lot less about any diplomatic incidents that might actually take place.

Returning to the triangular relationship outlined at the start of the chapter, the relationship between the diplomatic corps and the Nor-wegian society has developed from mutual suspicion and incompre-hension in the early decades, through acceptance and relatively advanced assimilation (at least of some diplomats) in the immediate postwar years to today's indifference on the part of Norwegian society. The two poles have come much closer to one another. The diplomats are assimilating to the extent necessary to do their job, but there is no pressure from society. The balancing act of the Ministry of Foreign Affairs is thus a lot easier than it used to be, as there is no perceived need for a filter that protects society against the diplomats. As there is less pressure on the diplomatic corps from society, it is also easier to ensure the special rights of the diplomats. Whereas the Ministry of Foreign Affairs spent the first years after 1905 trying to become more similar to the diplomats in the corps so as to gain acceptance, general diplomatic culture over the last 60 years has moved a lot closer to what are perceived as Norwegian values.

The trajectory of the Kristiania/Oslo diplomatic corps confirms many of the general expectations we have of a corps. It was more important when it was smaller, and when political ties were weaker. There have been few instances of concerted action by the corps, but the doyen has acted as intermediary in some of the more contentious cases. The inter-actions between the corps and the Ministry of Foreign Affairs and the Norwegian society also illustrate in varied detail how diplomacy is about so much more than representation. The corps has been con-cerned with greasing the wheels of interaction and ensuring privileges, and very seldom with power-issues. In short, it has been acting as an embodiment of international society.

Through its first century, the diplomatic corps of Kristiania/Oslo has transformed from a potential enemy within to seemingly just another group of foreigners living in Norway. This change, as demonstrated above, has not been due to successful assimilation from Norwegian society, but to a large extent stems from changes in how Norwegians see themselves and the world around them. While this more relaxed reaction to otherness is morally commendable, it has left the diplo-matic corps with not much more than ceremonial tasks. Toasting at royal dinners might be less arduous on the doyen than representing the corps in relations with a nationalist society and an upstart Ministry of Foreign Affairs, but the change nonetheless speaks volumes for the reduced importance of the corps specifically and diplomats more generally under peaceful and orderly conditions.

Notes

1   This article draws on research done for our history of the Norwegian foreign service (I. B. Neumann & H. Leira, *Aktiv og avventende. Utenrikstjenestes liv 1905–2005* [Oslo: Pax, 2005]), funded by the Norwegian Ministry of Foreign Affairs, research conducted in national archives in Oslo, Stockholm, Washington DC and London. A previous version was presented at the 46th annual ISA convention, Honolulu, Hawaii. We are thankful for the comments from the discussant, Paul Sharp, and our co-panelists.

2 The city was known as Oslo until 1624, then as Christiania until 1877 and Kristiania until 1925, when it was re-baptised Oslo.
3 Cf. F. H. Hinsley, *Power and the Pursuit of Peace: Theory and Practice in the History of International Relations* (Cambridge: CUP, 1963), p. 250n. Whereas 'new' corps were established with the unifications of Italy and Germany, these had direct precedents in the corps' to Prussia and Sardinia.
4 A polity called Norway had existed since the Middle Ages, but had been a part of a Danish-led conglomerate state from 1380 to 1814, and in a personal union with Sweden since 1814.
5 Cf. O. Riste, *Norway's Foreign Relations* (Oslo: Universitetsforlaget, 2005).
6 Swedish National Archives (hereafter SNA) 1P5-19, volume 106–7(a+b). All archival files are from the respective countries' Ministry of Foreign Affairs archives, unless otherwise stated.
7 The total population of Kristiania at the time was slightly above 250,000.
8 Norwegian National Archives (hereafter NNA) G7D 1/06, box 238. Translations from Norwegian and Swedish are by the authors.
9 SNA 1O10, volume 50–2.
10 SNA 1P5-19, volume 106–7(a+b).
11 The term used to refer to memos and notes in the Ministry of Foreign Affairs until the middle of the century.
12 NNA G3A 5/06, box 188.
13 SNA 1P5-19, volume 106–7(a+b).
14 *Ibid.*
15 NNA G6E 1/09, box 353.
16 *Morgenbladet*, 8 March 1911.
17 *Aftenposten* 20 July 1914, see NNA G6E 2/14, box 482.
18 The political climate made it of obvious interest how Norway positioned itself *vis-à-vis* the US. Added to this was the twist that the spat was over an anchoring site that had to be vacated because the yacht of the German emperor was expected.
19 NNA G6E 1/15, box 506.
20 In 1915 there were less than 1,300 cars in Norway.
21 NNA G6E 2/23, box 704 & NNA G7E1/16, box 524b. Prohibition in Norway was established temporarily due to rationing in December 1916, and was made 'permanent' as a result of a referendum in 1919. It was abolished after another referendum in 1926. Diplomats were exempt from it throughout.
22 The secretary-general was (and is) the highest ranking civil servant in the Ministry.
23 A similar case revolved around the the first Chilean diplomatic representative to Kristiania, Chargé d'Affaires Mundt Vasquez de Victoria, who was involved in more than one bootlegging-case between 1919 and 1924. What brought about his downfall was nevertheless the fact that his government discovered that he claimed a noble title that he had no right to. Mundt was thus not relieved of his duties until his own government reacted, and he left quietly, so that there was no scandal associated with Chile or the diplomatic corps of Kristiania. NNA G7E1/16b, box 524b.
24 NNA G7E1/16, box 524b.
25 Cf. *Morgenbladet* 12 January 1925.
26 NNA P2M14/17, box 5792.

27 From the autumn of 1940, the supreme authority in name and game in Norway was the German Reichskommissar. The Norwegian civilian structures were, however, mostly kept in place.

28 National Archives and Records Administration (hereafter NARA), RG 84, Norway, box 3. Biddle holds the record for multiple accreditations in the US Foreign Service, being accredited to the governments-in-exile in London of Belgium, Czechoslovakia, Greece, Luxembourg, the Netherlands, Poland, and Yugoslavia, apart from Norway.

29 NNA G5A 3/24, box 6888.

30 NNA 2.25/30, box 10051.

31 NNA 14.21/13, box 10155.

32 NNA 14.21/47, box 10159–60.

33 NNA 14.1/2, box 10124–6.

34 NNA 14.1/2, box 542–4. The last of the permanent legations were upgraded to embassies in 1961–2.

35 Both these numbers include Norwegian employees; the number of diplomats was usually around one quarter of the total.

36 NNA 2.25/30, box 445. Cf. 2.5/65, box 67–8.

37 British National Archives (hereafter BNA) FO 491/5, Foreign Office: Confidential Print Norway 1951.

38 NARA, RG 84, Oslo Legation and Embassy, General Records 350 66 01 01, Entry 3050, Box 1 (second series), File 301 – Diplomatic and consular representation.

39 NARA, RG 84, Oslo Legation and Embassy, Classified General Records 1956–61, 350 66 03 01-03, Entry 3054b, Box 10.

40 *Ibid.*

41 BNA, FO 371/66028, Heads of Foreign Missions in Norway 1947.

42 BNA, FO 491/5, Foreign Office: Confidential Print Norway 1951.

43 BNA, FO 371/66028, Heads of Foreign Missions in Norway 1947.

44 A. Ording (ed. G. Mordt), *Arne Ordings dagbøker, vol. 2* (Oslo: Universitetsforlaget, 2003), p. 79.

45 NNA 14.21/47, box 10159–60b.

46 *Arbeiderbladet* 29 October 1949.

47 NARA, RG 84, Oslo Embassy, Top Secret Records 1947–52, 350 66 02 06, Entry 3053, Box 2, Folder 9.

48 NNA 14.1/19, box 550.

49 NNA 14.7/9, box 10148.

50 *Ibid.* Emphasis in original.

51 NNA 14.6/6, box 10144.

52 BNA, FO 491/5, Foreign Office: Confidential Print Norway 1951.

53 The documents relating to drinking and driving can be found in NNA 14.7/6, box 561–2.

54 Ministry of Foreign Affairs current files 2.25/7.

55 This has happened in spite of the fact that the relative number of diplomats in Oslo has risen dramatically. In the first years after 1905 there were no more than 35 members (wives and children included) in the diplomatic corps, out of a total population of ca. 250,000. A century later, the population has doubled, while the number of diplomats with families is well over 1,000.

Part III

The Diplomatic Corps Recalled by Practitioners

6
Diplomacy in the East: Seoul, Beijing and Pyongyang, 1981–2002

J. E. Hoare

I was not a normal diplomat. I joined the British Diplomatic Service in September 1969 as a member of the Research Department, and remained formally a member of that cadre until I retired in January 2003. This Department was staffed by area specialists, as is its successor, Research Analysts. Their specializations might take them on overseas postings, but unlike mainstream officers, they would return to London to continue working in their area of expertise.[1] My specialization was East Asia and I completed my PhD just after joining the Diplomatic Service. I spent most of my time working on Chinese foreign policy. However, my grounding in diplomacy came from my doctoral thesis. Understanding and explaining the ways of the western powers in Japan in the 19th century, together with the mysteries of extraterritoriality and similar topics generated by their activities, provided the only theoretical training in the conduct of diplomacy that I ever received.

Seoul: 1981–85

I was appointed Head of Chancery and Consul for Seoul, Republic of South Korea (ROK) in January 1981. Seoul's diplomatic community in the early 1980s was somewhat distorted. Until 1905, Korea had been an independent kingdom, which had been reluctantly forced to open its doors to foreigners from the 1870s onwards. The Japanese had led the way in 1876, to be followed by the United States in 1882 and then a number of European countries. Korea was less important than either China or Japan in terms of trade, and the western foreign community was always small. When Japan declared a protectorate over Korea in 1905, the western presence declined even further, and the legations

105

closed. Some, including the British, reopened as consular posts, which continued after Korea became a Japanese colony in 1910. These posts remained small, and all were left vacant for long periods. The British consulate-general, in the heart of the city, occupied a position on a slight hill and was very much the centre of western social life until the outbreak of the Pacific War in 1941 led to the internment and eventual repatriation of the staff.[2]

Postwar Korea was very different. The peninsula was divided, and eventually two separate states emerged, the Democratic People's Republic of Korea (DPRK – North Korea), backed by the Soviet Union, and the ROK, backed by the United States. Despite a United Nations resolution that recognized the ROK as the only legitimate government on the peninsula, the Soviet Union and its allies recognized the DPRK, western states only the ROK. Britain revived its Seoul consulate-general in 1946. This became a legation in 1949, but Britain had no consular or diplomatic relations with the DPRK.[3] In June 1950, the Korean War overwhelmed the fledgling legation. The British Minister, Vyvyan Holt, George Blake (a later to be notorious member of the British Secret Intelligence Service, or MI6), and other foreigners were captured and held until 1953, when the survivors were released.[4] New staff were appointed to the legation, which spent the rest of the war years in the southern port of Pusan, where the ROK government had established itself.

After the end of the war, the diplomatic community moved back to Seoul. It was a relatively small body, and remained so until the 1990s. There were no communist states represented, and many other countries chose to side-accredit a representative from a neighbouring country, usually Japan. The United States embassy was by far the biggest, and there was also a huge American military presence. Whatever the formal position, the United States ambassador and his embassy were the pinnacle of diplomacy in the ROK. They had access at a level and a frequency that was denied to the rest of the diplomatic corps, a privilege reinforced by the military presence. The US ambassador in 1981 was Richard 'Dixie' Walker, a conservative academic appointed by President Reagan.[5] I met him rarely but came to respect his very capable staff, who covered all aspects of ROK politics with a thoroughness that the rest of us could only envy.

The relative smallness of the community meant that members of most embassies came across each other regularly at receptions and other functions. This could have its disadvantages. Britain did not recognize the 'Republic of China' (ROC) and we were not supposed to have contact with its diplomats. Our position was well established, since we had recognized the rival People's Republic of China (PRC) in January 1950, but many of us found ourselves regularly seated next to 'ROC' diplomats at functions. Our instructions allowed us in such circumstances to make small talk but nothing more. A couple of hours of small talk is not always easy to maintain!

No doubt there were occasional formal meetings of the ambassadors, but I have no recollection of these or of what they might have done. Neither can I remember the Doyen of the Corps ever taking any action. There was little need. The ROK government did not make life difficult for diplomats. During the years of the curfew, which only ended in January 1982, diplomats were exempt from its provisions – though one had to be careful of policemen who were unaware of this exemption. Parking infringements and other motoring offences were ignored. If by chance the ROK police did stop a diplomatic vehicle, they would usually profusely apologize and wave it on. The only exceptions to this leniency related to the regular air raid practices and the occasional blackout exercises. Failure to comply with these revealed a much tougher side to the Koreans.

I also found the Koreans much less formal than I had expected, and despite being a first secretary, I had relatively easy access to vice-ministers and directors-general. Perhaps the PhD helped in a society that attached much importance to learning and to titles. The biggest surprise I had was a telephone call from the then ROK foreign minister, who opened the conversation by addressing me as 'Jim', a level of informality that I would not meet again until Pyongyang.[6]

Among the diplomatic community, there were some co-ordinating groups. The ambassadors of the European Community (EC), as it then was, met from time to time, but I do not recollect other EC meetings. There were also occasional Commonwealth heads of mission meetings. The consular body met once a month over lunch at the American Embassy Club – this was very much a working group, which swapped experiences of attempted visa fraud and such like matters. Not all embassies would be represented and senior consular officers rarely attended in person except on first arrival.

Other groups were less formal. American, Australian, British, Canadian and New Zealand political officers met monthly for lunch under the auspices of a retired senior Korean journalist. The discussions were surprisingly frank and wide-ranging. After the 1983 attempted assassination in Rangoon of the ROK president, an attack which killed several of his cabinet and his senior advisers, the Commonwealth embassies held a series of meetings involving political and management officers to discuss evacuations in the event of conflict on the Korean peninsula. Some countries had already bilateral arrangements with the United States. Privately, the US embassy assured us that the United States' military would assume responsibility for all foreigners in an emergency. This was reassuring – until we realized that US evacuation procedures were based on those involved having American social security numbers. The problem had not been solved by the time I left the ROK in March 1985, but fortunately the plans have never been put to the test.

Postscript – Seoul in 1997

I returned to Seoul in 1997 for a spell of temporary duty. In some ways, not a great deal had changed. The embassy had grown bigger, with new sections but there had been no major change in its role. The context in which diplomats operated had changed considerably, however. The United States' embassy was still the most important, but there were many new embassies. Whereas once one needed to talk only to the Americans and the Japanese for a feel of what was going on, now Russia and China had large embassies, and a wise person sought their views. The old informality had gone with the growth of embassies. The traffic police no longer turned a blind eye to parking infringements, and foreign ministers no longer called first secretaries! Some of the old informal political nets survived, but European Union (EU) business had grown out of all recognition, with regular meetings at all levels, and a relatively high degree of policy coordination.

Beijing: 1988–91

In 1985, I returned to London and research, mainly on China, as before, but I now also had some expertise on Korean matters. It was suggested early in 1988 that I should go to Beijing (we still called it Peking in those days) with a position at senior first secretary level. My wife had served in the Beijing embassy in the 1970s and was eager to return. For anybody who had studied East Asian history, Beijing lay at the centre of the world. So we set off for Beijing in July 1988.

The British legation was established in Beijing in October 1860. From the beginning, it was the largest of the diplomatic missions in Beijing, and the site was much expanded after the end of the siege of the legations and the suppression of the Boxer movement in 1900. The

Boxer settlement also gave the Beijing diplomatic enclave a unique status, a miniature foreign city at the centre of China's capital, where Chinese jurisdiction did not run, and where Chinese could only enter by invitation. The Legation Quarter, a major sight for visiting tourists, was cut off from its surroundings by a wide-open space all around and protected by foreign troops. Effectively, diplomats in Beijing lived in a foreign ghetto, with little or no contact with the people of China. Even when the Chinese Nationalists moved the capital to Nanjing in 1928, the Beijing Legation Quarter continued to exist.[7]

The Second World War interrupted but did not end these arrangements. The Legation Quarter was placed on a new legal basis, and some of its formal privileges ended, but essentially, it carried on as before. But the establishment of the PRC in October 1949 marked the beginning of the end of the old system. The Chinese Communist Party was hostile to foreign privileges and determined to end them. Since many countries did not recognize the new government, several embassies, as the legations had usually become in the 1930s and 40s, were left empty. This included the American and French embassies. As noted above, the British recognized the PRC in January 1950, but the Chinese did not accept that this amounted to the establishment of diplomatic relations. British diplomats were allowed to move from Nanjing to Beijing, but were treated not as an embassy, but as a negotiating team. There then began a period which left one chargé, Humphrey Trevelyan (later Lord Trevelyan), feeling that he had been admitted to 'a superior mental home, provided with every comfort, but having no contact with the outside world beyond the limits of the British Embassy compound'. The mission's Notes, although sometimes acted upon, were never answered, the staff were not invited to Chinese functions and were, effectively, confined to their compound except when entering or leaving China.[8] Circumstances improved after the British foreign secretary, Anthony Eden, met his Chinese counterpart, Zhou Enlai, at the 1954 Geneva Conference. The British presence was formally recognized as a diplomatic mission. Its head remained *chargé d'affaires*, because of the continued presence of a British consulate in Taiwan, but was now appointed *en titre* rather *ad interim*. Business could now be conducted more normally, although the British (and the Dutch, also with a *chargé d'affaires*) were on the lowest level of the diplomatic community.[9]

The post-1949 world of Beijing diplomacy was very different from the past. British and later Japanese predominance had given way to the Soviet Union. The Western diplomatic missions had shrunk to a handful, for most Western states continued to maintain diplomatic relations with the Chinese Nationalist government on Taiwan. Contacts between diplomats from 'capitalist' and 'communist countries' were few, and very formal; they would remain so until the early 1990s. The diplomatic community grew in size as newly independent Third World countries opened embassies, but strong divisions remained.

The Chinese continued the process of reclaiming the Legation Quarter upon which they had embarked when the Communists had come to power. They regularly indicated that they intended to take the whole area, and to establish new diplomatic enclaves outside the then still existing city walls. The Legation Quarter might represent imperialism's oppression of the Chinese, but the idea of corralling diplomats away from the population was also seen as a good one. By 1959, and the planned remaking of Tiananmen Square, which abutted the Legation Quarter, the die was cast. The British, like the majority of other embassies, were forced to move to the eastern edge of the city. Only the Soviet and the tiny Luxembourg Embassy would remain within the old cities walls, then also in the process of disappearing as the Chinese modernized their capital.

It was a much reduced world that the British now occupied. The many acres and buildings of the old compound had shrunk to a mere two buildings on two plots, totalling one and a half acres. The move from the centre made direct contact with the Chinese more difficult. By the mid-1960s, as the Cultural Revolution began to take shape, such contacts became even more limited and working conditions grew steadily worse. Foreigners could still visit restaurants and markets, but they found more and more places off limits. Outside Beijing, travel was restricted, and the regular diplomatic tours came to an end. Before long, the Cultural Revolution began to affect the diplomats in more direct ways, as the Chinese retreated into xenophobia, and real or imagined slights against China and its leader played back into domestic politics. The emergence of the Sino-Soviet split in the late 1950s meant that some of the old divisions between communist and non-communist no longer applied, and the Chinese struggled against former friends as well as current foes. Soviet diplomats were roughed up along with Indian and others who were seen as hostile. By the summer of 1967, the Soviet, Mongolian, Kenyan and Sri Lankan embassies all had protesting crowds gathered outside.

In the British case,[10] events in Hong Kong, also affected by the Cultural Revolution, had their effect in Beijing. Demonstrations against the British began in May 1967 as a result of a labour dispute in Hong Kong. Huge protest groups gathered outside the British compound, and the Reuter's correspondent, Anthony Grey, the only other British representative in the city, also suffered demonstrations. During the Arab-Israeli Six Day War in June, the British were again attacked. The Queen's Birthday Party on 9 June saw further demonstrations, and only one member of the diplomatic corps, the Danish *chargé d'affaires* Arne Belling, managed to attend.

The pace of the demonstrations quickened in August, following the detention of three Chinese journalists in Hong Kong and the subsequent suspension of three newspapers. Grey was placed under house arrest, and would remain detained for over two years.[11] By now, the Foreign Ministry was in the hands of radical groups who orchestrated violent demonstrations against the British. On 20 August, a Chinese Note demanded the release of the journalists and the lifting of the suspension within 48 hours. The Note was delivered to Donald Hopson, then *chargé d'affaires*, at the International Club, since the ministry was apparently in chaos. Hopson tried to reject it, but was told to take special note of the deadline. In London, the Chinese embassy was reminded of the duty to protect diplomatic staff and premises, but in Beijing, the demonstrations continued. People's Liberation Army (PLA) troops surrounded the two compounds but did nothing to restrain the demonstrators who gathered in increasing numbers as the evening of 22 August and the expiry of the deadline grew nearer. The five women and 18 men inside the office building began to burn classified papers in anticipation of an attack, and as always, burning papers took a long time.[12]

The attack came 15 minutes after the expiry of the deadline. After holding out for some hours, fires forced the staff out. There they were attacked and beaten, but all were eventually rescued by the PLA and taken to the nearby residential compound. The Albanian embassy, directly opposite the British offices, firmly closed its gates to prevent any British taking refuge there. Other diplomats were more helpful. Together with Chinese soldiers, they prevented attacks on the British apartments and offered first aid and assistance. By dawn on 23 August, all staff were safe, though most had bruises and cuts, and some had been robbed of their watches and jewellery. The offices were a burnt-out shell, and the residence looted and empty.

For a few days, the Chinese left the British alone, and a makeshift office was established in the residence, from where semblance of a diplomatic mission operated for several months after. After an incident in London in which Chinese diplomats had spilled onto the streets carrying axes, conditions deteriorated. Staff were only allowed to move between the office and their apartments, and all exit visas, required to leave China, were cancelled. The Chinese arrested a number of Britons on spying charges, and Grey continued under house arrest. It was not until July 1968 that the Chinese lifted the ban on exit visas, and Hopson was finally able to go on leave. The wrecked offices sat empty until 1971, though they were used as a storehouse after some cleaning up. When they were being rebuilt, the Chinese premier, Zhou Enlai, obliquely apologized for the 1967 attack, which he said had never been official policy, but had been carried out by 'extremist elements' who had seized control of the Foreign Ministry. Zhou also indicated that the Chinese government would meet the cost of the repairs.[13] By then, the most violent phase of the Cultural Revolution was coming to an end, as the leadership used the PLA to reassert control.

The 1970s saw a steady improvement in relations. Britain and China agreed to exchange ambassadors in 1972, following the British decision to close the consulate on Taiwan. A military attaché and staff joined the new embassy, and a cultural section, ran by the British Council, also opened. Life in Beijing became relatively easier, with new embassies opening as more and more countries abandoned the Chinese Nationalists. The United States opened a Liaison Office in 1972, which would eventually become an embassy at the end of the decade. For the British, the arrival of the Australian and New Zealand embassies increased the opportunities for cricket, no small matter in a city where diplomats were still subject to many restrictions. China once again accepted foreign students, which added a new dimension to the foreign community. Some of the old tensions remained. Even though the events of the Cultural Revolution had for a time shown that diplomats were in the same boat, Cold War divisions persisted, so that relations with communist countries remained very formal, and would continue so until the fall of the Berlin Wall. Restrictions on internal travel remained, and the Chinese easily took offence at what they regarded as slights. A decision to allow Chinese staff to watch the British embassy Christmas pantomime backfired, when the performance was deemed insulting to the Chinese people; the experiment was not repeated.[14]

The 1967 attack was long in the past by the time we arrived in Beijing in the summer of 1988. The embassy was large, with whole sections that had not existed in Seoul, and there was a consulate-general in Shanghai, opened in 1985. Many staff spoke Chinese. While we were there, it became necessary to move the British Council staff to rented accommodation elsewhere in the city. This was resisted at first, but the increasing willingness of Chinese to drop in showed the benefits of separate premises. There were still travel restrictions but these were disappearing at a steady pace, and rusting signs in Chinese, Russian and English that had marked the limits for excursions outside the city were now ignored. Travel further afield was complicated, mainly due to the Chinese habit, in the days before computers, of not selling return tickets.

The Beijing diplomatic community was huge, and Beijing had much more of the feel of a world centre than Seoul. It was sometimes the site for third party negotiations, such as those between the United States and the DPRK which began in 1988 and between Japan and the DPRK from 1990.[15] But while China was a member of the Security Council Permanent Five, and at times the pace of work could be fast, in general Beijing in the late 1980s was no match for London, Paris, Washington, Tokyo or Moscow in terms of work. Hong Kong matters occupied much time, but there were colleagues whose sole role was Hong Kong; the rest of us usually did no more than make up dinner party numbers for visiting delegations. Odd tasks sometimes came our way. When Lesotho switched diplomatic relations from Beijing to Taipei in 1991, we found ourselves looking after a group of Lesotho students in the DPRK. Without diplomatic links or regular channels to the DPRK, this was complex, but the Swedish embassy in Pyongyang came to our aid, paying the students on our behalf and helping them when they finally left. The Pyongyang Swedish embassy also proved invaluable in 1991, when one of the British delegation to an International Parliamentary Union meeting in the DPRK ran out of money.

Beijing was more formal than Seoul. Chinese officials were very concerned about protocol, and rank (or sometimes title) mattered. However, ordinary Chinese were far friendlier than in the past, and there were opportunities for contact. The Chinese artistic world, in particular, welcomed links with foreigners. The large diplomatic community echoed Chinese behaviour. Ambassadors met ambassadors, first secretaries first secretaries. That said, there were a number of informal groupings which cut across strict rank; the 'old Commonwealth' and US ties were particularly strong. Personal contacts could also cut across the formality. We had known the Netherlands ambassador and his wife in Seoul, and others we had known there or in London also turned up. The EU met regularly at various levels from ambassador downwards, and the EU had a diplomatic office of its own. Several United Nations agencies also operated in Beijing, though in general we had little to do with them in work terms.[16]

The even temper of the Beijing diplomatic world began to waver in the spring of 1989. Even before the death of the former communist party general secretary, Hu Yaobang, on 16 April 1989, there had been signs that the authorities were concerned about growing unrest. Political activists came under pressure, some were detained and others forced to go abroad. We learnt quickly of developments that followed Hu's death on 15 April 1989. Most of the embassy, including the ambassador, were at my flat on 16 April when the BBC's James Miles arrived with news of memorial altars and other marks of remembrance erected to mark Hu's passing on the university campuses. Like most other embassies, it took us some time to realize the strength and wide scope of the movement that developed, but by mid-May, it was clear that it involved all sections of society. Police units joined in, and our embassy Chinese staff took part in one parade in the embassy lorry. We did not stop them demonstrating, but we had to stop the use of the lorry.

From the early stages, there was considerable cooperation between embassies to keep a track of what was happening. At the prompting of the North Atlantic Treaty Organization (NATO) and old Commonwealth military attachés, we noted military vehicle numbers, one of the signs that the authorities were intending an operation against the demonstrators that would involve army units from all over China.[17] By late May, with martial law declared, embassies began to engage in serious contingency planning. It was not that foreigners were thought to be either a prime or secondary target, but when there are convulsions in a big city, and it is placed under martial law, it is sensible to anticipate the worst.

Tensions increased among the diplomatic community following the PLA assault on Tiananmen Square on 3–4 June, and were increased when the dissident Fang Lizhi and his wife sought refuge in the American compound. Tanks with guns uncovered and pointing at the nearby diplomatic compound took up position on the Jianguomenwai interchange, just below our windows. From 5 June onwards, lorry loads of soldiers swept through the embassy areas. There was no obvious military need for either of these actions, apart from intimidation. On 7 June, troops entering the city from the east fired on the Jianguomenwai compound. Nobody was hit but there was much damage. They would later claim that there had been a sniper on the roof of one of the buildings. A Japanese tourist bus was shot at on the way to the airport, and roads were blocked by military control points. All through this period, embassies kept in close contact, exchanging information on developments and attempting a coordinated approach to the Chinese. The EU ambassadors met regularly; since none of our drivers reported for work, I drove our ambassador to a meeting at the Spanish embassy, weaving in and out of temporary roadblocks and burnt out buses. Most of the larger embassies decided that they should evacuate non-essential staff and dependents, and also to persuade their nationals to leave, as rumours spread of a possible battle between rival Chinese armies, and the shops and petrol stations closed. Since the demonstrations had begun on the universities, it was thought that foreign students might be especially at risk and great efforts were made to gather them up and send them home. Some were reluctant, but in the end, they all left. Airlines proved particularly helpful, many not charging for the special aircraft they sent for evacuation, and all were very flexible over accepting tickets.

Consular work took up much time. The MFA seemed to be barely manned and in any case, could do little with the city under military control. British embassies encourage residents and long stay visitors to register, which helps at times of crisis. However, few Hong Kong residents in China ever bothered to register and we had no idea of the numbers, except that there were thousands there in June 1989, and many now demanded help. To complicate matters, a number had come to support the demonstrations. We helped where we could, especially those who seemed to be in real danger, such as the trade union leader Lee Chuk-yan, forcibly removed from a Hong Kong flight on 5 June. We eventually secured his release, but there was much criticism in Hong Kong of the embassy's 'failure' to protect those from Hong Kong.[18]

The immediate crisis passed with the appearance on television of China's unofficial leader, Deng Xiaoping, on 9 June, and gradually Beijing returned to something like normal. But martial law continued until January 1990, and there were periodic shootings in the city well into the autumn. Diplomatic life became more constrained. The Americans, who had Fang Lizhi and his wife as guests for over a year, suffered some harassment, and it was generally harder to work with the Chinese. Social contacts were minimal and ordinary business was difficult. Hong Kong issues loomed large, as measures to bolster Hong Kong's economy met fierce Chinese objections. Unofficial contacts tapered off; there were no more invitations to art galleries. As time passed, however, the mood changed, and by the time I left Beijing in December 1991, not only were relations restored with the MFA but more casual contacts also resumed.

Pyongyang: 2001–02[19]

On 12 December 2000, Britain and the DPRK signed a document establishing diplomatic relations and agreeing to exchange diplomatic missions. Within minutes, the news was announced worldwide, but only Radio China International noted that Britain was the first Western permanent member of the UN Security Council to establish diplomatic relations with the DPRK.[20]

Britain and the DPRK had had little to do with each before 2000. As late as January 2000, the Foreign and Commonwealth Office (FCO) had announced that there was no intention of establishing diplomatic relations.[21] Britain had been a firm supporter of the ROK since 1948, and only recognized the DPRK when the two Koreas entered the United Nations in 1991. After 1991, there had followed a desultory political dialogue without much progress. Outside official circles, contacts had also been minimal, the DPRK team's participation in the 1966 football World Cup being a rare exception.[22] For the DPRK, Britain was in the imperialist camp, and DPRK comment about the country was hostile.

Kim Dae-jung's election as the ROK president in 1997 heralded a new South Korean policy of engagement with the DPRK. This had a wider effect, including Italy's decision to establish diplomatic relations with the DPRK in January 2000, and Australia's to renew relations in May 2000. Britain was not unaffected, and the head of the FCO's North-east Asia and Pacific Department visited Pyongyang in May 2000; one result was the establishment of an English-language teaching programme in the DPRK. Real momentum for change came from the meeting between Kim Dae-jung and the DPRK's Kim Jong Il in Pyongyang in June 2000. The Asia-Europe Meeting in Seoul in October 2000 provided the opportunity for Foreign Secretary Robin Cook to announce that Britain would establish diplomatic relations with the DPRK – a move that caught most officials by surprise.[23]

Following the December 2001 agreement, it was decided that I should be sent to Seoul as a counsellor dedicated to DPRK affairs and accredited to Pyongyang. After two exploratory trips, the ground was prepared for others, including Sir John Kerr, to visit in March 2002. Kerr decided to open a full embassy in Pyongyang, using offices in the German embassy that also housed the Swedish embassy and the Italian aid agency. Staff would live in hotels until other accommodation could be found. For the next 18 months, Pyongyang was home, and the Pyongyang diplomatic community my colleagues.

At first, two of us worked and lived out of the Koryo Hotel.[24] Then our offices were established at the German embassy in rooms originally earmarked for a United States liaison mission that had never material-ized. Because of a dispute with the DPRK about secure communi-cations, we abandoned the idea of our own premises, and stayed with the Germans, since there was also an accommodation building avail-able on their site. After six months in hotels, we were able to move into accommodation that was comfortable and more up to date than anything else in Pyongyang.[25]

Diplomatic life in Pyongyang had echoes of Seoul in the early 1980s. We were a small community of just over 20 embassies, plus several international agencies. Stronger were the echoes of Beijing in the early 1950s, however. Diplomacy had never been easy in Pyongyang, even when there were only communist embassies. Hungarian diplomats in Pyongyang in the 1950s and 1960s found the DPRK unwilling to share information or to allow high-level access. Diplomatic notes were often ignored until the time for action had passed. Even the Soviet and Chinese found the DPRK uncooperative.[26] Like the Chinese, the DPRK gradually forced most embassies to leave the centre of the city and to relocate to east Pyongyang, well away from party and government offices. By 2001, only the Soviet and Chinese embassies remained central.

The arrival of the first non-communist embassies in the 1970s saw no change. The DPRK welcomed what it regarded as signs of inter-national approval but did little to make the newcomers feel welcome. Business was difficult and controls tight. Cold War politics made rela-tions with most other embassies distant and formal. Despite the dif-ficulties, Sweden maintained a one-man office in Pyongyang until the early 1990s, but the Australian embassy was expelled in autumn 1975, after 18 months. 'Hooliganism' was amongst the charges against them – apparently a reference to eating ice cream on the street.[27] The welcome accorded to the international agencies that arrived in the mid-1990s after a DPRK appeal for international assistance was scarcely warmer. Staff were confined to the Koryo Hotel and only allowed out under escort. But the growing numbers of international staff and their move to accommodation in the diplomatic areas in east Pyongyang led to a relaxation of these rules in the capital, although they persisted in the countryside until after we left Pyongyang.

The number of embassies was the same as when the Swedes opened in 1975, although the composition had changed.[28] While we were there, Ethiopia and Yugoslavia closed, but others have since opened, leaving numbers still around 23. The Russians and the Chinese were by far the biggest and very self-contained. Indonesia, Nigeria and Poland came next. Most embassies were in Pyongyang to show solidarity and friendship. Some, such as Cambodia and Egypt, were once close to the DPRK because of personal rapport between their leaders and President Kim Il Sung, links that did not survive Kim's death in 1994; Kim Jong Il, his son and successor, was not interested. Some may have had military purposes; Egypt again, and possibly Iran, Pakistan and Libya. India and Pakistan admitted that their main role was to watch each other. The Swedes had re-opened in 1995, mainly to act for the United States. With only two staff, they had not been able to do much else except that they were unfailingly helpful to all visiting Western diplomats. The Germans were an interest section until March 2001. Large by local standards, with five people, they were not allowed to have formal contacts with Koreans or other Embassies. This changed when they established relations, especially after the arrival of the first ambassador in January 2002. With three EU embassies and the EU humanitarian ECHO office, it was possible to hold EU meetings, and to give an EU view of developments in Pyongyang. The Swedes, Germans, British and ECHO representative, together with the Polish, Romanian and Bulgarian embassies, would meet on a regular basis for discussion and to prepare reports for Brussels. The DPRK accepted that the EU was worth attention and the MFA's most useful briefing in my time, on the economic changes introduced in 2002, was given to the EU and UN representatives, even before the Russians and the Chinese.

Then there were the UN organizations. The UN Development Programme and the World Food Programme each had around 50 expatriates working for them, and a number of resident Non-Governmental Organisations (NGOs) were closely associated with the UN bodies. The Koreans treated the UN organizations somewhat differently from other diplomatic missions. The very tight controls of the past had gone, but they were still watched carefully, a process aided by the presence of Korean 'national officers' in UN organizations. The UN bodies wanted to modify the Koreans' attitude, and they made up the largest single group of foreigners in the country. But they could not push too hard if they wished to continue their programmes.

The North Koreans viewed us all with suspicion. They would have liked us to stay in our enclaves, preferably without contact with each other. If they gave something to one embassy, they always suggested that it should not be mentioned to others. They had provided clubs and a dedicated shop for diplomats, so in theory there was no need to go anywhere else. Communication was by Note, directed at the MFA's relevant geographical department or to the protocol or consular Departments. We issued 132 Notes between May and December 2001. They were rarely answered in writing when we first arrived, though this was beginning to change before we left. Long lead-ins were demanded for travel or other activities. Some calls were arranged with alacrity. Others moved in slower time, especially if anything out of the ordinary was requested. Protests were met by assertions that this was how it was done in the DPRK, and appeals to international norms fell on the deafest of deaf ears. Attempts to bypass the MFA by direct approaches to other organs or ministries were not welcome, though they sometimes worked as the MFA got fed up with our barrage of Notes.

Control was the name of the game, and control extended to all areas. Visiting delegations had their days filled with programmes that allowed for little or no deviation. Strenuous attempts were made to prevent visiting groups from meeting with their own diplomats. There were normally no briefings and no press conferences. Those requesting information were told to look at the press. We did this, and asked to follow up some stories, only to be met by a barrage of questions as to how we had got our information. Even Korean speakers could learn little. Links with the outside world were also limited. In the past, some embassies used radio; the masts are much in evidence but none seemed to be in use. The Koreans grudgingly allowed the use of e-mail. But lines were poor and contacts sometimes difficult. The internet was unavailable. The Koreans banned the use of satellite communications, including satellite phones, and threatened to enforce the ban if necessary. Mobile phones were not allowed. Telephone directories were secret so local staff had to ring the MFA for numbers. We had no contact telephone numbers for our staff. Theoretically, the MFA provided a contact service for out-of-hours crises, but the number never answered.

DPRK norms were imposed as much as possible. Diplomatic missions were expected to present flowers to Kim Il Sung's statue on formal occasions, and to send birthday cards to Kim Jong Il. The MFA helpfully printed these in advance. No major state anniversary was complete without a visit to the Great Leader's mausoleum. Failure to do so meant close questioning by the local staff – provided by the 'General Service Bureau for the Affairs of Diplomatic Missions' – whose main role was to keep a check on our activities. None of the long-established embassies felt it was any part of their role to challenge this strange world that the Koreans had created. Some bemoaned the lack of opportunities to travel – diplomatic tours had stopped in the 1990s – but did not do much about it, except to blame the Dean of the Diplomatic Corps for not pressurizing the Koreans. The latter, then the Palestine ambassador, was in a difficult position since it was assumed that the DPRK met the costs of his embassy. The exception was visiting the mausoleum, where there had been minor rebellions. The previous Nigerian Ambassador announced that seeing a corpse on 1 January would mean a bad year ahead. The Egyptian Ambassador announced at a dinner that unfortunately, he thought that he was going to be ill next day – he was. The corps did not meet formally, the Dean's activities normally being confined to arranging welcome and farewell dinners, and collecting money for the mausoleum flowers.

Into all this, the British had now come. Others greeted us with high hopes of bringing new ideas and a fresh approach. The diplomatic community was friendly, with political differences put aside, a welcome change from the 1970s.[29] One colleague from the Middle East was a devoted follower of the Royal Family, and constantly requested information on their doings. Our stand on communications was applauded, even if nobody else was trying the same thing, and few held out much hope of success – the Dean was a lone exception. Our English-language programme was seen as a positive development. Commonwealth diplomats greeted our arrival, hoping that there would soon be a British school under embassy auspices and a British Council library. We had to gently disillusion them.

In practice, while foreign visitors and especially journalists were often subject to very tight control, we found that were free enough in and around Pyongyang. In May and June 2001, I spent hours wandering about the town in the evenings and at weekends, often taking photographs, without once being stopped or questioned. Once we had the embassy cars, we extended our journeys into the surrounding countryside and even further. Nobody raised objections when I took the BBC's Brian Barron filming around Pyongyang. He also did a sympathetic interview, putting a positive spin on Britain's relations with the DPRK.[30] Even when we needed permission to travel, we found it relatively easy to do so. On one occasion, with less than 12 hours' notice, and without an interpreter, I accompanied a BBC correspondent to the east coast to look at flood damage. Other journeys were often arranged equally swiftly. In general, we found that the rules could be relaxed if you pushed. The Swedes, Germans and eventually the Poles joined us in these efforts. The Koreans did not object to us inviting academics and journalists as guests of the embassy. This worked not only for getting visas, but DPRK officials would actually help with the programmes for such visitors. These were small victories, but they did at least show that DPRK behaviour could be modified.

Our biggest victory, and probably the one that did most for the whole foreign community, was the decision to allow us to install secure satellite communications. Despite assurances in our negotiations that we could have such communications, on arrival in Pyongyang we were told that this was impossible, with the objections clearly coming from the security authorities. We persisted, using every opportunity to make the case, apparently to no avail. During a dinner party in May 2002, I took aside the UK desk officer and warned that the continued refusal might well jeopardize the future of the embassy. Whether this was the catalyst or not, we will probably never know, but the MFA informed us at the end of June that it had been agreed that we could install satellite communications. It was perhaps not appreciated in London how big a victory this was, but it seemed to surprise the MFA. We had got what the Koreans had denied to all other embassies, and to the UN organizations.[31] It was perhaps not surprising that our news was much welcomed by other missions and the UN organizations, which pressed for, and got, the same concession. Just after we returned to London, in December 2002, the head of WFP in Pyongyang sent me the first message on their new secure communications, which concluded 'You will be remembered for this'.[32] I suspect that is unlikely, but revisiting Pyongyang in 2004, we found that several embassies and all the UN organizations had satellite communications, diplomatic vehicles had two-way radios, and even our Korean staff had pagers for out-of-hours contact.

Before we left, we experienced DPRK methods of control one more time. Our main farewell party was to be a combined circus and dinner evening. All was arranged, but the Protocol Department intervened, and the circus became uncooperative. We might have changed some attitudes, but there was clearly a long way to go. A more subdued farewell dinner took place on 14 October at the Nationalities Restaurant, where we had a slight victory over the Protocol Department by refusing to organize a top table. On 15 October, we left Pyongyang for the airport for the last time with the flag flying. When the Air Koryo flight passed over the Yalu River into China at 09.40, my time as British *chargé d'affaires*, Pyongyang, was over.

Conclusion

My three posts were very different, though there were some similarities. Perhaps the most obvious change over the 20 years was the growth in EU cooperation. While the ideal of a common EU foreign and security policy is still far from achievement, EU cooperation seems far more advanced now then in 1981. Sharing physical space, as we did in Pyongyang, also seems more common and makes much sense in small posts.

This development is perhaps paralleled in the decline of the traditional diplomatic corps. There are many new diplomatic entities, including UN and other bodies, that do not fit into the traditional mould. The world of the large meetings of foreign representatives that were such a feature of Japan or China in the 19th century, now seems very remote. At the same time, the end of the Cold War divisions means that those who choose can have a much wider range of diplomatic contacts than was possible in the past. And of one thing I am convinced: despite the shrinkage of the world, the spread of the internet and politicians' constant travel, there still remains a role for traditional diplomacy.

Notes

1 Robert A. Longmire and Kenneth C. Walker, *Herald of a noisy world – interpreting the news of all nations: The Research and Analysis Department of the Foreign and Commonwealth Office* (London: Foreign and Commonwealth Office, 1995 – Foreign Policy Document (Special Issue), no. 263), p. 40; FCO 'About Research Analysts' and Richard Lavers, 'The role of Research Analysts in the FCO', Research and Analytical Papers, January 2001, both at http://www.fco.gov.uk/servlet/Front?pagename=OpenMarket/Xcelerate/Sho wPage&c..., accessed 4 November 2006.

2 J. E. Hoare, *Embassies in the East: The story of the British and their embassies in China, Japan and Korea from 1859 to the present* (Richmond, Surrey: Curzon Press, 1999), pp. 171–94.

3 Hoare, *Embassies in the East*, pp. 195–8.

4 'Foreign Civilian Detainees in the Korean War', in James Hoare and Susan Pares, *Conflict in Korea: An Encyclopedia* (Santa Barbara CA: ABC-CLIO, 1999), pp. 47–8.

5 There is a brief obituary at http://www.icasinc.org/2003/2003b/ b030722b. html and a fuller biography at http://en.wikipedia.org/wiki/Richard_L._Walker, both accessed on 11 November 2006.

6 This was Yi Pom-suk, who had transliterated his name as 'Lee Bum-suk', to the amusement of many foreigners. He was well aware of this, having an excellent command of English. He was one of those killed in Rangoon in 1983, when North Korean agents attempted to assassinate President Chun: Hoare and Pares, *Conflict in Korea*, p. 97.

7 Daniele Varè, *Laughing Diplomat* (London: John Murray, 1938), pp. 84, 86. For the early years of the British embassy, see Hoare, *Embassies in the East*, pp. 17–65.

8 H. Trevelyan, *Worlds Apart: China 1953–55; Soviet Union 1962–65* (Basingstoke: Macmillan, 1971), pp. 22–3, based on a dispatch, 'Life of a diplomatist in Peking', in the Foreign Offices records, FO371/11492/

FC1018/50, Trevelyan to Mr. Macmillan, no. 119, secret, 11 May 1955; see also Peter Lum (Lady Crowe), *Peking 1950–53* (London: Robert Hale, 1958).

9 Hoare, *Embassies in the East*, p. 72.

10 See Hoare, *Embassies in the East*, pp. 82–6, in turn derived from reminiscences and official papers, including Percy Cradock, *Experiences of China* (London: John Murray, 1994).

11 Anthony Grey, *Hostage in Peking* (London: Widenfeld and Nicolson, 1980).

12 The chemical device for destroying papers produced a neat uniform burnt edge around the documents, but otherwise failed to achieve its purpose.

13 A. M. Rendel, 'China to pay for sacking of British mission', *The Times*, 23 March 1971; letter from Sir Percy Cradock to J. E. Hoare, 10 March 1993.

14 The Beijing diaries of David Bruce, first head of the US Liaison Mission, have been published: Priscilla Roberts, ed., *Window on the Forbidden City: The Beijing Diaries of David Bruce, 1973–1974* (Hong Kong: Centre of Asian Studies University of Hong Kong, 2001). They give something of the flavour of Beijing in the 1970s, but more entertaining is diplomatic life through the eyes of a seven year old: Amélie Nothomb, *Le sabotage amourex* (Paris: Livre de Poche, 1993), translated into English by Andrew Wilson as *Loving Sabotage* (London: New Directions, 2000). One British diplomat's account is Roger Garside, *Coming Alive: China After Mao* (London: Andre Deutsch, 1981). Frances Wood, *Hand-grenade Practice in Peking: My part in the Cultural Revolution* (London: John Murray, 2000) is a student's more light-hearted account. I have also learnt much about these years from Susan Pares (second secretary 1975–6) and other members of the British embassy in the 1970s, and made my own first visit in 1976.

15 Briefly touched upon in G. R. Berridge, *Talking to the Enemy: How States without 'Diplomatic Relations' Communicate* (London: Macmillan Press, 1994), pp. 77–8.

16 James Lilley, with Jeffrey Lilley, *China Hands: Nine Decades of Adventure, Espionage, and Diplomacy in Asia* (New York: Public Affairs, 2004), especially pp. xi–xiv, 296–372; Lilley succeeded Richard Walker in Seoul, and became ambassador to China in May 1989; Hoare, *Embassies in the East*, pp. 88–90, and J. E. Hoare, 'Building politics: The British Embassy Peking, 1949–1992', *The Pacific Review*, 7, 1 (1994), 67–78; both contain more detailed references.

17 Lilley refers positively to the activities of the American military but is rather negative about their foreign colleagues: Lilley, *China Hands*, p. 326.

18 'Peking frees Hong Kong activist', *The Independent*, 9 June 1989. The US embassy also received criticism for 'failures'; Lilley, *China Hands*, p. 326.

19 This draws on J. E. Hoare, 'A Brush with History: Opening the British Embassy Pyongyang, 2001–02', *Papers of the British Association for Korean Studies*, vol. 9, 57–87, with references; J. E. Hoare and Susan Pares, *North Korea in the 21ˢᵗ Century: An Interpretative Guide* (Folkestone Kent: Global Oriental, 2005), pp. 199–225, has the text without references.

20 David Rennie, 'Britain signs diplomatic deal with North Korea', at http://www.telegraph.co.uk, 13 December 2000. (North) Korean Central News Agency (KCNA) 12 December 2000, BBC Summary of World Broadcasts (SWB) FE/4002/D2, 13 December 2000; 'The DPRK and the UK established diplomatic relations', Radio China International, 13 December 2000.

21 Hansard, House of Commons, Written Answers col. 325, 17 January 2000.

22 Warwick Morris, 'UK policy towards North Korea', in Hazel Smith *et al.*, *North Korea in the New World Order* (London: Macmillan Press, 1996), pp. 86–92; Hoare, 'Brush with History', 58–64.

23 FCO press release, 19 October 2000; Jonathan Watts, 'Britain opens links with North Korea', *Guardian*, 20 October 2000.

24 An account of the Koryo Hotel and its drawbacks is in James Church, *A corpse in the Koryo: a mystery* (New York: Thomas Dunne Books, 2006).

25 Hoare, 'Brush with History', 70 *et seq.*

26 Balázs Szalontai, *Kim Il Sung in the Khrushchev Era: Soviet-DPRK Relations and the Roots of North Korean Despotism* (Washington DC: Woodrow Wilson Center Press, 2005), pp. 54–7, 199–201.

27 Erik Cornell, *North Korea under Communism: Report of an Envoy to Paradise* (London: Routledge and Curzon, 2002). Sweden closed its embassy in Pyongyang in the early 1990s, but subsequently re-opened. In January 2002, the Swedish *chargé d'affaires*, Paul Beijer, became the first resident Swedish ambassador. Adrian Buzo, 'North Korea – Yesterday and Today', *Transaction of the Korea Branch Royal Asiatic Society,* 56 (1981), 1–27. Buzo was Second Secretary in the Australian embassy.

28 Cornell, *North Korea*, p. 25.

29 Cornell, *North Korea*, pp. 25–6.

30 Brian Barron, 'Britain moves into Kim's secret state', BBC News Online, 29 August 2001.

31 Catherine Bertini, head of WFP from 1992–2002, made four visits to the DPRK and each time asked that WFP be allowed satellite communications especially to communicate with its officers in the field. The requests were refused.

31 'Message for Jim Hoare', e-mail from Rick Corsino, WFP Pyongyang, to John Dunne, British Embassy Pyongyang, 7 December 2002.

7
Representing India in the Diplomatic Corps

Kishan S. Rana

Novelists often cast the diplomatic corps as a romantic freemasonry, its players busy schmoozing with one another at a succession of elegant receptions. The reality is more prosaic. This corps is a collection mainly of professional diplomatists (though envoys from outside the career ranks are also full members for the duration of their assignment); they are linked together, albeit notionally for the most part, in this entity, even though the work of diplomats is conducted at their own embassies.

The diplomatic corps varies in character from one capital to another, even while conceptually it is based on the same template – that is a voluntary, corporate body, ruled by diplomatic law and custom, consisting of all the accredited foreign envoys located in a single capital. Sometimes in the same country the diplomatic corps has varied in its activities at different historical periods. By tradition, the representatives of UN and multilateral agencies, who generally enjoy diplomatic status and privileges, are not treated as members of the diplomatic corps. That applies also to the representatives of regional organizations, including the EU and the Arab League, who bear the courtesy designation of 'ambassador' (the UN representatives are not designated with this title), but they too are not treated as full members of the corps.

The diplomatic corps is a guild of professional envoys who, as representatives of diverse and sometimes rival sovereign governments, behave both as competitors and collaborators, sharing a code of conduct, some of it unwritten. The 1961 Vienna Convention on Diplomatic Relations (Vienna Convention) lays down the framework of immunities and obligations of diplomatic missions and the receiving governments – though the Convention does not mention the diplomatic corps. Within its parameters, the host government lays down local procedures, which the diplomatic corps, as representatives of sovereign states are obliged to accept. The bulk of these rules are universal in character, in that they apply to all the embassies, but some rules are also applied on a bilateral or reciprocal basis, as we see below.

Collectively, the diplomatic corps in each capital symbolizes the international community and confirms the host state's membership of it. The corps deals with the host government on issues of immunity and privilege following the norms set by the Vienna Convention. It also deals as a group with the receiving state, through the protocol department of the foreign ministry, on logistics and administration; there is no clear line on the subjects that an embassy should take up on its own and those that concern the collective body; it may happen that if an embassy does not receive satisfaction on the issues it may have raised directly with the protocol department, it may 'kick the issue upstairs' to the corps.

Elements of unity and variation

What are the key determinants of how the corps is organized and operates in particular cases? As with other institutions and practices in international affairs, there is today a sense that the traditional bindings of this particular agency are weaker now than in the past. For one thing, the professional culture of diplomacy is more diffused than in the past, thanks to greater diversity within the world community, and a *laissez faire* attitude by some of the new states that do not fully subscribe to the old norms. A practitioner–scholar writes in a recent work: '...the old sense of binding common identity of the diplomatic corps is left for farewell ritual gatherings of departing colleagues'.[1] As we see below, this comment is over-drawn, but the issue remains – why has the sense of solidarity and united action weakened within the diplomatic corps?

Several factors have contributed. First, the number of embassies making up the diplomatic corps affects its operation. The wave of decolonization produced a huge growth in diplomatic representation in the 1960s and 1970s, and that has added to the diversity within the corps, although is it often the 'new' members who are the sticklers for old forms? One may categorize the corps into three clusters: the large diplomatic centres, where the number of resident embassies is in excess of 100 – including the major capitals such as Beijing, Berlin, London, Moscow, Paris, or Washington DC where more than 150 embassies congregate; second, the medium-sized capitals where the number of embassies is between 50 and a 100; and finally, the small capitals where the number is less than 50. One might even add a sub-category of capitals where the number of bilateral embassies is fewer than 15, as forming a special category. By a rough rule of thumb, the extent of mutual interaction within the diplomatic corps declines in inverse proportion to the growth in numbers.[2]

One factor affecting the work of embassies is that everywhere, the pace of bilateral action is more frenetic than ever in the past; for instance, a Chinese Embassy official in New Delhi said during an interview that the number of delegations they receive from ministries, provincial and local authorities, and state enterprises exceeds 100 in some months, forcing them to prioritize; this takes up much of their time. Further, the subjects under dialogue are more numerous and complex than before. In a word, an intensification of the bilateral process results in a low priority being assigned to the activities of the corps.

This means that the old courtesies of envoys making formal calls on colleagues, soon after their arrival in the capital, are now truncated; in busy capitals the newcomer may call on the dean and the regional dean, and perhaps another 15 to 25 colleagues, including the representatives of his neighbouring countries and the major powers. The practice of return calls now survives only in those capitals where the total number of embassies is very small. As we see below, this represents a functional loss for the newcomer.[3]

Second, the frequency of encounters within the corps has lessened. In Western capitals, as a result of the simplification of protocol procedures and improved communications, the opportunities for the entire corps to meet and interact collectively are generally fewer than in other capitals, though the winds of modernization also blow through the rituals of non-Western states, and we witness a progressive discarding of state ceremonies in an increasing number of countries. The receiving country usually hosts one or two events annually for the corps, such as a New Year reception to greet the head of state; at some places the corps hosts a dinner in honour of the foreign minister.[4]

In the large and medium category of capitals as identified above, the full corps seldom convenes for business meetings; the corps identity is now expressed through its regional groups, constituted on the usual UN-style geographic principles, but with local variations. Thus the groups of Arab and Islamic envoys cut across that principle, as does the Commonwealth group. Much of the interaction among envoys takes place within these sub-corps entities, including the customary monthly lunch meetings, and the farewell receptions for departing colleagues; a single omnibus reception hosted by the dean of the corps for departing envoys is a thing of the past in most capitals.[5] While nothing prevents the envoy from building close relations with his colleagues as he chooses, the regional cluster may become a closed circle for some. We thus witness a partial fragmentation of the homogenous corps.

Regional organizations that are advanced in their cooperation and integration, such as the European Union, ASEAN, the southern African SADC find their echo in the corps; these envoys meet extensively and at different levels, carrying out joint activities, including *démarches* to the receiving country, writing reports and other analysis on a joint or mutual exchange basis, and travelling in groups to places outside the capital.[6]

At some places, by happenstance or through individual initiative, regional clusters of envoys become especially proactive.[7] In Germany in the 1990s, an 'Asia-Pacific group' brought together the envoys of countries from Pakistan to Mongolia and Japan, including those from Australasia and the South Pacific. In place of the usual regional dean appointed on the basis of seniority, it selected a 'coordinator'. He helped the rotating host for the monthly lunches, where outside speakers were invited, and organized the group's two to three annual trips to different Länder and cities, often hosted by the local authorities and by large companies; it became a means for the joint marketing of business opportunities. Other regional groups watched in envy.

It is not just heads of mission who engage in these kinds of contacts. Other diplomats also engage in frequent professional exchanges with their counterparts in other embassies. Most capitals have informal groups of political, economic, and information officers, even those handling consular work, who meet periodically and exchange information. Which embassies are invited depends on whether the clusters are based on a regional organization, or are the product of someone's local initiative; the selection for the latter depends on the group itself. The underlying motive is to share experiences and information and when needed, to tackle local problems.[8]

The position of the head of the corps, traditionally called the 'dean', has also evolved. In principle, he is the longest serving envoy in the capital; among envoys, seniority is counted on the basis of the date on which the envoy presented credentials to the head of state of the receiving country.[9] It happens on occasion that the senior-most declines the deanship, if his embassy is too small to undertake the essential organizational tasks, or for personal reasons. This too is recent; in the past, the honour of representing the corps, and the local access that it provided would have been reason enough for almost any envoy to grab the position. It might also be noted that countries which rotate envoys from one assignment to another every three or four years – i.e., those that maintain strict human resource management norms – seldom hold the deanship in any capital; all too often, it is the ambassadors representing the smaller countries from Africa, the Arab world, and Latin America that hold these positions, some staying in one assignment for a decade or more.

A special arrangement exists in Catholic countries, in those that have a 'concordat' or special agreement with the Vatican, which ensures that the Papal Nuncio is permanently the dean of the diplomatic corps. While it ensures continuity, it also subtly affects the functioning of the corps; since this particular envoy has ecclesiastical responsibilities *vis-à-vis* the Catholic hierarchy of the receiving country, he tends to have less time for the corporate body of envoys. For instance, in Germany (where Catholics make up just under half the population, and are outnumbered by Protestants, after the 1989 Unification), the Nuncio is the dean of the corps; preoccupied as he is with representing the Vatican to the Catholic hierarchy in the country, he wears lightly his responsibilities to the corps.

Is such permanent deanship a good practice? Besides making for continuity; the corps' archives are preserved, and the institutional memory of the deanship is strong in such situations. When the position of dean rotates, recordkeeping suffers, as the thoroughness with which archives are kept is uneven; papers older than a few years may be untraceable. The collective memory is thus weakened. The downside is that a permanent dean is seldom inclined to be proactive, and may even become excessively solicitous of the local authorities. Further, the practice runs against the democratic principle that should govern any collective entity where the head plays a representative role.[10]

We should distinguish between the countries where normal work conditions exist, including basic safety and security, and the unfortunately growing number of locations where hazardous conditions obtain, which may make it difficult or impossible for diplomatic missions to function normally. Naturally this affects the way the diplomatic corps operates.

Where local conditions are harsh, in terms of security, standard of life, and availability of goods and services, the corps tends to draw together, in shared hardship. Conditions of travail also engender stronger mutual information sharing, even outside regional cooperation clusters, compared with the comfortable locations. Professional values also rise to the surface in such situations. Even in extreme conditions, each embassy is forced to look after itself, except for the countries that share special bonds (such as the Nordics), even while some solidarity persists. For instance, during the First Iraq War 1990–91, each embassy looked after its own problems, including the repatriation of refugees, but there was much information-sharing and informal assistance.

A further point regarding crises may be noted. In several African countries that have witnessed civil war and/or trans-border strife it is often the local diplomatic corps, or the activists among them, working in liaison with the local UN representatives, who have set the stage for peacekeeping activities that are undertaken under the sponsorship of the UN Security Council. In similar fashion, it is the resident African envoys that set the stage for similar peace efforts of the African Union. Such activity mostly takes place outside the gaze of the media.

Finally, we should differentiate between the bilateral capitals and the seats of multilateral activity, especially New York or Geneva. The links between the members of a multilateral diplomatic corps are tighter and more explicit than those of its more conventional bilateral counterpart. For the permanent missions located at these places, fellow diplomats are constant negotiation partners, who work jointly, cheek-by-jowl, and with a minimum of formality. Every diplomat creates his or her own network of contacts, primarily among the permanent missions, but also encompassing the UN or the specialized agency secretariat. What we see in operation is not so much a diplomatic corps working to formal regulations, as a flexible, pragmatic forum of permanent negotiators which spans different conferences, committees, and caucuses.

In the capitals where bilateral and multilateral activities coexist, be it Brussels, Nairobi, Paris, Rome, or Vienna, it is the multilateral activities that add to the proximity among the envoys and their staff.[11] Of course this operates among the envoys that wear multiple hats; the countries that designate separate ambassadors for each organization do not benefit from such professional proximity. Overall, this adds up to slight erosion in the collective personality of the corps, but not to the point where it undermines the concept or its operation. The *raison d'être* for the corps is as powerful today as before, and it is an unwise envoy who lets preoccupation with bilateral work overwhelm him to the point where he ignores the professional ties with fellow envoys in the corps.

Life within the corps

The envoy is the personal representative of one head of state to another, as the extravagant language of credential documents attests.[12] In monarchies, the diplomatic corps is an attachment to the royal court, though in modern democracies that have retained constitutional monarchs, this is not always apparent, since the notion of a royal court has faded. But colleagues who served in Morocco in the reign of King Hassan V have affirmed how they were required from time to time to travel to different cities, whenever the King travelled and wanted the company of the corps. Even in countries that have elected heads of state, that special link subsists in the convention that when convoked by the head of state, envoys are required to attend, even if they may be viewed as boring domestic ceremonies or other ritual gatherings. As we see below, even this custom has become weaker in practice in some places, and devalued in our times.

The first official task for a newly arrived envoy, immediately after assuming charge at a new post, is to call on the foreign ministry's chief of protocol, to discuss arrangements for his presentation of credentials; at that encounter, besides advising the envoy on the procedure (including the next pre-presentation formality, i.e., the handing over of the copies of the credential papers, usually to the permanent civil servant heading the foreign ministry), the chief of protocol customarily advises the envoy to call on the dean of the corps; once the envoy has called on the dean, he may begin his customary calls on fellow envoys.[13] Thus the meeting with the dean becomes virtually the second priority for the new ambassador.

As in the corporate world, the envoy is expected to hit the ground running. The normal rotation cycle of three to four years at each assignment does not permit him the luxury of gradually settling in during the first few months, keeping a low profile and learning the local ropes. One should also remember that convention forbids the presence of two envoys at the same embassy, so that the handover takes place remotely; usually, the new appointee has the chance to meet the predecessor in the home capital, for a personal briefing. Sometimes that is not possible, either because of a delay in naming a successor, or because the predecessor has already proceeded overseas for another assignment. The customary document through which the departing envoy narrates the key information for the successor is a 'handing-over note'. As a substantive document of some length, it is supposed to guide the new envoy on a host of issues; it also offers notes on personalities that the envoy will encounter, including fellow envoys, plus the working methods of the diplomatic corps.[14]

To an extent, it is the diplomatic corps which provides the framework that facilitates quick learning for the new envoy. The professional ethos permits him to seek and obtain useful advice from his counterparts, through the medium of courtesy calls and the first social encounters. Ambassadors are surprisingly relaxed about sharing information and opinions with one another, short of issues of vital importance to one's own country. Thus the corps and its regional and other affinity groups act as a support base; like any resource, it has to be used and exploited wisely, meaning that the envoy – and the other members of the embassy team – must invest time and effort in cultivating individuals, after identifying those that are likely to be particularly useful.

The protocol department of the foreign ministry is the permanent interlocutor and communications channel for the corps, handling issues of privilege, immunity, and the entire interface with the domestic authorities in the assignment country. Threats to security now loom high on the agenda; any incident or problem faced by an embassy concerns not only the affected entity but also the corps; the dean takes up issues of general concern, as well as individual cases where action is due. Considerable time is taken up with issues relating to taxation; while foreign envoys are exempt from paying taxes in the receiving state, in relation to sales tax or VAT on day-to-day purchases by diplomats, the exemptions offered vary from country to country; for instance, European countries do not give any special treatment to diplomats. In contrast, the US exempts diplomats from those countries that offer similar exemptions to US diplomats in their country, invoking the principle of reciprocity. For instance, in 2005 India moved to the VAT system, and initially offered exemptions to foreign diplomats, provided each sale voucher was for Rs.5000 or more (equivalent to $110); the Dean of the New Delhi corps took this up vigorously, and the exemption threshold was lowered to Rs.1500.

The above incident touches on another factor, the quality of the engagement between the corps and the host government. This varies from capital to capital. It is tempting to argue that in countries that take a tough attitude towards the corps, and do not permit it to engage in collective bargaining on behalf of the resident diplomatic missions, it is the host government that lays down the line and embassies comply. In the opposite case, where the host government shows accommodation, the corps often becomes demanding. There is probably a grain of truth in that. At the same time, the more influential factor is the pattern that each capital establishes; if dialogue and accommodation is the norm, the corps takes full advantage of that – one would put New Delhi as among the capitals where this happens. In places where the opposite circumstances obtain, the corps learns to live with the situation, and does not demand more.

An example will illustrate the point. In 1994, while Bonn was still the capital, the German President decided to signal Berlin's higher profile as the putative capital – though the formal transfer would not take place until 1998 – by holding his customary new year reception for the corps at his new Berlin residence, the Bellevue Palace. Unfortunately, a grave lapse in communication between the Foreign Office Protocol Department and the President's Office produced a day-long disaster. The envoys assembled at 0700 hours one cold morning in early January, at the military section of the Bonn airfield, attired in formal wear, which meant morning tailcoats and white ties for many. A special aircraft took them to Berlin, but with a singular lack of imagination, all that the flight served was orange juice and coffee. From the airport, the envoys were taken directly by bus on a sightseeing tour, to see the massive new construction underway, reaching the Bellevue Palace in the mid-morning. They then waited for the reception to commence; there were not even enough seats for the waiting envoys in the pre-reception salons. The Federal President arrived at 12 noon, and in strict protocol order, each envoy was formally presented to him; each was announced at the door, and walked a dozen steps to greet the president and exchange a few words, all of which took time, considering that some 130 envoys were involved. Champagne and fruit juice were on offer, plus a few trays of elegant hors d'oeuvres, but nothing that might count as lunch. As the reception ended, the envoys went on another bus tour, ending up at around 1600 hours at the city planning office where several models and other displays depicted the capital's master plan. Some kind soul had by then sent a distress message to the Berlin city authorities that the ambassadors had been without food since the morning; the platters of sandwiches that the hosts organized presented a welcome sight to this famished bunch. A while later, buses took the envoys back to the airfield for a flight back to Bonn; the ambassadors reached their homes late in the evening. Anywhere else, such treatment would have evoked howls of protest; at Bonn, there was not even a whimper of protest.

Take the more basic issue of the shift of the German capital, on which the Bundestag had voted in 1991; that was a complex compromise decision, and included the inducement that some ministries (e.g., Defence, Economic Cooperation) would remain in Bonn as before, even while the heads of those ministries and their senior staff relocated to Berlin. Another element in that awkward compromise: foreign embassies were given the option of staying on in Bonn. That political compromise ignored the simple reality that it would become increasingly difficult for envoys to operate out of Bonn. A handful of embassies, mostly African, stayed back and found themselves in a curious limbo, nearly a decade after the shift of the federal capital. The strange part is that the diplomatic corps, as the forum representing the collective interests of the resident envoys, did virtually nothing at all to plead the case of those embassies that could not afford the high real estate costs of Berlin; no effort was made to secure a concessional deal for them. Was it impossible for the German Federal authorities to locate land, say on the outskirts of Berlin or in the neighbouring state of Brandenburg, for a diplomatic enclave? The corps failed to even ask for this.

Relatively small diplomatic corps hold business meetings once a year, but there is no uniformity of practice. The large corps almost never meets at its full strength, and the meetings of the regional deans with the dean of the corps may take place once in several months. The issues covered relate mainly to communications with the host country's protocol department, formal and informal, and the organization of joint events of the corps, if that is the local custom. Debates over trade union types of issues are rare.

One factor that contributes to the uneven character of the corps–host country relations is that there is no sharing of experiences among different corps. The only transfer of knowledge that takes place is *via* the envoys themselves, as they move from one capital to another. Of course their parent agencies, the foreign ministry, and its protocol department are aware of the situation in different capitals, but not in any detail. Immersed as any typical protocol department is in its immediate tasks in each capital, it has little time to look over its shoulder and consider the modes of functioning of the corps in other places. One might imagine that the Vatican, through the deanships held by its envoys in the catholic states has such a database of comparative information, but no outsider has access to this.

Vignettes

Some sketches from life in the diplomatic corps, drawn from personal experience, may illustrate its ethos and mode of operation. When I reached Beijing on my first substantive assignment in 1963, the diplomatic corps consisted of barely 32 embassies; that, plus our shared task of understanding an enigmatic China, produced an extraordinary sense of kinship among the diplomats; by the time I returned to Beijing in 1970 on a second assignment, the number in the corps had swelled to about 60, but the atmosphere of mutual cooperation had not changed. The usual principle was that one guarded closely all important issues revolving around one's own bilateral political relationship, but most of the other information could be shared with others, on a reciprocal basis. We Indians, smarting from our bruised egos following the 1962 border clash with China, seldom had much of our own information to put into the pot, but using analytical skills, and fixing bits of the jigsaw puzzle into a holistic picture, we became experts at this game. At all levels, from the head of mission, the deputy chiefs of mission to the second secretaries, we had our contact networks and exchanged visits continually. In 1964, six of us as second and third secretaries from Asian, African, and West European embassies established a monthly lunch club, which grew and was capped at a membership of a dozen; my head of mission, a little miffed at the long afternoons we spent at these 'official' lunches, named this the 'tails of mission lunch club'; we gladly accepted that honorific. Revisiting Beijing in 1999, I was delighted to find that this club had survived, even if it was divided up into its political, economic, and other clusters.

My heads of mission at the two spells at Beijing, Jagat Mehta and Brijesh Mishra respectively, both held the rank of Minister and functioned as *chargé d'affaires* a.i. (India and China withdrew ambassadors in 1961 when relations deteriorated);[15] they were treated by the corps as full ambassadors, regularly exchanging visits with key counterparts. Each had a few trusted contacts that even sometimes showed them their outgoing cipher telegrams; such mutual confidence is rare in the profession, especially for countries that do not belong to alliances or kinship groups. In those days, partly to compensate for the travel restrictions that were in force,[16] the Chinese Foreign Ministry used to organize two annual 'diplomatic tours' to which they invited the head of mission and his or her spouse from each embassy, accompanied by one other diplomat; substitution was permitted, so in effect most diplomats had opportunity to join one tour or another. Travel was mainly by special train, and in convoys of cars, and some remarkable places were covered in this fashion, including interior rural areas and places of scenic or historical importance. Those of us who spoke Chinese could usually slip away from our official minders and ask a few questions to the officials and staff at the factories, museums, and other places visited, garnering small bits of pertinent information. The arrangements were impeccable; even in 1963–64, when China had barely recovered from the 1958 Great Leap Forward disaster and the ensuing famine, we were invariably treated to lavish hospitality.[17]

In the first chaotic year of the 1966–70 Cultural Revolution, when the Foreign Ministry was taken over by Red Guards, and for a while the foreign embassies became the target of xenophobia engineered by Jiang Ching and others, the diplomatic corps was tested as seldom before in recent times. Noisy, stone-throwing demonstrators besieged a succession of embassies – representing East Europe, Mongolia, Burma, and India among others – but they did not cross the property line into physical violation of the embassy. The line was transgressed with the sacking and burning of the British mission in August 1967; other embassies watched helplessly, sheltering fellow diplomats that jumped over walls to seek temporary respite, and providing succour in other ways. When diplomats from the Soviet Union and India were declared *persona non grata* and expelled, the corps, cutting across political groupings showed its solidarity by seeing them off at the airport, braving the demonstrating crowds of Red Guards.

That crisis period produced a strange episode. The dean at the time, an Asian ambassador, found the going too hot, and sent out a note to all embassies to the effect that he was unwell, handing over the responsibility for representing the corps to the deputy dean, a West European envoy. The latter attempted to organize the corps to collective action, and circulated a series of notes to all of them for this purpose. At that point, the Asian ambassador resurfaced with a circular to the effect that he was resuming charge, and proceeded to repudiate the actions of the deputy dean! Beyond the personalities and the myopic reaction of a few, was the fact that the corps as a whole simply did not have a channel to communicate with the only authorities that wielded real power, Mao and Premier Zhou.

The diplomatic corps in Prague (1979–81) seemed staid, mostly inactive. It followed the tradition of presenting a silver salver to departing ambassadors, provided that they had participated in the contributory gift fund collection, and if they had completed two years at the post. Barely six months after arrival, I entered into what proved to be a futile exchange of letters with the dean, over my simple suggestion that if an envoy left before completing two years, as long as he had contributed to the gifts offered to others, he should receive a token gift from the corps, perhaps a coffee-table book; the dean stuck to the two year rule and I withdrew from the gift funding process, as a personal protest. An element of prescience may have been at work, because I left that assignment after barely 19 months, to take up a job in the office of Prime Minister Indira Gandhi. In the panoply of corps-related annual rituals, the President of Czechoslovakia made a unique offering to the envoys based in Prague each December, an annual pheasant shoot at one of his many castles, Konopiste, followed by a grand banquet. A few of us who enjoyed hunting also received invitations from the then Foreign Minister to accompany him on the occasional duck shoot, and once to hunt for wild boar. Meticulous arrangements were made, typical of East Europe in those days, in the hospitality offered, and in the provision of guns and supervision by professional hunters to avoid accidents.

One corps related incident at Prague remains vivid, a diplomatic tour planned by the Foreign Ministry in early May 1981, the first they had organized in many years. A heavy unseasonal snowfall delayed our departure by some hours; subsequently, as the aircraft, a Soviet built TU-104 began its take-off, midway it hit accumulated patches of snow, and the pilot decided to abandon the take-off; the plane came to a juddering halt, right at the end of the runway. Several ambassadors and their spouses were shaken. As we descended, the Turkish envoy asked the Pakistan Ambassador, a former air vice marshal, if we had been in danger; the latter replied somewhat laconically: 'Well, the pilot had about ten seconds to make the right decision, and he did that!' The Foreign Ministry, having taken us to the edge of becoming an air industry statistic, abandoned the tour.

At the next two assignments, Nairobi (1984–86) and Mauritius (1989–92) life in the corps was uneventful, in the former with some 70 resident embassies, and the latter with just 15. At neither places was the corps particularly active; when an airport tax was imposed by the finance minister at one of these places, the corps took it in its stride, with no protest over the fact that if designated as a 'tax' it ran counter to the exemptions stipulated in the 1961 Vienna Convention (of course, if presented as a service charge, it is unexceptionable). At Nairobi, President Daniel arap Moi followed a quaint custom; every time he travelled abroad, a welcome ceremony was organized for him at a purpose-designed amphitheatre adjoining the ceremonial section of Nairobi airport. Several thousand tribal singers and dancers were mobilized to greet him, and the entire cabinet plus senior officials had to attend. The diplomatic corps was also invited. A good quarter of the corps often skipped attendance; this could sometimes evoke a comment from the chief of protocol that he had not seen a particular envoy for a while, but no other sanction was applied. I found it useful to attend, if there was some pending business with a cabinet minister of high official, since one could always buttonhole the target for brief discussion.

Serving as a Consul-General in San Francisco (1986–89) provided a different flavour. US cities compete to attract foreign representation, and take considerable pains to make the resident foreign consuls welcome, organizing a number of activities for them each year, through voluntary 'host committees' and the like, which gives the resident consuls access to interesting local personalities. For instance, Los Angeles and San Francisco see themselves as rival locations for consular representation, which means that consuls-general usually get an opportunity to join the Bohemian Club – an extraordinary American institution, misogynist and a *bête noire* for some, but also a collection of talented people who congregate each summer for a three-week retreat at 'the Grove'.[18] A similar situation obtains in Texas between Houston, the state capital and Dallas; Dallas even annually hosts Washington DC-based ambassadors for a very pleasant weekend, flying them in on a charted aircraft. The mayors often have a part-time 'chief of protocol' on their staff, usually a retired State Department official. The consular corps socializes with the city elites, and holds the usual lunch meetings, with a small difference, in that the honorary consuls are also invited to the contributory lunches.

At Bonn (1992–95) the flavour of the corps was very different; some 120 diplomatic missions, each preoccupied with its own bilateral relations reduced the time for interactions within the corps. Besides the incidents narrated above, some points stand out in memory. Once again, it was the British Ambassador that offered a valuable insight at my initial call, giving his advice that Germany was one of the few countries where an astute envoy could actually influence a decision by the host government, provided he tracked the developments closely and intervened at the right time. One could usually find someone who was willing to share information on how a bilateral issue was shaping up; one could say this was a feature of the plurality of the country's political–bureaucratic system. This turned out to be true, as subsequent experience with a couple of issues important to my country showed.

India was a member of three sub-groups within the diplomatic corps: the SAARC group of South Asia (five of the then seven member-states had resident embassies in Bonn); in 1994 we did something that was perhaps a first for this rather un-united group, in which the persisting differences between India and Pakistan have stunted regional co-operation. In 1994, we sought a joint meeting with the Federal Labour Minister Blum, to impress on him our opposition to the raising of the issue of labour standards at the WTO, which was a bee in the bonnet for this particular long-standing political associate of Chancellor Helmut Kohl. When the Pakistan Ambassador pleaded his inability to attend, owing to a 'prior engagement' in the neighbouring city of Köln, as the rotating chair of this group, I urged him to send a senior representative, who should participate in the discussion and not simply register pro forma attendance.[19] That worked well; we had a substantive meeting, and while we could not move the Labour Minister from his fixed views, the German Foreign Office saw as a positive development the very fact that SAARC envoys had presented a joint *démarche*. We later found that such activism was rare for the SAARC group; colleagues who served contemporaneously at places such as Bangkok and Brussels confirmed this.

The Commonwealth group in Bonn, like at almost all other capitals, was little more than a friendly lunch club, where some information-sharing took place, but seldom any deeper professional activity, unless the rotating host took the trouble to invite a guest speaker. As narrated earlier, the Asia-Pacific group, the third sub-corps entity where India was a member was far more purposeful and productive.

Conclusion

The corps remains a useful, relevant forum for the resident envoy, but one should posit its role in a balanced fashion, taking care not to exaggerate its importance. Take for example, the role today of representational diplomatic entertainment and how this relates to the corps. One general consequence of an intensified bilateral process is that ambassadors and other diplomats now target their official entertainment at official and non-official contacts of the receiving country, much more so than in the past. With more varied local entities now included among their outreach partners, the capacity of ambassadors and other embassy officials to socialize with fellow diplomats stands correspondingly reduced. This in turn diminishes the intra-corps encounters.

At the same time, these social-functional encounters do not fall below a certain threshold, even in the very large diplomatic capitals, because envoys need one another. The corps remains an active entity, a safety net and a professional, information-exchange brotherhood, used by all envoys, ignored at their peril.

Notes

1 Jagat S. Mehta, *Negotiating for India: Resolving Problems Through Diplomacy* (Manohar, New Delhi, 2006), p. 13.
2 As one envoy in a capital that has 13 resident missions put it, an absence from a corps-related function is noticed immediately; in contrast, where a 100 and more envoys jostle for space, one may not even recognize by face all one's colleagues.
3 In the case of pairs of countries that enjoy close ties, sometimes the new envoy and spouse may call jointly on their counterparts. It signals a desire to enter into professional and social relations.
4 In Germany the annual end of year reception hosted by the Federal Chancellor and the Federal President's New Year reception were two fixed events on the calendar. Prime Minister Indira Gandhi, annually hosted three or four tea parties where she spent a few minutes with each ambassador; she usually received resident ambassadors when they made an express request. While serving on her staff in 1981–82 I ventured to mention to her that in most capitals our envoys did not enjoy such access, to be told: 'Why, I receive ambassadors all the time!'
5 The traditional silver salver or box that fellow envoys offer to departing colleagues, through joint subscription, is now given by the regional groups; at some places the departing envoy is allowed to choose the gift he prefers.
6 Groups of envoys that travel together invariably receive far greater attention and access from provincial and local authorities, and even private entities, compared with those that travel individually; besides the EU and ASEAN, SADC is one group that uses a similar formula in some capitals. This practice is spreading.
7 Rana, *The 21ˢᵗ Century Ambassador: Plenipotentiary to Chief Executive* (DiploFoundation, Malta, 2004; Oxford University Press, New Delhi, 2005), p. 30.
8 In Germany the author experimented with creating a cross-regional monthly discussion lunch group in 1994–95 of a dozen compatible colleagues; it worked well, but died away later on.
9 When more than one envoy present credentials on the same day, the same chronological sequence of presentation determines the seniority.
10 In Algiers in 1977–79, I witnessed a situation where the Papal Nuncio became the dean by right of seniority; viewing this a signal honour in an Islamic country, the dean conducted himself with humour and wisdom, winning praise from the corps and the local authorities for his sound leadership.
11 Based on my experience at Nairobi (headquarters of United Nations Environment Programme (UNEP) and United Nations Human Settlement Programme (HABITAT)), and discussions with colleagues at other similar posts.
12 The language is unchanged over some centuries, since the days of royal courts and the notion of personal representation; the envoy is extravagantly praised for his personal qualities, and the head of the receiving state is assured that he may repose full trust in this individual.
13 By custom, the new envoy may call on fellow-ambassadors even before he has presented credentials. Once the copies of the credential papers have

been handed over, he may also begin contacts with other officials in the foreign ministry and elsewhere, but by old tradition he could not meet ministers and other personalities at a political level. This restriction has fallen by the wayside in some capitals, in part because the presentation of credentials sometimes takes place several months after the envoy's arrival and it is unreasonable to restrict his functioning for such a long period.

14   At five ambassadorships and one post of Consul-General, my handing over notes averaged about 100 pages in length; speaking at a book launch function in September 2005, Foreign Secretary Shyam Saran who was my successor in Mauritius in mid-1992, noted the value that my note had provided to him in the initial months. A few countries (Australia and Norway among them) strangely do not use this method of knowledge transmission.

15   The two countries sent back their ambassadors in 1976, when the process of normalization of relations gathered momentum.

16   In the 1960s diplomats were restricted to a 20 km radius from the centre of Beijing, with three exceptions, the Ming Tombs and the Great Wall to the West of the city and the airport to the East; travel to all other places required formal authorization from the Protocol Department. By the 1970s some relaxation was in place; visits to about a dozen cities needed just a formal notification 48 hours in advance; other places still needed authorization.

17   On the diplomatic corps' long car trips to the interior, such as the 1963 visit to the Huang Shan in Anhui province, the cars conveying the ambassadors were arrayed in strict protocol order, with the dean's car bearing the number 1. Curious about the number of the car that bore the vice foreign minister who accompanied us, I went to the very head of the convoy to check; his car bore the number 0!

18   It is hard to describe San Francisco's Bohemian Club in a few words; its members do not speak of it much; googling it provides information, though not all of it is accurate.

19   Notwithstanding the convoluted and often hostile relationship between India and Pakistan, ties between the envoys of the two countries, and even more so between their spouses, are often cordial (with the exception of the hot-house atmosphere of a place such as Beijing). This often puzzles observers not familiar with the cultural and linguistic identity of the two countries.

Part IV
The Diplomatic Corps in Action

8
The Kathmandu Diplomatic Corps: In Search of a Role in Times of Transformation

M. Humayun Kabir[1]

The diplomatic corps in Kathmandu[2] has been intimately linked with major turning points in recent Nepali history. The members of the diplomatic corps played a catalytic role during the anti-Rana regime struggle in 1950–51 and during the campaigns for more democracy in 1960 and 1990. The massive display of people's power in April 2006 and the ongoing transformation in Nepal have also attracted considerable attention from the members of the diplomatic corps in Kathmandu.[3] Indeed, despite some scepticism,[4] members of the diplomatic community became involved with various political and social actors in an effort to move the situation in a positive direction. Not much attention has been devoted at the academic level to the systematic exploration of this sort of activity. In order to help fill this gap, therefore, I will explore how the members of the Kathmandu diplomatic corps responded to the difficult political situation in Nepal, both collectively and individually, and how elements of Nepalese society responded to their efforts.

I shall argue that despite the problems generated by the domestic power struggle, it is likely that Nepal will maintain its position as a member of international society and continue to make its own distinctive contribution to the maintenance of that society. The part played by the diplomatic corps in achieving this state of affairs, I shall argue, has been generally restricted to the promotion of norms of good government and governance, rather than being instrumental in having them translated into practice. This is so because the perceptions of its members have not always accorded with the facts on the ground, as these have actually existed in Nepal. Nonetheless, and despite an uneven performance, I shall argue that the diplomatic corps is likely to remain a useful interlocutor for facilitating interactions between Nepal and the international community. In support of my contention, I will focus on the role of the corps in developments in Nepal following the Royal proclamation at the beginning of February 2005 and the consequent political upheaval leading to the popular revolution in April 2006, which dramatically transformed the political landscape. Two areas, in particular will be investigated. The first will be the perceptions of the members of the diplomatic corps regarding the nature of the transformation taking place in Nepal, and how the members of the corps played their role in terms of managing the response of their governments, for example, in terms of conducting mediation between Nepal and the international community, framing the issues, individually and collectively, socializing the Nepalese actors to universal values, and facilitating the resolution of political crisis. The second will be Nepalese perceptions of this role and its contribution to strengthening the values and practices of democracy, the resolution of conflict through peaceful means, and respect for human rights and the establishment of the rule of law as norms of international society.

The diplomatic corps, international society and Nepal

The diplomatic corps has been defined as 'the collective body of foreign diplomats accredited to a particular country.' By virtue of their appointment, the members of the corps generally represent their respective states to the host country. Berridge defines the role of the diplomatic corps as follows:

> It serves as a lobby in defense of diplomatic privileges and immunities, fosters common professional standards, helps to keep down the temperature in many dangerous conflicts, develops friendships that may prove useful down the line and in its wings some important negotiations still take place.[5]

Others have noted how, through the performance of its traditional functions as the collective voice of the diplomatic community in a capital, the corps also provides one of the few concrete expressions of the way in which the international society of states is constituted. Individually, its members serve the states they represent, but together they represent the society of which their host is a member.[6] That society can be conceived in a number of ways, for example, in terms of a common culture, in terms of certain functions performed within it, and in terms of the character of its members. Should it be seen as a society of states or as a society of different sorts of human relationships, and can we define patterns and processes of change in these terms? Janine Kissolewski, for example, understands an international society as a '...socially and politically constructed phenomenon with normative principles underpinning the construction process'[7] where 'common rules, social institutions can be established, reproduced or transformed respectively by dialogue and consent.'[8] It is in these terms that the sense of a pressure 'from below' seeking to inject and strengthen a stronger respect for democratic norms, human rights and the peaceful resolution of disputes in the conduct of international relations may be best understood. An international society formed primarily of states, is being transformed into one in which civil society actors are increasingly claiming a role as actors and, indeed, members. If this is so, then the upheavals in Nepal not only reflected the effects of external pressures upon a traditional national or state society, they also could be said to be contributing to changes in that external world itself, thus a two-way process in which the role of the Kathmandu diplomatic corps was important and possibly central.

The process by which Nepal became a fully integrated member of the modern contemporary international society got underway in the 1950s. Before that, Nepal had maintained limited relations mainly with its neighbours. This opening had mixed consequences. Nepal began to contribute to the evolution of agenda and discourses in the international society, participated in international efforts to maintain global peace and security, particularly through participation in the United Nations peacekeeping efforts, helped strengthen international normative regimes through becoming party to a number of UN Covenants, Conventions and Treaties, and succeeded in getting elected to various international bodies.[9] It also received considerable financial assistance from the international community, although the motives for such assistance varied significantly.[10] In the process, Nepal became exposed to global and regional interactions that opened the way for the inflow of new ideas and interactions. More interactions with the outside world, led the people of Nepal to becoming more aware of their socio-economic conditions, raised their expectations about how they should be treated and resulted in new patterns of social organization which challenged existing arrangements. Although the 1990 Constitution of Nepal proclaimed democratic principles and upheld fundamental human rights under the broad framework of twin principles of constitutional monarchy and multiparty democracy, many analysts believed that the new power arrangement could not adequately meet the emerging aspirations of the people. A Department for International Development/World Bank study in 2005 also identified several systemic shortcomings, including the continuation of non-inclusive structures, values and behavioural norms and expectations throughout the system, and reluctance on the part even of aid agencies to require a 'fundamental change of the rules of the game'.[11] Although the House of Representatives of Nepal adopted changes to address some of these challenges in May 2006, it remains to be seen how they will be put into practice on the ground.

Arguably the transition toward democracy during the 1990s created a new and difficult political climate in Nepalese society. High expectations imposed huge pressures on the political system leading to the unravelling of political compacts worked out between the monarchy and political parties. Consequently, political turmoil increased in Nepal by the mid-1990s. The organization of people in multiple social, professional and political groups and the radicalization of social and political discourse contributed to this development.[12] The growing demands for social equality and inclusion challenged the traditional system of power, and the authority of the state was challenged through violent means from the bottom. As the insurgency under the leadership of the Communist Party of Nepal (Maoist), (henceforth referred to as Maoists), continued to spread, successive governments were unable to handle the evolving political situation. Accordingly, the monarchy reasserted itself. On the advice of the then Prime Minister, Parliament was dissolved in May 2002, and this was followed by the dismissal of the Sher Bahadur Deuba government in October 2002. Thereafter, three successive governments could not make much headway in legitimizing their rule, breaking the political deadlock, or addressing the Maoist insurgency effectively. In this vacuum, political observers argued that a new informal power structure was emerging in Kathmandu.[13]

In his proclamation of 1 February 2005, King Gyanendra stressed the values of democracy and the rule of law and expressed his commitment 'to eliminate terrorism in her [Nepal's] own interest as well as in the interest of democracies around the world.'[14] Regarding democracy, he observed, 'It is our desire that democracy be a way of life, politics be conducted in keeping with democratic norms and value...It is our belief that upholding human rights not only preserves and promotes democratic values but also enhances a way of life and civilizational values commensurate with the 21st century.'[15] It is noteworthy that he not only reaffirmed the commitment of his government to universal values, norms and practices, but also interpreted them from a deeper perspective in civilizational terms. He reiterated his commitments to 'meaningful democracy' during his proclamation on the anniversary of his direct rule on 1 February 2006 and his message to the nation on Democracy Day on 18 February 2006.[16] King Gyanendra's initiative, although not unexpected, introduced a completely new dimension in Nepalese politics with long-term ramifications.

The diplomatic corps in Kathmandu was caught in the middle with basically three challenges. First, despite rhetoric to the contrary, there was a clear indication that the Royal government would pursue a policy of 'war for peace,' if required, to deal with the Maoist insurgency.[17] Secondly, a sense of 'exceptionalism' based on a strong dose of nationalism was used to justify and sustain the new power arrangement;[18] and thirdly, democracy was portrayed as a goal apparently with a roadmap set by the Palace, which could include the holding of elections to local and national bodies, among others.

As the mainstream Seven Party Alliance (SPA)[19] with support from the Maoists announced peaceful agitation beginning on 6 April 2006 to end monarchical rule and to restore democratic rights, including reinstatement of the House of Representatives, another new challenge confronted the diplomatic corps. There was a palpable fear among some of its members that the Maoists might infiltrate the peaceful agitation and engineer a violent overthrow of the government.[20] The announcement of a unilateral ceasefire by the Maoists in the Kathmandu valley and their assurances that they would participate in the agitation peacefully did not reassure some influential members of the diplomatic corps. They continued to strongly advocate reconciliation between the so-called constitutional forces, i.e., between the monarchy and the mainstream political parties, virtually along the roadmap suggested by the King.[21] Perhaps as a part of this move, major countries quickly welcomed the Royal declaration of 21 April 2006,[22] by which the King had invited the political parties to 'recommend a name for the post of Prime Minister,'[23] and actively lobbied with the political parties to accept the offer.[24] There was a faint hope that if the constitutional forces could cooperate, then the Maoists could be isolated. As thousands of protestors thronged the streets in Kathmandu and in other cities around the country, major political parties decided on 22 April 2006 to reject the Royal offer, leaving the diplomatic corps scrambling to catch up with the fast unfolding political situation in Nepal.

The SPA and the Maoists intensified their cooperation and signed several agreements that raised the prospect of a peaceful transition for

Nepal towards a competitive multiparty democracy. This would be accomplished by drafting an interim constitution, by forming an interim government, and holding elections for the constituent assembly. Nevertheless, important members of the corps continued to express their concerns, particularly about the commitment of the Maoists.[25] Obviously, while such moves might strengthen the moral position of the SPA, some analysts feared they might actually complicate the process of transition toward peace.[26] Nonetheless, the newly formed SPA government under Prime Minister Girija Prasad Koirala reaffirmed its commitment to universal values and ideals. While briefing the diplomats on 19 May 2006, the Deputy Prime Minister and Foreign Minister K. P. Sharma Oli said,

> Nepal has once again joined the community of democracies. In this changed context, Nepal's foreign policy will be guided by the universal values of democracy, human rights and fundamental freedoms, and the rule of law, in addition to the established guiding principles and norms of international law. By upholding these eternal values we are determined to play an active role in the multilateral institutions, including the United Nations.[27]

He reiterated these commitments at a meeting of the Human Rights Council in Geneva and said that the respect for democracy, rule of law and promotion and protection of all human rights were the foremost priorities of the government of Nepal. As the government and the Maoists moved ahead with their agenda, however, new challenges appeared.

The diplomatic corps as an actor in the evolution of the domestic political process

From the outbreak of the Maoist insurgency in February 1996, security concerns gradually climbed to the top of the national agenda, and as the insurgency continued to spread, the members of the diplomatic corps by and large shared the perception of the threat as defined by the government. Accordingly, they tried to help the government address this challenge by a variety of means. Several of their governments offered military assistance to the Royal Nepalese Army (RNA)[28] and support to strengthen the existing state institutions, including a variety of assistance to the political parties. They also offered diplomatic support to the government.[29] However, acts of both omission and commission by members of diplomatic corps created some unintended consequences for the evolution of the power struggle in Nepal. Since the dissolution of Parliament in May 2002, problems with the legitimacy of the government, the terms for settling the Maoist insurgency, and possible reform measures dominated the political agenda. While the efforts of the diplomatic corps gave clarity to many of these issues, outlining possible solutions, in most cases its efforts did not produce desired results. Various domestic actors interpreted the corps' efforts in their own ways and there was a general belief that everyone was engaged in promoting their own partisan objectives.

At this stage, the first and foremost priority of the diplomatic corps was to help restore the legitimacy of the government. This would be achieved, they agreed, by ensuring the participation of major political parties represented in the last Parliament,[30] by encouraging the formation of an all-party government, and by holding credible elections to the House of Representatives as soon as possible. In this context, members of the corps consistently urged reconciliation between the Monarchy and the political parties[31] so that a legitimate government could be formed and elections involving all democratic parties be held in a climate free of intimidation and violence.[32] While there was some degree of appreciation for the efforts made by the diplomatic corps to restore the democratic process, its apparent sympathy for the King, which was perhaps generated by the strong desire for maintaining systematic stability and order, posed problems.[33] Occasional initiatives by members of the corps to foster the political process also produced mixed results. The pressure exerted by some members of the corps on the political parties in September 2003 serves as an example of how such efforts could prove counterproductive.[34] This episode, as some political observers pointed out, badly exposed the limits to their understanding and appreciation of the dynamics of the political struggle underway in Nepal at that time.[35] Subsequent efforts by the diplomatic corps after the appointment of Sher Bahadur Deuba as Prime Minister in June 2004 did not prove to be of much help in improving the situation. Two factors perhaps stymied their efforts. First, actual power was concentrated in the hands the King with the rest of the government enjoying little effective power. Some political leaders alleged that the King was merely preparing the grounds for a complete takeover during that period. Secondly, the Deuba government suffered from internal bickering and was immobilized by pressure from both inside and outside.

The Royal takeover in February 2005 accentuated the division within the diplomatic corps. A large segment of the diplomatic corps expressed great reservations, considering the move as 'constituting a serious setback to the cause of democracy in Nepal'[36] and violating the 'two pillars of political stability in Nepal,' namely constitutional monarchy and multiparty democracy. This group used public statements issued both at home capitals and in Kathmandu,[37] although it is not clear if various diplomatic missions coordinated their moves in this regard. The reactions generally took strong exception to the arrest of political leaders, journalists and civil society activists and expressed hope that political detainees would be released soon and that constitutional rights would be restored and fundamental human rights safeguarded. Several envoys, as a first step, were also recalled to their headquarters in home capitals for consultations,[38] as a demonstration of concern against at the Royal decision. Symbolic and formal protests were also lodged. At the other end of spectrum, however, some countries defended the Royal action by invoking the concept of the sovereign rights of each country to manage its internal affairs without outside involvement. Although not all of them directly supported the Royal move, countries belonging to this group in general justified their stance on the issue by arguing that it was an internal matter and they expressed the hope that the people of Nepal would be able to manage their affairs without external interference.[39] Some members offered to supply military hardware, if Nepal so requested.[40] It was possible that many members of this second group were concerned that any endorsement of external involvement in Nepal could negatively impinge on their respective claims to handle their own internal situation without external interference. Yet there were also members of a third group who, although unhappy about the Royal takeover, preferred to express their views by 'quiet diplomacy.' They conveyed their strong preference for the restoration of democracy and constitutional rights privately.[41]

Members of the diplomatic corps signalled their governments' strong disapproval of the takeover in other tangible ways as well. For example, some members of the corps announced the suspension of military assistance to the RNA until democracy was restored.[42] Others subsequently joined in this action.[43] Economic assistance was also reduced or suspended altogether. Citing developments after 1 February 2005 as a 'serious setback in regards to multiparty democracy, to constitutional monarchy, to human rights, and to finding a peaceful solution to the ongoing violent conflict,' some members decided to reduce the planned bilateral financial assistance for 2006.[44] Several other members froze assistance.[45] Practically, such decisions affected support for specific high profile projects as well as general economic assistance. No one, however, wanted to precipitate an economic crisis, and there was a general tendency to maintain humanitarian economic commitments. Even those countries that kept the issue of military assistance to Nepal under constant review announced that they would continue to offer other economic assistance. However, in the wake of the takeover, donors shifted their focus to human rights, democracy and peace from the earlier priorities of development, good governance and anti-corruption measures. As the new democratic government under the SPA assumed power in April 2006, donors reversed their decisions and in some cases increased their assistance.[46]

Mixed signals from the diplomatic community continued to affect the political process in Nepal. Analysts identified several trends. While the twin pillar theory, centring around constitutional monarchy and multiparty democracy was promoted as a basis for reconciliation between the King and political parties, excluding the Maoists from the calculation was interpreted as undercutting the prospects for peace.[47] The ambiguous position of certain members of the corps *vis à vis* the Maoists further added to the confusion. Again, some analysts argued that linking the Maoist insurgency with global terrorism made it easier to adopt the paradoxical and perhaps cynical concept of a war for peace.[48] Initial reluctance to acknowledge the violation of human rights by some actors, some analysts alleged, led to continued abuse of human rights. Yet, a large group of members was 'in favour of peaceful resolution of Nepal's problems within the framework of the rule of law, respect for human rights, and multiparty democracy,'[49] and some members saw the ongoing Nepalese turmoil as a threat to their territorial integrity,[50] but declined to share the position of others *vis à vis* the Maoist insurgency. Certain member states also supported the government position from their belief that a strong government could perhaps resolve the insurgency problem.[51] Indeed, in the post-February 2005 period, four major developments intensely tested the role of the diplomatic corps. The announcement of a unilateral ceasefire by the Maoists on 2 September 2005, the holding of municipal elections on 8 February 2006, the signing of a 12-point understanding between the mainstream political parties and Maoists in November 2005, and the resulting popular uprising that dislodged the King from power in April 2006 all evoked mixed reactions from the members of the corps along predictable lines. Some members of the corps shifted positions[52] advocating untenable formulae for resolution of the conflict in Nepal.[53] These were not seen as helpful gestures. The massive public rejection of the

Royal offer for reconciliation on 21 April 2006, which had been strongly supported by influential members of the corps, demonstrated clear limitations in their grasp of public sentiment.

Clearly the response of the Kathmandu diplomatic corps was not uniform. Despite a general consensus around international norms, some, it was alleged, were perhaps engaged in pursuing a parallel strategy within the turmoil to promote their own national strategic interests in Nepal, at times ignoring the aspirations of its people as these were articulated by popular protest. It would perhaps be naïve to think that actors in Nepal did not seek advantage in the opportunities presented. A prominent Nepali politician articulated this thought further when he observed that all sides could play their cards suitably.[54] However, some clearly tried to calibrate their responses to the Nepalese situation on the basis of their normative commitments to universal values. They tried, as best they could, to promote higher goals that could strengthen human security by restoring peace and democracy as well as ensuring social justice and equality. Others, in contrast, conveyed the impression of reluctance to engage in Nepal's problems despite the pressure 'for something to be done' being exerted in all quarters. Indeed, apart from the United Nations, only a few countries[55] expressed their readiness to extend their good offices for addressing the problem in Nepal up until the April movement of 2006. On their part, of course, the Nepalese authorities were similarly reluctant to seek or accept 'help' directed at helping them reform. Regarding the Maoist insurgency, in particular, members of the corps differed on the approaches to ending it. Some members supported strategies for their military defeat or complete surrender. They also made it clear that the Maoists could not be considered as a legitimate political force and that no dialogue should be initiated with them until they completely renounced violence.[56] This hard line persisted in some quarters even after the new government had initiated peace talks with the Maoists.[57] Others advocated a conciliatory course so that the Maoists could be enticed back into dialogue and negotiations directed at ending the insurgency through peaceful means.[58] As the prospects for reconciliation between the SPA government and Maoists brightened, even the latter showed signs of hesitation about the details of how this was to be accomplished in the context of the new developments.

The new SPA government and Maoists signed an eight-point agreement on 16 June 2006, which included the formation of an interim government in which the Maoists were likely to participate. Such a possibility posed a serious question for important members of the corps about how to deal with Maoists, whom they regarded as 'terrorists', but were now informal negotiating partners of the government. As the pressure from the Maoists to form an interim government intensified, some members of the corps became worried at the possibility of their armed presence in a future government.[59] The possibility of their merger with the Nepalese army, suggested by the Maoist leaders, also became a contentious issue posing yet another challenge for members of the diplomatic corps.[60] The corps was, however, almost united in urging both the government and the Maoists to respect human rights and international humanitarian laws. Almost all members of the corps repeatedly expressed their concern over the resumption of human rights violations by both sides in the conflict and called upon the government and the Maoists to respect human rights and humanitarian laws.[61]

On the issue of mediation, the UN expressed its readiness to facilitate or support any effort to find a peaceful way out of the ongoing conflict in Nepal. Some members of the diplomatic corps resisted such an idea, while others strongly supported it.[62] On its part, until the signing of an eight-point agreement with the Maoists, the Nepalese government rejected all such suggestions. However, the government eventually showed some flexibility. They and the Maoists both agreed to request 'the United Nations to help manage the armies and weapons of both sides and to monitor it in order to ensure free and fair elections for the constituent assembly.'[63] Nonetheless, scepticism about the modalities and value of inviting the United Nations persisted among domestic political actors. At the same time, the reservation of certain members of the corps on the mediation issue was also obvious despite the fact that Nepalese Prime Minister G. P. Koirala on his return from New Delhi on 9 June 2006 said, 'India suggested to invite UN – only for management of arms and rehabilitation.'[64] The government eventually asked the UN to monitor and manage the weapons and forces of the government as well as those of the Maoists. The Maoists contested this on the grounds that they had not been consulted and Maoist leader Prachanda subsequently wrote a separate letter to the Secretary General of the United Nations.[65]

In general terms, the reasons for the division in the diplomatic corps during the Royal rule were all too clear. Countries from the developed world (including India) largely opposed the Royal move, out of fear of the unknown consequences of any major change in the power structure and perhaps a genuine desire for democracy in Nepal. Other countries generally from the developing world defended the right of a country to manage its internal affairs, although many of them did not explicitly support the Royal move of 1 February 2005. Indeed, competing policy prescriptions by various members of the diplomatic corps helped to widen the gap among the domestic actors, and sometimes contributed to deepening the crisis. Perhaps too much emphasis on institutional power arrangements had blinded them to shifting political realities and the degree of polarization that had developed. Therefore, one could come to a reasonable assumption that members of the diplomatic corps remained as divisive in framing the issues as in articulating their response to the evolution of the situation in Nepal. Perhaps narrow interpretations of national interest may have influenced their vision, but members of the corps achieved some success in establishing international standards as markers in the internal struggle, even if their performances as facilitators was at best lacklustre.

Nepalese views of the diplomatic corps

The actions of members of the diplomatic corps during the crisis generated a variety of responses from major actors in Nepal. From the government side, these took several forms. As the majority of the diplomatic corps declined to endorse the Royal proclamation of 1 February 2005, King Gyanendra himself expressed disappointment over the initial response of the international community.[66] Diplomats were blamed for conveying the wrong message to the international community and creating misperceptions about Nepalese realities. Some members of the government even accused members of the diplomatic community of encouraging violence.[67] Such criticism was not however unique to Nepal; it also happened in Skopje during the crisis of 2001.[68] Given the charged environment, the intense scrutiny of the role of the diplomatic community may continue to increase if the political problem persists. In addition, envoys were summoned to hear the displeasure of the government whenever their views were not considered to be helpful. Two envoys were summoned to the Ministry of Foreign Affairs on 20 May 2005 to hear protests against their alleged 'interference' in Nepalese internal affairs.[69] Earlier, on 8 May 2005, the Ministry of Foreign Affairs sent a Note to all Diplomatic Missions in Kathmandu urging them to understand the sensitivities of the situation when they tried to meet persons being held in detention. The activities of some envoys were also closely monitored.[70] Indeed, there were rumours that tougher action would be taken against some of them.[71]

Nevertheless, forceful *démarches* by the diplomatic corps at the highest level yielded at least some modest results, particularly in the post-Royal proclamation period. Political leaders and other detainees were released; emergency provisions were allowed to expire and media restrictions were lifted within a 100 days of their imposition. Other anticipated policies of the government were also adjusted in the light of possible reaction from the members of the diplomatic corps. In the mean time, the Nepalese government under Royal rule continued its efforts to widen its space for diplomatic manoeuvre and to diversify its sources of military supplies.[72] Furthermore, in the face of a strong demand for the exclusion of the RNA personnel from UN peacekeeping efforts for alleged violation of human rights,[73] the government tried to demonstrate that the army was addressing claimed shortcomings in this area.

The mainstream political parties maintained an ambivalent attitude to the diplomatic corps despite its professed sympathy for their cause and predicament. During Royal rule, this ambivalence was manifested in a number of areas. Although the confidence level improved somewhat after the members of the diplomatic corps welcomed the restoration of democracy, following the events of April 2006, sensitivities were still apparent on both sides. On the eve of the visit of Prime Minister G. P. Koirala, members of the reinstated House of Representatives warned the Prime Minister not to sign any deal with India.[74] Likewise, so too did the Maoist leader Prachanda. He also warned that the peace negotiations between the government and the Maoists might breakdown, as some of Koirala's ministers were 'agents' of India and the US, trying to keep the Monarchy alive in Nepal.[75] At a later date, Maoist leaders also strongly criticized the United States and India for 'not grasping the ground reality of the people's 19 days of peaceful movement.'[76] This apparent ambivalence clearly limited the ability of the diplomatic community to extend any tangible support to the parties during the Royal regime. Thus, after a meeting with a British official on 16 February 2006, who reportedly urged Nepali Congress leader G. P. Koirala to abandon the 12-point understanding between the political parties and Maoists, Mr. Koirala was reported to have commented that the 'Foreigners do not understand.'[77]

As the talks between the government and Maoists were progressing following the signing of the eight-point agreement on 16 June 2006, Deputy Prime Minister Amik Sherchan echoed similar sentiments when he said, 'In my meeting, Ambassadors from several countries to Nepal have expressed their own interests, and they are not all happy with the new changes... Problems for the peace process could come not only from the regressive forces but also from international causes.'[78] Earlier, the Maoist leader Krishna Bahadur Mahara also shared similar views when he had observed, 'If what US Ambassador Moriarty said is the official voice of the US, we urge the US to review it since it is against the aspirations of the Nepali people and the entire democratic forces. It was up to the people of Nepal to decide what should be done to resolve Nepal's political problems and restore peace.'[79] The Leader of the Communist Party of Nepal (UML) Bhamdev Gautam also expressed his dissatisfaction over the comments made by some important members of the diplomatic corps.[80]

The ambivalence of their political partners notwithstanding, the Maoists, themselves, repeatedly called for the UN and other international organizations to take an active role in monitoring human rights, negotiating ceasefires and even mediating a resolution of the conflict in Nepal.[81] After the signing of the eight-point agreement, where it was agreed to seek the support of the United Nations for arms management, the Maoists intensified their lobbying of both the mainstream political parties and the members of the diplomatic corps.[82] They sought to convince them of their commitment to competitive and democratic politics against the backdrop of growing controversy over the issue of disarming. In particular, the issue of whether the Maoists should be allowed to join the interim government before they surrendered their arms became a burning topic of debate. Again, how far such interactions were able to dispel the lingering suspicion about the Maoists remained to be seen at the time of writing.

Members of Nepalese civil society, while remaining united in their pursuit of restoring peace and democracy appeared to be divided on the role of the diplomatic corps in Kathmandu. A large section of Nepalese civil society believed that the diplomatic corps had not been helpful in finding a way out of the conflict; rather they believed that some members of the corps had indeed been pursuing narrow interests based on traditional conceptions of power politics with a view to promoting their narrow national and strategic interests. There was also a strong sensitivity among some civil society leaders about accepting any significant role for certain members of the corps in the resolution of Nepalese problems because their 'credentials' were judged questionable.[83] In general, there remains a feeling that some members of the diplomatic corps were hypocritical and pursued double standards.[84] In addition, there was also a feeling that they placed the need for order over justice in supporting the *status quo*. As the people's movement grew in intensity and the important members of the diplomatic corps welcomed the Royal proclamation of 21 April 2006, 18 detained civil society leaders and activists wrote an open letter to the Ambassadors of the United States, India, China, and to the representatives of the European Union and the United Nations urging them to recognize political realities and to support the people's attempt to restore democracy under a new concept of Nepali nationhood.

The achievements of the diplomatic corps assessed

It may be seen that the members of the diplomatic corps offered their services in variety of forms. As I have argued, the members of the diplomatic corps acted as a conveyer belt of ideas about international standards and expectations to the participants in the dispute. Almost as importantly, however, they mediated between local events and external expectations. Many members of the corps either openly or discreetly supported the struggle for peace and democracy, thereby encouraging and conferring a measure of legitimacy on those demands and the people who made them. In addition, they offered general suggestions to all parties about how to proceed and possible solutions while signalling what, in their view, would be unacceptable courses of action because they violated international norms. To this end, many individual diplomats engaged directly, if informally, with cross-sections of Nepalese society. In so doing, they tried to sensitize Nepalese actors about the importance of universal values and norms in their interactions with the international community while, at the same time, providing the international community with direct information about the forces in play. During the unilateral ceasefire period observed by the Maoists in late 2005, for example, several envoys visited eastern, central and western regions of Nepal and met different people from those areas.

Such a process clearly helped to connect people at the grassroots level with the idea of universal human values and offered insights into the general position and role of the international community on the situation in Nepal. In addition, the diplomatic corps offered 'the collective expression of those states on the ground,'[85] and a convenient point of access for the local actors to the international community. Indeed, everyone recognized that the presence of the diplomatic corps in Kathmandu served to confirm Nepal's membership of the international society as an independent and sovereign state. Perhaps, this explains why the recent expansion of the diplomatic corps, with addition of Malaysian and Danish representation at Ambassadorial level and European Commission at *Chargé d' Affaires* (CDA) level in recent years was so welcomed.[86] The eagerness of the government and all political actors[87] to maintain regular contacts with the members of diplomatic corps also testifies to their continued relevance and importance. As in the case of the Skopje diplomatic corps in 2001, events in Nepal have clearly shown the potential of the diplomatic corps as a catalyst for facilitating the political and social evolution of a country at times of great internal difficulty.

However, the multiple imperatives under which the members of a diplomatic corps necessarily function limited the Kathmandu corps' effectiveness in this regard. At the practical level, the ability of the diplomatic corps to influence the course of events was always modest. Divisions within the diplomatic corps usually prevented the members from adopting a practical position unanimously that might have resulted in more effective pressure on the parties to the dispute. Offsetting this *sui generis*, but important, constraint, however, was the fact that they were able to muster a degree of declaratory solidarity about international norms and expectations which did help moderate the conduct of the dispute. Accordingly, therefore, and notwithstanding their similarly fragmented response to the efforts of the corps, domestic actors did recognize its value in keeping their window to the outside world open with an immediacy and official quality which no other agent was able to match.

Notes

1 An earlier version of the Paper was presented at the 47th Annual Convention of the International Studies Association, San Diego, California, USA, 22–25 March 2006. The author expresses his gratitude to Professor Paul Sharp for his encouragement, and valuable comments on the first draft. At the same time, the author also expresses his deep appreciation to Prof. James Mayall, University of Cambridge, Professor John D. Stempel, University of Kentucky and Evan H. Potter, University of Ottawa for their helpful observations on the paper. Mr. Sufiur Rahman, Director, SAARC Secretariat in Kathmandu and Mr. Mehdi Hasan, First Secretary in Bangladesh Embassy in Moscow also deserve a word of appreciation for taking the trouble to go through the initial draft and making useful comments. The views expressed in this paper are those of the author only, who is a senior diplomat from Bangladesh who served in Kathmandu from 2003–06.

2 The diplomatic corps in Kathmandu is reasonably large. As of June 2005, there were 20 resident Missions at Ambassadorial level plus one Mission at *Chargé d' Affaires* (CDA) level, 2 offices of International and regional organizations, namely SAARC and the UN, 42 concurrently accredited Missions, five Donor Agency offices, 21 UN Agencies and Specialized offices, 15 Aid

Agencies offices in Kathmandu. On its part, Nepal has 21 resident Missions around the world capitals plus three Consulates-General.

3 Former Prime Minister Surya Bahadur Thapa articulated the role of the diplomatic community in Nepal in one of his recent statements. He said that there were four parties to the conflict in Nepal, namely the Monarchy, political parties, Maoists and the international community. For details see, 'Thapa pushes his own formulae to end Nepal crisis', *The Telegraph Weekly*, 2 November 2005.

4 Questions have been raised recently about the utility of diplomacy and resident diplomatic missions as means of communication among various states. For a pessimistic perspective see, Hans J. Morgenthau, *Politics Among Nations: The Struggle for Power and Peace*, 4th Edition (New York: Alfred A. Knopf, 1967), 527. For a different view see, Alec Solomita, 'Who needs diplomats', *Harvard University Gazette*, 2 May 1996. In Nepal, proponents on both sides have strong views on the role of the diplomatic corps in Kathmandu. For general understanding on the evolving role of diplomatic corps see, G. R. Berridge and Nadia Gallo, 'Role of the Diplomatic Corps: the US-North Korea talks in Beijing 1988–94', in J. Melissen, ed., *Innovation in Diplomatic Practice* (Basingstoke: Macmillan, 1999); Paul Sharp, 'Who Needs Diplomats?', *International Journal* (Winter 1997–8), pp. 609–34.

5 G. R. Berridge and Nadia Gallo, 'The Role of diplomatic corps: the US-North Korea talks in Beijing, 1988–94', in J. Melissen, ed., *Innovation in Diplomatic Practice* (Basingstoke: Macmillan, 1999).

6 Sharp *Ibid.*

7 Janine Kissolewski, 'Norms in international society: English School meets constructivists', Paper prepared for the workshop on European Integration II at BISA Conference, Bradford, 18–20 December 2000.

8 *Ibid.*

9 For a good understanding of Nepal's relationship with the United Nations see, Nishchal N. Pandey, Keshav R. Jha and Bishwa K. Maskay, *Nepal and the United Nations* (Kathmandu: Institute of Foreign Affairs, Nepal Council of World Affairs and the United Nations Association of Nepal, 2005).

10 For details see, Ram Saran Mahat, *In Defense of Democracy: Dynamics and Fault lines of Nepal's Political Economy* (New Delhi: Adroit Publishers, 2005).

11 *The World Bank and The Department for International Development*, 'Unequal Citizens: Gender, Caste and Ethnic Exclusion in Nepal-Summary Report', Kathmandu 2005, 14.

12 International Crisis Group, 'Nepal's New Alliance: The Mainstream Parties and the Maoists', *Asia Report* no. 106, 28 November 2005, 9.

13 See, Hari Roka, 'Militarization and Democratic rule in Nepal', *Himal South Asian*, November 2003; On the role of unified command see, C. K. Lal, 'Defusing the pressure cooker', *The Nepali Times*, 19–25 May 2006.

14 Proclamation by King Gyanendra Bir Bikram Shah Dev of Nepal on 01 February 2005, *The Kathmandu Post*, 2 February 2005.

15 *Ibid.*

16 RSS, 'King calls to resume democratic process', *The Himalayan Times*, 18 February 2006.

17 According to some analysts 'war for peace' strategy reached a new threshold since the beginning of 2003. For detail see, Rita Manchanda, 'War for Peace' in Nepal promises bloodshed', *The South Asia Tribune*, 5 January 2003.

18 Following Royal takeover in February 2005 Ministers in the Royal government and their supporters regularly played on the issue of national feeling and its vital link with the institution of monarchy.

19 The Seven Party Alliance (SPA) includes mainstream political parties, such as the Nepali Congress, Nepali Congress (Democratic), Communist Party of Nepal (UML), Janamorcha Nepal, Nepal Majdur Kishan Party, Nepal Sadbhawana Party (Anand Devi), Sangjukta Bam Morcha Nepal.

20 The US Ambassador was most vocal on this point. Other Western Ambassadors also largely shared this view. For details see, International Crisis Group, 'Nepal: From People power to Peace?' *Asia Report* no. 115, 10 May 2006.

21 For an understanding of US position see, 'American considerations on Nepal changing?', *The Telegraph Weekly*, 19 April 2006; for an Indian position see, Post Report, 'Ball in King's Court: Dr. Singh', *The Kathmandu Post*, 21 April 2006.

22 Post Report, 'We salute people of Nepal: US', *The Kathmandu Post*, 22 April 2006; 'King has taken bold step: Karan Singh', *The Kathmandu Post*, 22 April 2006; Post Report, 'UN, UK, Canada welcome Royal address', *The Kathmandu Post*, 23 April 2006; 'India with people, for twin pillar', *The Kathmandu Post*, 23 April 2006.

23 'King invites seven parties', *The Kathmandu Post*, 22 April 2006.

24 Himalayan News Services, 'Envoys press parties to accept King's invite', *The Himalayan Times*, 23 April 2006.

25 Rekha Shrestha, 'Maoists to give up arms forever: Bloomfield', *The Himalayan Times*, 24 June 2006; Himalayan News Service, 'Moriarty flays Maoists violence', *The Himalayan Times*, 29 June 2006.

26 Ajaya Bhadra Khanal, 'Invisible hands and Resistance', *The Kathmandu Post*, 29 June 2006.

27 Opening remarks of Mr. K. P. Sharma Oli, Deputy Prime Minister and Foreign Minister at the briefing organized for the Heads of Diplomatic Mission in Kathmandu, 19 May 2006.

28 The US, UK and India regularly offered military and military-related supplies to the RNA to fight Maoist 'terrorism.' For details of military supplies offered by various countries see, 'The role of the international community', *Annual Report*, Human Rights Watch, 2004.

29 In a bid to support the government efforts to tackle Maoist insurgency, UK, US and India endorsed the concept paper prepared by the government during peace negotiations with the Maoists in August 2003. However, reportedly government side made no serious effort to engage with Maoist proposals. See, Rita Manchanda, 'On the warpath again', *The Frontline*, 24 October 2003.

30 Sir Jeffrey James, Special Envoy of UK during his visit to Nepal in September 2003 emphasized on the need of involvement of 'all interested parties' to keep the principles and practices of constitutional monarchy and multi-party democracy operational. See, Rita Manchanda, 'On the war path', *The Frontline*, 24 October 2003.

31 See, Jan Sharma, 'Rocca stresses unity', *The Himalayan Times*, 18 December 2003; Christina Rocca, 'New Horizons in United States Relations in South Asia, Statement made at the University of Pennsylvania, reprinted in *The Telegraph Weekly*, 28 April 2004; Statement by James F. Moriarty, US Ambassador at the Nepal Council of World Affairs on 9 August 2005. On its part, India also called on for such reconciliation.

32 Niraj Aryal, 'Sir Jeffrey James favours and rejects elections concurrently', *The Telegraph Weekly*, 31 March 2004.

33 S. D. Muni, 'On a hot tin roof', *The Hindustan Times*, 30 August 2004; Post Report, 'Rocca mum over US support to parties', *The Katmandu Post*, 21 December 2003.

34 When the major political parties announced mass agitation to force King Gyanendra to restore democracy in Nepal in September 2003, the Indian, US and British Ambassadors in Kathmandu met the leaders of Nepali Congress and Communist Party of Nepal (UML) and persuaded them to postpone their agitation. Political leaders alleged later on that Ambassadors had misled them to believe that King Gyanendra would respond positively to their demands for restoration of democracy in exchange for their decision to postpone agitation, which did not materialize. Such diplomatic *démarche* may have also led the King into a false impression that the international community had virtually abandoned the political parties, and would go along with him in his effort to maintain order, even ignoring political parties, and to fight Maoist 'terrorism'; Hari Roka, 'Militarization and democratic rule in Nepal', *Himal South Asian*, November 2003.

35 For detail see, Asian Center for Human Rights, 'Deal for International Inaction on Nepal in Geneva', Weekly briefing paper on the key Human Rights concerns in Nepal, 7 April 2005.

36 Ministry of External Affairs, New Delhi, 'Statement on Developments in Nepal', 1 February 2005.

37 India, UK, USA, Germany, Canada, European Union, Norway, Denmark, Japan, Republic of Korea, Russian Federation, China and Pakistan made public statements in the wake of Royal takeover on 1 February 2005.

38 The British, German, Norwegian, Danish CDA and other Ambassadors from EU countries posted in Kathmandu were recalled to Headquarters for consultations. The US Ambassador also left Kathmandu for about ten days following 1 February takeover, although the US Embassy in Kathmandu characterized it as a routine visit on leave. For detail see, Embassy of the Federal Republic of Germany in Kathmandu, 'Press Release no.1/2005', 15 February 2005.

39 For detail see, Diplomatic correspondent, 'China, Pakistan, Russia Support Royal Action', *The People's Review*, 10–16 February 2005; Embassy of Republic of Korea, 'News and Commentary from Korea', 16 February 2005.

40 See the statement by former Ambassador of Pakistan to Nepal, Press Trust of India, 'Pak Offers Nepal Arms, Information', *The Asian Age*, 12 March 2005.

41 Bangladesh and Sri Lanka, for example, fell in this category of states.

42 *The Asian Age*, 'Military aid is stopped by India', 14 February 2005; Siddharth Srivastava, 'India Hits Nepal where it hurts', *The Asia Times Online*, 22 February 2005.

43 Post Report, 'US arms assistance embargo to continue', *The Kathmandu Post*, 13 September 2005.

44 Press Statement, 'The Government of Norway decides to reduce development assistance to Nepal', The Royal Norwegian Embassy, Kathmandu, 20 July 2005.

45 Denmark froze assistance worth about USD800 million; Canada about USD50 million; Sweden about USD33 million; and Switzerland Rupees 1.7 billion. The World Bank and ADB also froze about USD1.75 billion and USD800 million respectively. For details see, 'Costly Year', *The Himal Khabarpatrika*, 29 January 2006.

46 Post Report, 'Denmark to provide Rs.2 billion additional aid', *The Kathmandu Post*, 30 May 2006; Post Report, 'US increases assistance by $12 million, but won't support a Maoist-included govt in present situation', *The Kathmandu Post*, 29 June 2006.

47 For various perspectives see, Himalayan News Service, 'Moriarty warns agitating parties of Maoists' designs', *The Himalayan Times*, 16 February 2006; Editorial, 'American paranoia', *The Kathmandu Post*, 17 February 2006; Post Report, 'Leaders object to Moriarty's remarks', *The Kathmandu Post*, 17 February 2006; Editorial, 'Kiss me Kate', *The Himalayan Times*, 17 February 2006; Vijaya Chalise, 'US Roadmap: Ignoring basic reality of Nepali politics', *The Himalayan Times*, 1 Mach 2006.

48 See, Bharat Bhushan, 'Big Brother is in the neighbourhood', *The Telegraph*, Calcutta, India, 20 January 2003.

49 For details on EU position see, 'Report on Nepal's Foreign Affairs (2002–2003)', Institute of Foreign Affairs, Kathmandu, March 2004, 94. For UK position see, International Crisis Group, 'Nepal: Beyond Royal Rule', *Asia Briefing* no. 41, 15 September 2005, 12.

50 Quoted by M. R. Josse, 'Nepal's Insurgency: Chinese View', *The Kathmandu Post*, 21 August 2004.

51 See, farewell statement of former Russian Ambassador to Nepal, which appeared in *The Telegraph Weekly*, 1 June 2005.

52 Post Report, 'US cautiously welcomes', *The Kathmandu Post*, 24 November 2005.

53 The press statement issued following the 24-hour visit of Admiral William J. Fallon, commander of the US Pacific Command to Kathmandu on 1 February 2006, he said, 'considering the...violence, Maoists cannot be considered as legitimate political group.' For details see, 'Reconciliation must: US Gen', *The Himalayan Times*, 3 February 2006. A flurry of reactions, mostly critical, emerged following US Envoy's warnings on 15 February 2006 on 12-point understanding between the seven political parties and Maoists. For details see, Damakant Jayshi, 'Behind Moriarty's phobia', *The Kathmandu Post*, 20 February 2006; Bhola B. Rana, 'US Re-think on 12-point Accord', *The Rising Nepal*, 20 February 2006; 'US Gunboat Diplomacy', *The Asan Bazar*, 20 February 2006; Baburam Bhattarai, 'On Moriarty's pontification', *The Kathmandu Post*, 23 February 2006; WM Correspondent, 'US jostles parties out of their illusion', *The Weekly Mirror*, 23 February 2006; C. K. Lal, Professor Moriarty strikes again', *The Nepali Times*, 24 February–2 March 2006; Himalayan News Service, 'Leaders irked at Moriarty's "rethink" advice', *The Himalayan Times*, 25 February 2006;

Moriarty's Feb 15 speech 'a bolt from the blue to seven party con-glomerates', *The Weekly Telegraph*, 22 February 2006; Vijaya Chalise, 'US Roadmap: Ignoring basic reality of Nepali politics', *The Himalayan Times*, 1 March 2006.

54 Damaru Lal Bhandari, 'After China card, here's Nepal card', *The Himalayan Times*, 26 December 2005.

55 The Norwegian envoy expressed the readiness of his county to help Nepal in informal discussions and Norwegian Embassy arranged a seminar in Kathmandu entitled 'Sharing Norwegian Experience in Conflict Resolution and Mediation', in association with Nepal Council of World Affairs on 5 March 2006; Manish Chand, 'India not worried by Swiss diplomacy in Nepal', *The New Kerala.com*, 9 December 2005; Dikshya Thakuri, 'Finns wish to replicate Aceh success here', *The Himalayan Times*, 9 December 2005.

56 See, editorial, 'Hard line', *The Himalayan Times*, 22 October 2003; Also see, Himalayan News Service, 'Government offers amnesty to Maoists giving up before February 12', *The Himalayan Times*, 19 December 2003. Even after the Maoist leader Prachanda has offered to return to mainstream political process following the municipal elections in Nepal, government policy remained same. For detail see, Himalayan News Service, 'EC will call upon parties for parliamentary polls: Dr. Giri', *The Himalayan Times*, 11 February 2006.

57 Post Report, 'US wary of Maoists', *The Kathmandu Post*, 19 May 2006.

58 The EU has been consistently advocating for dialogue and negotiations between the government and Maoists for peacefully resolving the insur-gency. In their February 2003 statement EU 'strongly encourages the GON and Maoists to enter into a cease-fire agreement and to initiate a "peace process"'. See, 'EU calls for "establishment" of multiparty government', *The Telegraph Weekly*, 4 February 2004.

59 Dinesh Regmi, 'US ready to help create conducive atmosphere', *The Kath-mandu Post*, 7 June 2006; 'How Maoists will fare with India and US when in power?', *The Telegraph Weekly*, 24 May 2006.

60 Surendra Phuyal, 'The Indian Dilemma', *The Kathmandu Post*, 21 June 2006; Tilak P. Pokhrel, 'UN, UK envoys welcome pact: US with people', *The Kath-mandu Post*, 18 June 2006; Rekha Shrestha, 'Maoists must give up arms forever: Bloomfield', *The Himalayan Times*, 24 June 2006.

61 *Ibid*; also see, 'EU Members take to task govt. and Maoists', *The Telegraph Weekly*, 31 March 2004; US government also repeated their call in this regard. See for example, James F. Moriarty, 'US assistance has HR element attached', *The Telegraph Weekly*, 21 July 2004.

62 See, Suman Pradhan, 'Long and winding road to UN mediation', *South Asia Intelligence Review*, 18–24 July 2005; Gert Meinecke, 'Nepal's rejection of UN offer is just the latest in a long chain of depressing events', *The Telegraph Weekly*, 31 March 2004.

63 Tilak P. Pokhrel and Yuvraj Acharya, 'Agreement of Peace signed', *The Kath-mandu Post*, 17 June 2006.

64 Himalayan News Service, 'Delhi backs UN monitoring: PM', *The Himalayan Times*, 10 June 2006.

65 THT Online, 'Prachanda Writes to UN, Objects to Govt. Letter', *The Himalayan Times*, 24 July 2006.

66   Post Report, 'I am disappointed with international community: HM', *The Kathmandu Post*, 19 April 2005; *Time Magazine*, 25 April 2005.

67   King Gyanendra himself alluded to foreign interference during a meeting with Chairman and vice-chairmen of eight districts of Bagmati zone in Jawalakhel on 22 September 2005. For detail see, Post Report, 'Foreign fund fuelling unwarranted activities', *The Kathmandu Post*, 23 September 2005; Pushpa R. Pradhan, 'Nepalese people will unmask trouble making foreigners, their stooges', *The People's Review*, 29 September–5 October 2005; Kalyan Dev Bhattarai, 'Say no to foreign interference!', *The People's Review*, 29 September–5 October 2005; Post Report, 'Press blamed for being foreigners' puppet', *The Kathmandu Post*, 23 September 2005. For a different perspective see, Editorial, 'Foreign bogey', *The Himalayan Times*, 30 September 2005; Post Report, 'Parties, media, foreigners behind Maoists: Thapa', *The Kathmandu Post*, 3 February 2006.

68   See Paul Sharp, 'The Skopje Diplomatic Corps and Macedonian Political Crisis 2001', in this volume.

69   Dhruba Adhikary, 'Nepal Losing its Way', *The Asia Times Online*, 27 May 2005.

70   At least two European Ambassadors complained against this measure after 01 February 2005 in informal exchange of views with other members of the corps.

71   For detail see, Saurabh Sukla, 'The Gulf Widens', *India Today*, 19 September 2005.

72   Himalayan News Service, 'China Pledges Rs.72 million military aid', *The Himalayan Times*, 26 October 2005.

73   See, Sushil Pyakurel, 'Crisis in Nepal and Response from the International Community', Director-General for External Policies of the Union, Directorate B, The European Union, Brussels, 15 February 2006.

74   Himalayan News Service, 'Sign no deal in India, MPs tell Koirala', *The Himalayan Times*, 5 June 2006.

75   Sudeshna Sarkar, 'Do not sign pact with India: Maoists', *The Asian Age*, 7 June 2006.

76   Himalayan News Service, 'Glued, in spite of international pressure, says Prachanda', *The Himalayan Times*, 17 June 2006.

77   Rekha Shrestha, 'Maoist ties will hurt parties: Top UK Official', *The Himalayan Times*, 17 February 2006.

78   Himalayan News Service, 'Sherchan hits out at some foreign envoys', *The Himalayan Times*, 1 July 2006.

79   Post Report, 'Moriarty did not understand ground reality: Mahara', *The Kathmandu Post*, 29 June 2006.

80   Himalayan News Service, 'US envoy's comment loaded, says Bamdev', *The Himalayan Times*, 30 June 2006.

81   For details of Maoist appeal for international support see, Himalayan News Service, '4-month ceasefire is now history', *The Himalayan Times*, 3 January 2005.

82   Tilak P. Pokhrel, 'Rebels court foreign envoys', *The Kathmandu Post*, 29 June 2006.

83   Bijen Jonchhe, 'Support for Democracy', *The Rising Nepal*, 21 October 2005; 'India's moral support: At what price?', *The Telegraph Weekly*, 26 October

2005. Following a television interview by Indian Ambassador to Nepal on 8 January 2006, a flurry of articles appeared in Nepali media, largely criticizing some positions articulated by the Envoy. For detail see, Editorial, 'Intention to incite', *The Weekly Mirror*, 19 January 2006; Maila Baje, 'Nepalese sovereignty and Indian soreness', *The Weekly Mirror*, 19 January 2006; K. Kailali, 'Dysfunctional Diplomacy in Indo- Nepalese Relations', *The People's Review*, 26 January–1 February 2006; Dr. Trilochan Upreti, 'Understanding Intentions', *The Rising Nepal*, 3 July 2005; Bihari K. Shrestha, 'No Sermons, Please: Foreign Meddling Impedes Nepal's Democratic Development', *The Nepali Times*, 8–14 July 2005.

84 In recent years both the government as well as members of civil society increasingly shared this perception that there are 'foreign hands' in 'shaping' political developments in Nepal. After the Royal takeover, King Gyanendra and Ministers of his government have been repeatedly talking of double standards pursued by the international community, particularly on terrorism. Civil society activists have also been expressing their unhappiness about the role of the diplomatic community. For reaction to British Ambassador's high profile activity even before the Royal takeover see, 'Foreigners told to keep off Nepal affairs', *The Himalayan Times*, 7 June 2003.

85 'Sharp', this volume.

86 While the European Commission set up its office at *Charge d' Affaires* (CDA) level in 2002, Malaysia and Denmark sent their Ambassadors to Nepal in 2005.

87 Minister for Foreign Affairs, Government of Nepal regularly invites the members of diplomatic corps to brief them on the position of the government. Likewise, political leaders occasionally invite the members of the corps for the same purpose.

9
Genocide in Rwanda and the Kigali Diplomatic Corps: Consultation, Cooperation, Coordination[1]

Joyce E. Leader[2]

When I arrived in Kigali, Rwanda, in August of 1991 as Deputy Chief of Mission at the US embassy, three complex social transitions were in progress: from an oligarchic to a democratic political system, from one-party to multiparty politics, and from war to peace.[3] The first two transitions – from rule by one man and a coterie of collaborators from his home region and from single-party to multiparty politics – were aimed at liberalizing the political process. These transitions held the promise of breaking the monopoly of power exercised for nearly 20 years by Hutu President Juvenal Habyarimana, his close collaborators (known as the Akazu, or 'little house'), and his omnipresent political party over the political, economic and social systems of the country. The transitions offered a way to end the regime's discrimination against the Tutsi minority and against Hutu from regions other than the president's. Under pressure from the international community, particularly French President Mitterrand, President Habyarimana had reluctantly opened the door to changes that were stimulating broader participation in the political process. His summer 1990 commitment to reform was followed a year later by constitutional changes legalizing a multiple party process. Six months later, in April 1992, a multiparty government headed by an opposition Hutu Prime Minister took office. The president's monopoly on power was broken. He could no longer exercise unfettered control over governmental decisionmaking. Power sharing was launched, albeit primarily among the majority Hutu with little participation from the minority Tutsi.

The third transition – from war to peace – aimed to end the conflict between government troops and the Rwandan Patriotic Front (RPF), an armed group comprised primarily of Tutsi refugees in neighbouring Uganda. When it invaded Rwanda from Uganda in October 1990, the RPF announced that it was fighting for refugees to be allowed to return, a right long denied them by President Habyarimana on grounds there was not enough land to accommodate them all. Hundreds of thousands of Tutsis had become refugees or exiles as a result of earlier ethnic violence in Rwanda. The invading RPF also wanted to ensure full Tutsi participation in the announced democratization process. Low intensity fighting simmered at the Ugandan-Rwandan border for one and a half years while the diplomatic community's efforts to promote a ceasefire and dialogue between the two sides made little progress in ending the conflict. Only after President Habyarimana installed a multiparty government led by an opposition prime minister did both the government and the RPF decide that talks were in their interest.

The international community and its diplomatic representatives in Kigali fully supported the subsequent negotiations, known as the Arusha peace process after the town in neighbouring Tanzania where the talks occurred. Spanning just over a year, from July 1992 through July 1993, the negotiations resulted in a series of agreed protocols known collectively as the Arusha Accords. This revolutionary document, signed in August 1993 by President Habyarimana and his RPF counterpart, Alexis Kanyarwengwe, provided a blueprint for Rwanda's future that detailed power-sharing arrangements in new political, military and security institutions. The arrangements, however, guaranteed a substantial role for the Tutsi-dominated RPF and the mostly Hutu opposition parties while, at the same time, significantly diminishing the power of the president and his party. The losers in this arrangement, namely those around the president who would lose power and privilege, totally rejected the peace accord and its power-sharing provisions. These Hutu extremists saw no hope of retaining or restoring their monopoly on power under this agreement. A united Kigali diplomatic corps, believing that implementation of the accords would provide a framework for containing these potential spoilers, exerted enormous pressure on the parties to implement the agreement as quickly as possible. But, the diplomats failed to convince the parties that implementation was in their own best interest. With no strategy other than implementation of the accords for containing the potential spoilers, the diplomatic corps contributed significantly to the failure to avert the catastrophe that followed. The genocide that cost the lives of over 800,000 Tutsi and Hutu opposition leaders began before the power-sharing protocol was implemented.

The Kigali diplomatic corps

Composition

The diplomatic corps in Rwanda in the early 1990s was sizeable and quite active for a small, land-locked country in central Africa. The size reflected the interest of the World Bank and international aid agencies in the country's development and economic prosperity during the 1980s when Rwanda was considered a responsible development partner and had a reputation among development workers as 'the Switzerland of Africa'. The activity reflected the importance the Kigali diplomatic corps attached to the issues at hand, namely increasing violence and insecurity and the prospect of addressing them through promoting democratization and peacemaking.

In the early 1990s, the diplomatic corps in Kigali consisted of several distinct groups: the western donors; neighbouring and other African states; the United Nations aid agencies; the European Commission delegation; and the delegation of the International Committee of the Red Cross (ICRC). Most active among the western group were the Belgian, French, American and German embassies and the Canadian and Swiss aid missions. The Russians had an embassy and the Chinese, an aid mission, but neither was active on the political front. Britain and the Netherlands operated in a low-key manner through their Honorary Consuls. Neighbouring Uganda, Zaire, Burundi and Tanzania played active roles at varying times depending on the issues, while Egypt and Libya were present, but kept low public profiles. The United Nations Development Program (UNDP), the United Nations Children's Fund (UNICEF), and the Office of the UN High Commissioner for Refugees (UNHCR) were quite engaged, reflecting the UN's development, relief, and refugee interests, respectively. The ICRC delegation, consisting of only four persons in 1991, grew substantially in response to escalating violence and growing humanitarian need as numbers of internally displaced persons increased. Following conventional practice in predominantly Catholic countries, the Vatican's representative, the Papal Nuncio, was, by agreement between Rwanda and the Holy See, the permanent dean of the diplomatic corps. As dean, the Papal Nuncio played a critical role in forging common positions among the states in the diplomatic corps; he was also actively involved in promoting track two mediation involving leaders of the Catholic Church.[4]

Functioning

Member states of the Kigali diplomatic corps adhered to the same rules of conduct and followed the rituals and protocols of diplomatic practice, giving the corps a degree of cohesion and marking it as part of a unique institution on the Rwandan political scene. Likewise, there was general support among the states represented for the broad policy goal of assuring peace and stability by supporting the political liberalization process and promoting a negotiated end to the conflict. The western group with its resources, investments and access to the power brokers had a much greater impact, at least initially, than did the African group that engaged in a more traditional state-to-state relationship. Nevertheless, despite similarities in their behaviour and policy goals, the diplomatic corps was by no means a homogeneous unit. There were substantial differences among the corps members on several dimensions.

Belgium, the former colonial power and principal investor in development, and France, with its substantial and critical military assistance, were the lead diplomatic actors in Rwanda between 1990 and 1994. Their policies, however, frequently put them at odds with each other. Both sent troops in the fall of 1990 following the RPF invasion. The Belgians, who withdrew their troops shortly thereafter, were viewed as supporters of political reform, and thus perceived as favouring the Tutsi. The French, who had been gradually replacing the Belgians as military and political advisors to the president since the late 1980s, retained a substantial force presence, creating the perception that they supported the *status quo* and thus favoured the Hutu. This perceived division created tensions within the diplomatic corps. Informal groupings developed around the French and Belgian positions. Zaire, whose president, Mobutu Sese Seko, was a close advisor and confidant to President Habyarimana, tended to align itself with the French, while Uganda, often accused of aiding and abetting the RPF, was closer to the Belgian position. The United States supported democratic reforms, consistent with Belgian priorities, but, at the same time, viewed the French emphasis on security as vital for the stability necessary during the transition period.

None of these positions or alignments, however, was static. The way the diplomatic corps functioned in Rwanda between October 1990 and April 1994 changed over time. The African role and that of the international institutions, namely, the United Nations (UN) and the Organization of African Unity (OAU), predecessor to the current African Union (AU), gradually grew in importance. This evolution reflected in part Tanzania's appointment by the parties to the Arusha peace talks as 'Facilitator' of the negotiations. It also reflected the critical roles played by the OAU and the UN in supporting the peace process, both by helping bring the peace talks to conclusion and by fielding observer and peacekeeping troops, respectively. Additionally, tensions within the diplomatic community began to subside as the Arusha peace talks got underway and helping assure a successful outcome emerged as a common policy priority. Close cooperation that marked the diplomatic corps during the negotiations evolved into close coordination following the 1993 signing of the Arusha Accords as diplomatic interests coalesced around the goal of ensuring implementation of the peace agreement.

Between 1990 and 1994, the functioning of the diplomatic corps can be divided into three fairly distinct but not mutually exclusive periods, each characterized by a dominant *modus operandi* among the member states and between them and the Rwandan authorities. The first period, from the October 1990 RPF invasion until July 1992, when the Government and the RPF began negotiations in Arusha, can be described as 'The Period of Consultation'. The next period, from the beginning of the Arusha talks until the signing of the Arusha Accords in August 1993, can be labelled 'The Period of Cooperation'. The third phase, from the signing of the Arusha Accords until the onset of the genocide in April 1994, can be called 'The Period of Coordination'.

The period of consultation: October 1990–July 1992

In the year and a half following President Habyarimana's announced liberalization of the political system and the RPF's invasion, states in the diplomatic corps in Kigali tended to interact bilaterally with the government of Rwanda on the principal issues of democratization and peacemaking and to consult among themselves on their respective policy priorities. Even though the envoys were by and large advocating similar goals – democratization, respect for human rights, a negotiated settlement to the border war – each country pursued its own diplomatic agenda. The positions of the three principal western countries represented in Kigali are illustrative of this.

Belgium's policy priorities centred on its role as Rwanda's principal economic and development partner. In this context, Belgium supported Rwanda's political liberalization and was a staunch advocate of respect for human rights. It also continued to provide significant security assistance through its military training programme with the gendarmerie, or territorial police. Belgium's historical ties to Rwanda gave it special standing with the Rwandan president, his government, and the Rwandan people as well as with the Kigali diplomatic community.

Although France had insisted at the 1990 Francophone Summit in Baule that French-speaking African countries begin to democratize, its policy priority in Rwanda was stability. It pursued this policy by providing technical and material support for the Rwandan security forces. After the 1990 RPF invasion, the Rwanda government depended for its security on several hundred French troops present in the country. The French military presence aimed to protect French nationals, to provide military trainers linked to the six-fold increase in the size of the Rwandan army, and to serve as military advisors who worked closely with the Rwandan military authorities.

The United States policy priorities and diplomatic efforts focused on promoting political reform, democratization and respect for human rights on the one hand and peaceful resolution of the conflict between the Rwandan government and the RPF on the other. This made US policy goals more convergent with those of Belgium than with those of France. The US agreed with the French that stability was important and appreciated the French troop presence, but it directed its diplomatic efforts toward democratization and peace as the means for achieving the desired stability.

These differing policy perspectives resulted in differing approaches to Rwanda's problems and precipitated divisions both within the European group of countries represented in Kigali and within the larger diplomatic community, with some African countries gravitating toward the French and others toward the Belgian position, as noted above. The three principal western diplomatic actors did not see themselves as a coherent group that coordinated approaches or acted in concert. Indeed, sometimes their diplomatic initiatives were contradictory. At one point, for example, when the United States and others were advising government officials to open an in-country dialogue with RPF representatives, the French had instructions, we learned later, to urge the Rwandan government against participating in any such discussions.[5]

This is not to say there was no communication between and among the Kigali diplomatic missions. To the contrary, there were frequent informal bilateral and multilateral contacts. The US ambassador met regularly, individually and collectively, with his Belgian and French counterparts. There were a number of *ad hoc* heads of mission gatherings, often hosted by the Belgian ambassador, usually involving western group representatives but sometimes including African ambassadors as well. My Belgian and French counterparts and I met together regularly, and I periodically called on several of my African colleagues. The purpose of these numerous communications, however, was to compare information, analyses, and policies rather than to coordinate them.

There were two notable exceptions to the predominantly bilateral state-to-state functioning of the Kigali diplomatic corps during this period. They concerned the reaction of the diplomatic corps to human rights violations that followed the RPF invasion. After mass arrests of Tutsi citizens, claimed by the government to be 'collaborators' of the invaders, western group envoys made joint representations to the president, relevant ministers, and other government officials urging fair treatment in accordance with the rule of law or release for those in custody. When Bagogwe (a Tutsi subgroup) were slaughtered in the north in early 1991 and Tutsi killed south of Kigali in March 1992, western Ambassadors went together to the president to protest these massacres. Even so, diplomatic representatives also made bilateral interventions to protest these and other human rights abuses. The United States, for example, made numerous unilateral démarches to government officials in a variety of government departments not only protesting the mass arrests of Tutsi generally, but also seeking the release of Tutsi embassy employees who had been arrested.

Promoting peaceful resolution of the conflict between the Rwandan government and the RPF became a common policy priority of foreign office officials in capitals and diplomats in Kigali following the 1990 RPF invasion. Initial peacemaking efforts, however, were conducted outside Rwanda with the Kigali diplomatic corps playing a supporting role. Almost immediately Rwanda's African neighbours resorted to collective efforts and multilateral diplomacy to encourage an end to the fighting and to broker ceasefire agreements, relying on regional summits and meetings of regional and sub-regional organizations as fora in which to press their case and underscore to the Rwandans the urgency and importance they attached to ending the conflict. Western capitals also launched some peacemaking efforts of their own. In response to this regional and capital-centred diplomacy, the Kigali diplomatic corps employed traditional bilateral state-to-state diplomacy to support the African or western initiatives. These efforts, however, had short-lived results, came to naught, or made little impact on events on the ground.[6]

Bilateral diplomacy, coupled with a degree of cooperation between the US and France, was instrumental in the spring of 1992 in finally bringing the warring parties to the negotiating table. In May 1992, US

Assistant Secretary of State for Africa, Ambassador Herman J. Cohen, held discussions in Kampala, Uganda, with Ugandan authorities and RPF leaders and in Kigali with President Habyarimana and newly installed opposition ministers in the government. This bilateral diplomatic intervention helped convince all parties that the time was ripe for negotiation.[7] From Rwanda, the US Assistant Secretary for Africa went to Paris where he consulted with his French counterpart about the situation in Rwanda, sharing his assessment that the parties appeared ready to negotiate. On the heels of this exchange, the French invited both parties to Paris to discuss how, when, and where to conduct talks. Tanzania and Zaire both offered to host the talks.

Weeks later, in July 1992, what became known as the Arusha peace process got underway. Peace talks began in earnest in Arusha, Tanzania, between delegations from the government of Rwanda and from the rebel RPF. Observers representing the countries in the Kigali diplomatic corps as well as several international organizations were on hand to monitor their progress. The diplomats' role throughout the period leading up to the Arusha talks had been to cajole and convince while creating opportunities for the two sides to meet and discuss. Only the parties themselves had been able to decide whether and when they would talk.

The period of cooperation: July 1992–August 1993

Once peace talks got underway in Arusha, diplomatic missions in Kigali gradually embraced support of the Arusha peace process as their common policy priority. As they did so, cooperation emerged as the dominant *modus operandi* of the diplomatic corps, even though independent bilateral diplomacy continued on this and other issues. The diplomatic corps was able to achieve this unity of purpose in part because each state believed that its own national interests would be best served by securing a negotiated peace agreement as soon as possible. The Belgians and the Americans wanted to advance political liberalization and social equity. France no longer believed government forces could win a military victory and wanted an exit strategy for its troops that had shored up the Rwandan government since the 1990 RPF invasion. So, even though their reasons differed, the states in the Kigali diplomatic corps were strongly motivated to help broker a successful outcome to the Arusha talks and, as a result, were willing to set aside individual differences in order to cooperate on achieving the goal they shared.

Another factor that helped unify the Kigali diplomatic corps around the policy goal of successful peace talks was their adherence to a shared diplomatic culture[8] that led them to believe a negotiated settlement would provide the basis for a stable peace in Rwanda. The Kigali diplomatic corps shared a common vision for the peace talks: the Rwandan government and the RPF would conclude a workable agreement that would end their conflict and establish a framework for resolving future differences peacefully. This convergence of views reflected shared norms and values relating to the conduct of negotiations that diplomats both in capitals and in Kigali projected onto their expectations for peace talks. Implicit among the diplomats was the shared belief that once parties to a conflict agreed to negotiations, they were signalling their commitment to resolving their differences peacefully through dialogue and compromise. Further, diplomats believed that a decision to negotiate implied that the parties would strive for agreements they were committed to implementing and that could be sustained over time. As a result of this set of shared norms, diplomats had a common set of expectations not only for the process of the negotiations in Arusha, but also for the behaviour of the parties during the course of the negotiations.[9]

Despite this common set of implicit beliefs that helped unify the Kigali diplomatic corps around the policy goal of a successfully negotiated peace agreement, the diplomatic community did not share a common vision of the content outcome of the talks. The positions of the various states toward the substance of the negotiations continued to reflect their sense of their individual national interests which in turn had long shaped their attitudes toward both the conflict and the parties involved. France favoured compromises and agreements that would not unduly disadvantage the Hutu president and his ruling party. Uganda, on the other hand, tended to support the negotiating positions of the RPF. Other states represented in the Kigali diplomatic community fell somewhere between these two positions. The United States sought a balanced agreement that would lead to sustainable peace and would favour neither side over the other. Despite these differences on substance, the Kigali diplomatic corps shared a common commitment to a successful peace process. Because of these differences, however, Kigali diplomats continued with their bilateral interventions with Rwandan authorities.

While diplomats in Kigali continued their bilateral interaction with Rwandan officials, they found a growing list of issues on which to cooperate. They saw a two-fold role for themselves to promote successful peace talks, their primary policy focus. First, the Kigali corps was involved in helping the disparate political players in Kigali forge common negotiating positions for the fractious Rwandan government delegation to take to the negotiating table. The government delegation, led by the opposition party foreign minister, was deeply divided between the president's pro-Hutu representatives and moderate Hutu and Tutsi opposition leaders. Second, Kigali diplomats encouraged Kigali officials and other actors across the spectrum of Rwandan opinion to accept and honour the outcomes being negotiated at Arusha. Bilaterally, but sometimes collectively, the diplomats met frequently in informal discussions and occasional formal démarches with key Rwandan officials, or with persons influential with them, to deliver their diplomatic messages. At the beginning of the talks, for example, they urged Kigali players to implement the ceasefire agreed by the parties in Arusha and to accept an OAU ceasefire monitoring group as called for in the ceasefire agreement. Though the latter issue was complicated by the government's perception that the OAU was biased toward the RPF, the government did finally agree to letting the OAU field a monitoring force. The Kigali diplomatic corps continued this sort of diplomatic pressure throughout the Arusha talks in support of the negotiated compromises and decisions.

Security in and around Kigali was another issue of common concern to the diplomatic corps. As the peace talks began, political violence was escalating. In particular, inter-party violence prompted by party youth groups that were in the process of being transformed into political party militias was creating considerable insecurity. Party youth regularly used violence to disrupt rallies of rival political groups and to brake up opposition demonstrations. Diplomats lobbied jointly and independently for the government to improve security in Kigali and elsewhere in the country, arguing in part for the Rwandan government to fulfil its obligations to protect foreign nationals.

In addition to finding common policy grounds for cooperation around the peace process and over security issues, Kigali diplomats also found common cause in support of Rwanda's economy. France, Belgium, Switzerland, Canada and the United States, in concert with the World Bank, cooperated closely on continuing economic support to the country. Keeping Rwanda's sagging economy viable was considered an important complementary goal to ensuring a successful peace process. Even though the Arusha process was considered a positive development, diplomats and the World Bank, nevertheless sometimes used threats of aid cuts at key points in the process to maintain momentum and keep the process moving forward.[10]

As the Arusha peace talks continued, the Kigali diplomatic corps confronted a number of new elements that changed the diplomatic dynamic. First, the Kigali diplomatic corps was no longer the only focal point for diplomatic activity in support of peace and democratization. A 'shadow diplomatic corps' emerged in Arusha consisting of the observers to the talks, namely, western countries and neighbouring African countries represented in Kigali along with several international organizations.[11] This 'shadow diplomatic corps' in Arusha shared the same goals and expectations for the peace talks as did their counterparts in Kigali, but its role and its functioning were somewhat different. The growing cooperation evident among the diplomats in Kigali was even more apparent among the observers in Arusha. They saw their collective role as one of facilitation, helping the negotiating parties, namely, the Rwandan government and the RPF, find common ground and forge compromises on the issues under discussion. This attitude of the diplomatic observers in Arusha and their interpretation of their 'shadow corps' role reflected the policy priority attached by their capitals and the Kigali diplomatic corps to ending the conflict between the Rwandan government and the RPF through a successful Arusha peace process. As was the case in the Kigali diplomatic corps, however, observers in Arusha often held disparate positions on the issues under discussion, but their interest in encouraging agreement took precedence over their differences. The 'shadow corps' diplomats were on the front lines, entrusted by their governments with responsibility for helping bring the two sides to common understandings that would result in agreements and move the peace process forward. Of necessity the 'shadow corps' observers worked closely together, developing a genuine camaraderie that transcended their policy differences and the various diplomatic groupings. While Kigali diplomats were helping one side at the negotiating table, the fractious government side, consolidate its position, the 'shadow corps' was working with both parties to the talks – the government and the non-state RPF – to facilitate agreement.

In a second new element, the two major policy issues that had dominated diplomatic dialogue in Kigali, democratization and ending the conflict, became joined in the Arusha peace negotiations when the issue of Rwanda's political future became the centrepiece of the peace talks. As a result, the centre of gravity on democratization and political liberalization shifted from state-to-state discourse between Rwandan government authorities or party leaders and primarily western country diplomats, to the negotiations between the Rwanda's diverse government delegation to the talks and the disciplined RPF. The president and the party leaders essentially lost control over this issue. They were no longer the sole decisionmakers about the course of political liberalization. This made the generally shared policy goal of promoting the transition to democracy much more complicated for the Kigali diplomatic corps.

For example, the critical political issue during the first six months of peace talks was how to distribute power in the transitional government. Political parties became the agreed basis for sharing cabinet posts and legislative seats, but negotiators could reach no agreement on how to distribute those posts and seats. Talks were suspended to allow discussion and decisions on the issue in Kigali. The US ambassador spent endless hours with opposition political party leaders listening to their ideas and discussing pros and cons of each. He also worked with the president's people, urging them toward acceptance of a power-sharing formula that would inevitably reduce their grip on power. One issue became the stumbling block not only at this juncture, but also in the days and weeks just before the genocide. That issue was representation for the hard line Hutu party, the Coalition for the Defense of the Republic (CDR).[12] Western diplomats in Kigali stood united on principle: the new Rwandan government should be inclusive rather than exclusive. Diplomats argued that all political tendencies in Rwanda, including the Hutu supremacists represented by the CDR, should have a voice and thus a stake in Rwanda's future government. By taking this position, however, the diplomatic corps was supporting President Habyarimana who insisted on CDR representation for his own reason: to bolster his much reduced power within the proposed government structures.

Opposition parties and the RPF adamantly opposed the president's ploy and unanimously rejected including the CDR. When discussions moved from Kigali back to Arusha in December 1992, the government and the RPF delegations, disregarding the advice of the diplomats and the preferences of the president and his close associates, agreed on a power-sharing formula for the government that excluded the CDR, gave equal representation to the president's party and the RPF, and put the balance of power in the hands of the opposition parties. Reaction in Kigali was swift. Even though the arrangement was immediately codified in the power-sharing protocol signed by the delegations in January 1993, leaders of the president's party and the CDR resoundingly rejected it. This power-sharing agreement, which essentially transferred power from the president and his party to the opposition and the RPF, triggered widespread communal violence against Tutsi in northern Rwanda. This, in turn, handed the RPF its rationale for breaking the six-month-old ceasefire and fighting its way almost to Kigali before another ceasefire took hold.

A third change in the diplomatic corps' dynamic was the significantly increased visibility and importance of African diplomats, particularly in Arusha, where Tanzania, as 'Facilitator' of the talks at the request of the two sides, became the *de facto* leader of the 'shadow diplomatic corps'. Also, their observer status gave representatives of neighbouring African states standing equal to that of the western diplomats in seeking resolution of the conflict.

African diplomats in Arusha had a strong impact on the process of the talks and on the way the observer corps functioned. This was due mainly to the leadership of the Tanzanian diplomat delegated the responsibility of Facilitator,[13] his diplomatic colleagues, and the Tanzanian officials who lent their weight and their periodic presence to the negotiations. When the talks hit a snag, the Facilitator would assemble the observers, discuss with them the sticking points, and seek their counsel on possible ways to break the logjam. The observers might agree among themselves on a suggested strategy for the Facilitator to pursue with each side. They might also settle on who among them would be most likely to sway one party or the other and then dispatch that diplomat in an effort to move the talks forward. Each negotiating side carefully calculated into its negotiating strategy the nature and the source of support it might be likely to garner for its positions from the diplomatic observers. Consequently, diplomatic interventions could be critical in nudging the parties toward compromises on the issues either by encouraging restraint in their demands or by urging acceptance when it appeared the deal was the best that could be expected.

The degree of unity among the observers on specific contentious issues, therefore, often had a significant impact on the outcome of the negotiations. For example, in the talks on the organization of the security forces, the RPF insisted on disbanding the territorial police (gendarmerie), institutionally part of the military that would remain under the jurisdiction of the president's party. Instead, the RPF favoured a police force independent of the military housed in the interior ministry that was to come under RPF control. The 'shadow' diplomatic corps unanimously opposed the RPF position: there must be no split in control of the forces under arms. The RPF eventually dropped its demand.[14] Close cooperation between African and Western observers was critical to this outcome.

Another contentious issue, under the rubric of military integration, did not find similar unanimous support from either the diplomatic corps in Kigali or from the observers in Arusha. That was the issue of force proportions: what percent of the officers and soldiers in the new Rwandan army should be allocated to each side? Diplomats in both Kigali and Arusha held a variety of views on the optimal outcome of the negotiations on this issue. The RPF's initial demand for more than a half of the posts at each level exacerbated these differences. In the absence of a common position among the diplomats, finding common ground and reaching compromise at the negotiating table remained elusive. Talks were suspended at one point while the Facilitator and some high-level envoys from the Tanzanian capital travelled both to Kigali and to the RPF headquarters in northern Rwanda to offer a proposed compromise for consideration and to impress upon each side the importance of reaching agreement on this issue. RPF intransigence and the government's unwillingness to capitulate kept the issue from being resolved for several more weeks and caused the talks to break down altogether for over a month before the two sides finally accepted the Facilitator's compromise proposal as the best deal they could expect at the time. The final agreed position went beyond what some in the diplomatic corps, in particular, the French, thought reasonable, but the corps closed ranks in support of the agreed position and individual states used their influence with the parties to encourage its acceptance. Their independent calculations of their own national interests led the states represented in Kigali and Arusha to promote agreements even though they disliked some of the specific terms, in lieu of risking collapse of the talks. None lost sight of the common goal: a negotiated settlement. This convergence of goals, regardless of variations in motivations, made collective diplomatic action possible.

A fourth element that changed the diplomatic dynamic in Kigali was the increasing importance of multilateral institutions as observers in Arusha. The OAU, as joint sponsor of the peace talks with the Tanzanian Facilitator, and the UN, which joined the Arusha observer corps nine months into the talks, played significant roles in the peace process. They actively engaged in providing both political and military advice to the negotiating parties which made them important members of the 'shadow' diplomatic corps of observers.

The OAU invested considerable political and financial capital in the peace process. A representative of the OAU president (at the time Senegal's President Diouf) and an official from the OAU secretariat were present in Arusha throughout the talks. The OAU also established a presence in Kigali once it dispatched to Rwanda the Neutral Military Observer Group (NMOG), a small but significant contingent of cease-fire monitors. Like the Facilitator from Tanzania, both the OAU and the UN Observers served as neutral advisors and sounding boards to members of both negotiating teams, helping them find common ground and compromise. Anticipating a post-conflict role in Rwanda as implied in the Dar es Salaam agreement that restored the broken ceasefire in March 1993, the UN assigned a military advisor as Observer to the military portion of the talks and sent a political advisor period-ically from New York to Arusha.

The presence of both the OAU and the UN was particularly critical during the prolonged and highly emotional debate over which of the two organizations – the OAU or the UN – should field a military force to help implement the peace agreement following the conclusion of the talks. The Rwandan government favoured a UN force while the RPF insisted on an OAU force, both wary of what they believed to be nega-tive bias toward them in the other organization. The diplomatic corps in Kigali and the 'shadow' corps in Arusha generally supported a UN force because of the UN's experience and funding capacity. The US, on the other hand, advocated an OAU force to strengthen the OAU's conflict mechanism. After the OAU declined to take on the task, however, negotiators agreed to seek a UN post-conflict peacekeeping force and made a formal request to that effect. Nevertheless, it was the OAU's NMOG soldiers, already in country as ceasefire monitors, who became the first forces to come under the UN command upon arrival of the UN force commander.

A fifth challenge to the diplomatic dynamic in Kigali was the changed status of the RPF once it came to the negotiating table and became in essence a partner for peace. Although capitals had been in periodic, low-profile contact with rebel RPF leaders since the 1990 invasion, the advent of the peace talks made the RPF an official participant in the diplomatic discourse and elevated its status to one of equality with the Rwandan government. Diplomats in the Arusha 'shadow' corps dealt directly with members of the RPF delegation throughout the talks. Capitals began having more overt contacts with the RPF at significantly higher levels. Only after the peace accord was signed did the RPF become a permanent feature of the political scene in Kigali, though Kigali diplomats did make occasional visits to the RPF headquarters across the ceasefire lines in northern Rwanda during the course of the negotiations.

A sixth factor affecting the Kigali diplomatic corps' functioning was having the peace talks take place at a venue outside and distant from the country. This presented diplomats with two key problems: maintaining cohesion between the diplomatic corps in Kigali and the 'shadow corps' in Arusha and assuring consistency in the messages to interlocutors in the two sites. No instant communications were available between the two locations. No e-mail (government delegates and observers, unlike the RPF, did not even have computers!) and no traditional cable facilities existed. As US observer for over two months, I had to rely on faxing my reports on the talks to our embassy in Dar es Salaam for subsequent transmission to Kigali and Washington. Nothing sensitive could be passed in such a channel. Conversely, I was totally cut off from official communications emanating from Washington and Kigali. Only once, when I made the four-hour bus trip to Nairobi, Kenya, did I see classified cable traffic from Kigali and Washington. I depended on erratic, open telephone lines to connect me to my ambassador in Kigali or to the Rwanda desk officer at the State Department in Washington, again restricting the content of the communication. Not surprisingly, I found that my Arusha perspective on the progress of the peace talks was quite different from that of my ambassador in Kigali. Arusha diplomats focused on the process as well as the content of arriving at agreements. While we celebrated agreements in Arusha, some were heading in directions totally at odds with the thinking in Kigali. There the Ambassador was getting a daily dose of resistance to the content of the Arusha agreements from his government interlocutors who viewed most compromise deals as too unbalanced in favour of the RPF.

With the diplomatic corps increasingly united in support of the success of the peace talks, cooperation among diplomatic missions became common in both Kigali and Arusha. However, the sense of being one team with one goal was more apparent in Arusha than in Kigali. Group differences remained strong in Kigali and bilateral diplomatic interaction with government interlocutors continued during the period of the peace talks. In Arusha, on the other hand, unity of purpose pushed diplomatic 'shadow corps' observers into close collaboration regardless of group affiliation or preferred policy outcomes. Despite inevitable differences among the states they represented, all were allies in the priority task of facilitating agreement between the two negotiating parties. The efforts of all reached fruition in July 1993 when the parties to the talks reached agreement on all outstanding issues. The Arusha Accords were signed the following month.

The period of coordination: August 1993–April 1994

On August 4, 1993, Rwanda's president and the RPF president along with all but one political party, the Hutu supremacist CDR, signed the Arusha Accords that were intended to end the war between government and rebel forces and usher in power sharing in the government, the military, and the security services. Diplomats from the Kigali diplomatic corps were on hand in Arusha to witness the event. They heralded the peace agreement as a great diplomatic accomplishment that promised peace and security for Rwanda. While the diplomats recognized that difficulties that lay ahead in implementing the accord, in particular, the power-sharing protocol, they counted on overcoming any impediments by building on the momentum of apparent good will that had enabled the parties to go the last mile to achieve the agreement. The United States believed that the president's signature on the peace agreement signalled, finally, his support for the power-sharing arrangement and counted on him to bring the Hutu hard-liners from among his close collaborators into the process.

Between the signing of the accord and the beginning of the genocide eight months later, the Kigali diplomatic corps focused individual and collective diplomatic interventions on encouraging implementation of the Arusha Accord. All believed that the agreement offered an acceptable and workable power-sharing framework for ending the conflict and setting the country on a sustainable course to democracy and peace. French leadership on Africa in Paris and at the Embassy in Kigali was committed to implementing the Accord, bringing France's Rwandan policy into full alignment with the rest of the Kigali diplomatic corps. The diplomatic agenda was full. It included promoting early deployment of a UN peacekeeping force, urging rapid installation of the transitional government, and supporting planning for the integration of the two armies, including developing strategies for disarmament, demobilization and reintegration of fighters. Cooperation that had marked the interaction of the Kigali diplomatic corps and the Arusha 'shadow corps' during the Arusha negotiations increased. Once UN personnel arrived in Kigali, coordination on policy messages and policy priorities became the norm.

It soon became clear that there may have been more good will within the Kigali diplomatic community than between the parties to the peace accord. Managing the unending setbacks to prevent collapse of the Arusha process quickly consumed the diplomats. The US ambassador spent hours and hours encouraging competing leaders of fractured political parties to overcome their differences in order to select unified slates of representatives to the transitional government and national assembly, as required by the Arusha Accords. Kigali diplomats lobbied capitals in support of a robust peacekeeping force, but they faced reluctance from their respective headquarters to commit resources to a large operation. The October 1993 assassination in neighbouring Burundi by Tutsi military officers of the first elected Hutu president provided new grist for Rwanda's Hutu supremacist propaganda mill, forcing moderates who supported power sharing to reconsider their position. Diplomatic démarches failed to convince government authorities to take steps to tone down or shut down the hard-line Hutu propaganda arm, a new radio station known as RTLM. Diplomatic interventions, individual and collective, only temporarily dampened escalating violence. Grenade attacks, mine explosions, assassinations and massacres occurred with increasing frequency, and, as before, with impunity. Within a week of the UN establishing its mission in Rwanda in November 1992, unknown assailants killed close to 70 persons, some in close proximity to the UN forces.

By early 1994, cooperation among the members of the diplomatic corps had evolved into full-fledged coordination under the leadership of the dean of the diplomatic corps, the Papal Nuncio. As the political and security situation deteriorated, the corps shared a sense of urgency about implementation of the accord. By joining forces and speaking with one voice, the members hoped to impress upon the Rwandan parties the critical significance all attached to their honouring their Arusha commitments. The Nuncio summoned the diplomatic corps to a meeting on New Year's Day morning. The result was a collective decision for three joint démarches to the three central players: the Rwandan president, the RPF president, and the prime minister designate, who also represented the opposition parties. These joint démarches, aimed at pressing broadly for installation of the transitional government and ending the distribution of weapons to civilians, became more and more frequent. The strategy of joint démarches, however, quickly moved beyond the general to the specific, involving the diplomatic corps in details of the issues preventing the parties from moving forward.

As in the protracted negotiations preceding the unpopular Arusha decision over distribution of government portfolios, the key sticking point again revolved around the role of the hard-line Hutu supremacist CDR, this time in the transitional national assembly. The president's side was adamant that the CDR should occupy the one assembly seat accorded to it by the Arusha agreement. The RPF was just as adamantly opposed. Again the diplomats opted for the principle of inclusion, arguing that inclusion of the CDR would be a means of containing the extremist group and holding it accountable for abiding by the code of conduct for political parties set out in the Accords, in particular the renunciation of violence. Diplomatic interventions, however, failed to sway the RPF leaders who categorically refused to consider this option. They maintained that the CDR had not renounced violence and could, therefore, neither sign the peace agreement nor take up the seat accorded to it. The issue was pending when the president's plane went down and Hutu extremists unleashed the genocide.

The role of multilateralism in the diplomatic community greatly expanded with the arrival in Kigali of the UN Secretary General's Special Representative (SRSG), Cameroonian Roger Booh-Booh, and the Commander of the UN peacekeeping force (UNAMIR), Canadian General Romeo Dallaire. The diplomatic corps, individually and collectively, consulted closely with the UN mission mandated by the Security Council to assist in the implementation of the peace accord. In addition, the diplomats ensured that their frequent coordinated, joint diplomatic interventions with Rwandan authorities conveyed a message consistent with that of the UN. This arrangement actually gave the UN a dominant role in the search for a solution to the implementation quandary. While this may have had its benefits, it also had its drawbacks. As we now know, UN headquarters instructed General Dallaire to use diplomacy instead of his military resources after he advised them that he was about to seize a weapons cache.[15] Furthermore, Dallaire and the SRSG did not always see eye to eye, thus reducing the clarity of the UN message to both the government players and diplomatic corps.

Emphasis during this period on having the diplomatic corps speak with one voice may have been, in some instances, counterproductive.[16] Although intended to maximize the impact of the message and increase the pressure on the Rwandan parties, it actually may have reduced the leverage of some key diplomats by restraining their bilateral contacts with players over whom they might have exerted private influence. In one instance, when the US ambassador made a particularly strong unilateral intervention with Rwandan authorities on a time-sensitive issue, he felt obliged to apprise the UN SRSG of this initiative; his very presence in the country made him the international community's key interlocutor with the Rwandan government, superseding the traditional diplomatic corps. In another example, a collective diplomatic corps intervention with the president led by the Papal Nuncio pre-empted one proposed by the four key western countries – Belgium, France, the US, and Germany – on the same subject. Although the western diplomats were able to interject their individual points, the overall message was diffuse and lacked the clarity it might have had if the western diplomats had intervened alone. As a result, at a particularly key juncture in the implementation process, the president felt less pressure to alter his course than he might otherwise have. In another case, the diplomatic corps collectively presented the Rwandan parties with an ultimatum that may have made them feel cornered in lieu of a less confrontational approach advocated by one key diplomat that aimed to leave the way open for continuing dialogue over the implementation stalemate. Shortly after, the president's plane was shot down and the genocide ensued.

Why did diplomacy fail?

The Kigali diplomatic corps was fully engaged in conflict mitigation and preventive diplomacy during the three years prior to the 1994 genocide in Rwanda. States represented in the diplomatic corps in Kigali vigorously pursued policies aimed at supporting Rwanda's three simultaneous, complex transitions: to multiparty politics, democracy, and peace. Their goals were lofty: to prevent escalation of not only the simmering war at the border but also the pervasive civil violence in the country while helping to shape a sustainable peace that would stabilize Rwanda and the region. But this prolonged and at times intense diplomatic effort at conflict management through peacemaking and democratization failed with catastrophic consequences. Diplomacy failed to avert the escalation of a low-intensity conflict into mass violence and genocide.

Bruce Jones, a former UN staff member who has written widely on the Rwandan genocide, argues that diplomacy failed not because of a failure to act, but because of a failure of the actions taken.[17] To what extent can the 'actions taken' trace their roots to diplomatic culture itself and to the nature of diplomacy? Indeed, the shared norms and values of the diplomats exercising their trade in Kigali and Arusha shaped the positions, actions, and advice of the Kigali diplomatic corps in the years prior to the genocide. Did the norms, values and the structure of the diplomatic corps contribute to mistaken assumptions and misjudgements? Did the commitment of diplomats to the success of peace and democratization contribute more to the escalation of the conflict than to containing or resolving it? Though acting with the best of intentions, could diplomats, in retrospect have been hampered by their own diplomatic perspective?

One of the most serious flaws of the Arusha Accords was the absence of any strategy to keep the potential spoilers engaged in the peace process. The Kigali diplomatic corps had consistently advocated the 'principle of inclusion', as first the democratization process, then the peace talks, and finally implementation of the peace accord stalled over whether Hutu extremists should participate in the new political institutions. When an inclusive power-sharing model was rejected at each stage, it became increasingly clear that the hard-line Hutu extremists, who claimed they were being relegated to 'permanent minority' status, had the potential to become 'spoilers'. Nevertheless, once the RPF and government negotiators had agreed in Arusha to a power-sharing arrangement, diplomats embraced the agreement despite adamant public opposition from Hutu extremists and an escalation of anti-Tutsi violence. The principles of diplomatic negotiation led diplomats to expect that, if the president signed the agreement, he and his people would abide by the radical changes it called for, even if they found them distasteful, and that they would proceed in good faith to implementation. So, instead of pressing negotiators to address the issue of the 'losers', the diplomatic corps pressed the president to accept the agreement. Diplomats strongly advised against reopening the power-sharing protocol on grounds it could lead to collapse of the entire peace process. Collapse, they argued, would inevitably open the way for return to civil war, an option no one wanted to risk. Collapse would also mean diplomatic failure, an outcome unpalatable to the diplomatic corps. Although diplomatic counsel against reopening the disputed portions of the agreement kept the peace process moving forward, it also contributed to locking the parties into a flawed agreement that contained within it the seeds of the genocide. The position of the diplomatic corps allowed the architects of the power-sharing arrangements – the RPF and moderate Hutu negotiators – to avoid reexamining their deal in light of its potential consequences. Hutu extremists who had been the 'losers' at the negotiating table became the 'spoilers' who launched the genocide.

Another key problem was the serious underestimation of the lengths to which the 'losers' would go to defeat the Arusha process with its power-sharing arrangements that they abhorred. While diplomats were concentrating their attention and effort on assuring a peace agreement, Hutu extremists were planning and executing a progressively more elaborate and violent strategy for holding on to power. Unable to win on the battlefield, they had agreed to negotiations. Unable to prevail at the negotiating table, they turned to political machinations aimed at gaining the allegiance of political party representatives in the new institutions. When that ploy failed, they used delaying tactics to prevent implementation of the peace agreement. With that route nearing an end, they resorted to the only alternative they knew for eliminating their enemies: unleashing their loyal militia, an effective killing machine that they had organized and trained while the peace process was underway.

Why did the diplomatic community misjudge this situation so badly? Although diplomats had factored these twists and turns into their analyses along the way, they failed to see the bigger picture. First, they focused squarely on the success of the peace process because they believed the extremist problem could be 'managed' within the framework of the peace agreement. Thus, their policy priorities and diplomatic energy focused almost exclusively on securing a peace agreement and its implementation. Second, genocide seemed inconceivable. While some Rwandan interlocutors had tried to suggest this as a possibility, there were many more who downplayed this outcome and were themselves caught off guard. On the one hand, the diplomats' analysis probably suffered from a short-term perspective. Generally diplomats are assigned to a diplomatic mission for two to four years at most, giving them a rather myopic view of conflicts such as the Rwandan one that stretch back decades, if not farther. On the other, diplomatic missions, especially small ones with few resources, tend to focus primarily on positive developments at the expense of negative ones. The small US embassy in Kigali focused its energies and reports to Washington on progress in democratization and the peace process rather than on the violence that accompanied each success. Emphasis was on the achievements rather than on the known impediments to them. This attitude likely contributed to downplaying or neglecting the significance of clearly threatening negative developments: the militia build-up, the continuing distribution of weapons to civilians, and the impact of the private 'hate radio' station that spewed ethnic hatred over the airwaves.

Some critics have argued that, in retrospect, there should never have been any attempt at democratization in Rwanda while a civil war was underway. At the time, however, diplomats, heavily invested in promoting democratization, reasoned that the prospect of participating in a liberalized political system as a political party on equal footing to the others would offer the RPF an incentive to lay down its arms and join the new political process. In retrospect, there were two basic problems with that expectation. First, the RPF had grander goals that became clear only after the Arusha negotiations were well underway. Instead of joining the political process as a political party of a minority ethnic group, the RPF wanted a complete reorganization of the institutions of power to ensure substantial Tutsi representation in the decisionmaking process at all levels. Second, the incipient liberalization of the political system changed the power dynamic among the ruling elite, weakening the president and strengthening the moderate opposition. This change in power relationships elevated Hutu moderates to government leadership positions both in Kigali and at the negotiating table, creating the political opening that convinced the RPF to enter a negotiation process it had long eschewed. Because of the incipient democratization process, there was a group of moderates – Hutu and Tutsi – within the government negotiating team. The RPF no doubt realized it could make common cause with them on a number of issues because they shared a common goal for the peace agreement, namely, to prevent the president and his party from continuing their monopoly over political, military, and security decisionmaking. Thus, diplomatic support for democratization inadvertently set the stage for the unbalanced peace accord that provided little incentive for those required to cede power to stay engaged in the process.

Many analysts of the Rwandan genocide have argued that a show of force at the onset of the genocide by the UN peacekeeping force, UNAMIR, or by some other troops, such as those who came to evacuate foreigners, could have prevented escalation of the killing and kept it from spreading throughout the country.[18] The Security Council authorized a force seriously reduced in size and mandate from that recommended by the UN's own reconnaissance mission. Indeed, Council members with missions in Kigali were acting against the recommendations of their own embassies. Kigali diplomats supported the rapid arrival of a strong UN peacekeeping force with a broad security mandate, as called for the Arusha Accords. The US embassy had argued to Washington for months that once the peace agreement was signed, quick deployment of a robust force with a strong mandate would be critical to successful implementation of the peace agreement. However, repeated embassy arguments underscoring the critical urgency of this issue failed to register in Washington or to rise above the level of the Assistant Secretary for Africa in the State Department. Higher officials were consumed with a myriad of other crises – Bosnia, Somalia, Haiti, and Cambodia, to name just a few – that out-ranked Rwanda on the scale of US interests.[19] In addition, there was growing scepticism in Washington over the creation of new UN peacekeeping missions. Already in the development stages was PDD 25, a presidential directive issued in May 1994 that set out strict, narrow criteria for US support of peacekeeping missions. Consequently, US diplomats in Kigali, like those of other nations, were unable to convince decisionmakers in their capitals to authorize the robust force they believed was needed to consolidate the success of Arusha.

This inability of the Kigali diplomatic corps members to convince their headquarters to support a robust peacekeeping force highlights the policy impact of the differing perspectives that often arise between diplomatic missions abroad and their headquarters at home. Diplomats in a given foreign capital can only report and recommend policy directions based on what they observe and determine from the situation on the ground. Decisionmakers in the capital filter this through their larger lens and weigh the recommendations within their important framework of domestic, fiscal, and broader foreign policy considerations. Furthermore, there are no mechanisms diplomats in the field can use to ensure that their recommendations reach top decisionmakers. This becomes especially difficult when the recommendation aims to prevent a potential crisis, even one that appears to be looming just around the corner. Preventive diplomacy to avoid deterioration of a situation or to avert a future catastrophe rarely resonates in crisis-driven headquarters. Securing additional resources, of either personnel or funding, for such eventualities is nearly impossible.

Conclusion

In the years prior to the genocide in Rwanda, the Kigali diplomatic corps was fully engaged in using the diplomatic tools at its disposal in an effort to prevent conflict in Rwanda from escalating into mass violence. The *modus operandi* of the corps members evolved from loosely aligned bilateral efforts at supporting political liberalization and promoting dialogue to end the conflict into full cooperation around the goal of facilitating a successful negotiated settlement, particularly among the 'shadow corps' diplomats at the peace talks in Arusha. Once an agreement was reached, revolutionary though it was, the diplomatic corps was united in its efforts to ensure its implementation and fully cooperated in this enterprise. The more their national interests converged, the more diplomatic corps members cooperated to present a collective front and common message to their Rwandan interlocutors. Despite all their diplomatic activity and their concerted diplomatic interventions, and despite seemingly clear evidence along the way that success was at hand, peace and stability in Rwanda eluded them.

Diplomacy failed in Rwanda at least in part because the Kigali diplomatic corps was a victim of its own diplomatic culture. The Kigali diplomatic community and the 'shadow' observer corps in Arusha were so committed to the success of the Arusha process, as a way of both ending the war and bringing democracy to Rwanda that they failed to see or to comprehend the warning signs that the process was not leading to peace. Diplomats believed that the parties to the peace agreement had made good faith efforts to forge compromises acceptable to both sides, that their signatures on the peace agreement indicated they were committed to working together to implement it, and that they were ready to resolve their future differences through peaceful means within the framework set out in the accord. To the diplomatic corps, the Rwandan peace agreement, promised an end to the war and provided a blueprint for political and military power sharing, signalling a diplomatic success. Diplomats recognized that there were flaws in the agreement, but they did not consider them fatal. They knew that the Hutu extremists had rejected the Arusha Accord over the political power-sharing and military integration arrangements. Nevertheless, they believed these potential 'spoilers' could and would be 'managed' within the framework of the agreements once they were implemented. Their calculus failed, however, to give enough credence to 'dark side' elements threatening this success and the implementation of the agreement: the formation and training of militia forces, the distribution of arms to civilians, propaganda demonizing the Tutsi, the emergence of the brazen 'hate radio' station.

Ambassador Herman Cohen, Assistant Secretary of State for Africa in the early 1990s, cautioned in retrospect that diplomats should resist regarding a signed peace agreement as the basis for peace. When he launched his book on his peacemaking efforts in Africa, he said that perhaps his biggest mistake was putting too much faith in negotiated peace agreements. Flawed agreements, he said, should have been denounced even if the parties were willing to sign them, as in the case of Rwanda. 'Frequently', he wrote, 'such flawed agreements signal that the peace process is just another aspect of war for some protagonists, a resting and regrouping period between battles rather than a peaceful new beginning.'[20]

To avoid in future the kinds of mistaken assumptions and misjudgements that contributed to the failure of diplomacy in Rwanda in 1994, diplomats will need to become much more aware of the traps lurking within the structure and norms of their own diplomatic culture. There is no intention here to suggest that diplomatic culture and its impact on negotiations at Arusha can alone explain diplomacy's failure. Indeed, other structural and process variables undoubtedly contributed equally to the flawed outcome and the catastrophic consequences. Nevertheless, if diplomats could become more aware of the impact their collective perspective is having on the course of negotiations, give due weight to negative factors that can impede positive achievements, and generally look more objectively at their own assumptions, they might be less likely to play inadvertently into the hands of negotiators eager for a one-sided agreement in their favour.

Notes

1 This chapter is based on a paper entitled 'Genocide in Rwanda and the Kigali Diplomatic Corps' that Ambassador Joyce Leader presented at the Annual Convention of the International Studies Association (ISA) in Honolulu, Hawaii, 1–5 March 2005. The Institute for the Study of International Migration (ISIM) at Georgetown University in Washington, D.C., where Ambassador Leader is a Senior Research Fellow, supported her participation in the 2005 ISA Convention. The author alone is responsible for the views expressed here.

2 Ambassador Joyce E. Leader served as Deputy Chief of Mission in Rwanda from August 1991 until the genocide began in April 1994. Her book, *Rwanda's Struggle for Democracy and Peace, 1991–1994* (Washington: The Fund for Peace, 2001), analyses the US response to Rwanda's internal conflict.

3 During colonial rule in Rwanda, first Germany and then Belgium gave preferential treatment in education and employment to the Tutsi minority, exacerbating existing tensions between them and the Hutu majority. At independence in 1962, Belgium shifted its allegiance and handed the reins of power to a Hutu-controlled government. Periodic Hutu violence against the Tutsi minority during the 1960s and early 1070s resulted in thousands deaths and the flight of cumulative total by 1964 of 336,000 refugees, according to official 1964 figures of the UN refugee office (see below Prunier, p. 62). A Hutu-led military coup in 1973 ushered in a period of prosperity and growth but also a period of institutionalized discrimination against Tutsi and informal discrimination against Hutu not from the president's northern region. Tutsi refugees failed in several attempts to fight their way back into Rwanda in the 1960s and had their 1988 request to return peacefully denied by the president. Under pressure from the Ugandan government to quit the country, Tutsi refugees and other exiles, including some Hutu, formed the Rwandan Patriotic Front (RPF), an armed group that invaded Rwanda from Uganda in October 1990. This move, that coincided with the president's announced policy of political liberalization, launched a war that simmered at the border until the Rwandan government

and the RPF agreed in July 1992 to a ceasefire and to negotiate an end to the conflict. The resulting Arusha Accords, signed in August 1993, spelled out political and military power-sharing arrangements that would greatly reduce the power of the president and his entourage. In a misguided effort to preserve their power and privilege, a powerful few around the Hutu president, who found the agreement totally unacceptable, launched the systematic and targeted killing of Tutsi civilians and moderate Hutu. Over 800,000 people were brutally murdered in just 100 days in this genocide before the RPF routed the government army and its militias and took control of the country in mid-1994. Since then, a government led by minority Tutsi has ruled the country. For more detail on the historical background to the genocide see Gerard Prunier, *The Rwanda Crisis: History of a Genocide* (New York: Columbia University Press, 1995); Alison Des Forges, *Leave None to Tell the Story* (New York: Human Rights Watch, 1999); and Bruce D. Jones, *Peacemaking in Rwanda: The Dynamics of Failure* (Boulder: Lynne Rienner Publishers, 2001).

4   Jones, 2001, p. 87.
5   Private communication in January 2005 with Robert Flaten, United States Ambassador to Rwanda, 1990–93.
6   For a detailed account of early peacemaking efforts, see Jones, 2001, pp. 53–68.
7   Ambassador Cohen recounts these discussions in Herman J. Cohen, *Intervening in Africa: Superpower Peacemaking in a Troubled Continent* (New York: St. Martin's Press, 2000), pp. 169–71.
8   The existence of a common diplomatic culture across national boundaries has been noted by both practitioners and scholars. Sir Harold Nicolson, a British diplomat considered an expert on the subject of diplomacy, notes in a collection of 1953 lectures that professional diplomatic services consisted of 'officials representing their governments in foreign capitals (who) possessed similar standards of education, similar experience, and a similar aim. They desired the same sort of world...As Callières has already noticed in 1716, they tended to develop a corporate identity independent of their national identity.' See Harold Nicolson, *The Evolution of Diplomatic Method* (London: Constable & Co., 1954), p. 75.
9   For more on culture in relation to negotiations see Peter Berton, Hiroshi Kimura, and I. William Zartman, *International Negotiation: Actors, Structures/Process, Values* (New York: St. Martin's Press, 1999). In a chapter entitled 'Cultural Aspects of International Negotiations', Guy Oliver Faure discusses the influence of culture, 'a system of widely accepted beliefs and assumptions', on key aspects of negotiations, including actors, structure, strategies, process, and outcome, noting that people, including those involved in negotiations, 'tend to act according to beliefs and values provided by their culture'. (See pp. 12–13.) In another chapter entitled 'Negotiating Cultures', I. William Zartman, a specialist in international negotiation, notes that multilateral or multinational structures often create their own cultures. He could have been referring to the diplomatic corps instead of the United Nations when he writes: 'The homogenizing socializing culture of the United Nations often seems to override component national cultures and to be a creation of its own, not just a larger sum of its parts'. (See p. 4.)

10 Des Forges, 1999, p. 24.
11 The diplomatic observers at the Arusha peace talks tended to came either from embassies in Tanzania's capital, Dar es Salaam, from their home capitals or, in the case of the UN and the OAU, from headquarters. Some stayed for the duration of the talks while others were present periodically. Some countries had more than one observer present depending on the nature of the discussion. Military officials often supplemented or replaced political observers during discussions of military issues. Several officials represented the United States over the course of the year-long negotiations: during the ceasefire negotiations, then military advisor and later Acting Assistant Secretary for Africa Charles Snyder and then State Department lawyer Ambassador John Byerly; during political power-sharing talks, Ambassador David Rawson; for initial talks on power sharing in the military, Lt. Colonel Tony Marley; and for the balance of the military and subsequent refugee talks, the author. All US observers but the author, who remained in Arusha from April through June, 1993, came from Washington.
12 The CDR, or Coalition for the Defense of the Republic, was the first of several political parties formed in support of President Habyarimana as counterweights to the three main opposition political parties. The CDR's virulent pro-Hutu, anti-Tutsi pronouncements, put it farther to the right on the political spectrum than President Habyarimana and his ruling MRND party. Speculation among Rwandans and diplomats alike was that the CDR was created to give voice to radical, pro-Hutu thinking prevalent among many in the president's entourage which would have been 'politically incorrect' coming from the president himself or from his political party. The president's wife was closely associated with the CDR and its leadership although the president's connections were less clear. Those subscribing to the CDR's anti-Tutsi, anti-power sharing, and anti-Arusha peace process philosophy were among the masterminds behind the 1994 genocide. CDR ideologue Jean-Bosco Baryagwisa was among three persons convicted in 2003 by the International Criminal Tribunal for Rwanda (ICTR) of inciting the genocide for his role in founding and using the 'hate-radio' station, RTLM to promote genocide.
13 Ambassador Ami Mpungwe, Director for External Relations/Africa at the Tanzanian foreign ministry served as 'Facilitator' for much of the Arusha negotiations. He was acting on behalf of President Mwinyi, officially designated 'Facilitator' of the talks by the two sides at the Paris meeting that launched the negotiations.
14 Not long after ending the genocide and installing an RPF-led government, the RPF disbanded the territorial police, or gendarmerie, managed by the Ministry of Defense and replaced it with a national police force under the auspices of the Ministry of the Interior.
15 See Des Forges, 1999, pp. 150–1 and 172–4; Romeo Dallaire, *Shake Hands with the Devil: the Failure of Humanity in Rwanda* (Toronto: Random House Canada, 2003), pp. 145–7.
16 Ambassador David Rawson, Ambassador to Rwanda 1994–96, introduced the author to this concept and the examples cited in private conversations in August and November 2006.

17 Jones, 2001, p. 3. Jones provides in this book an in-depth analysis of the failure of diplomatic actions in Rwanda. He first put forward this concept in an earlier piece co-authored with Astri Suhrke. They wrote: 'It is not the failure to take preventive action that characterizes the international role in the period leading up to the genocide but the failure of actions taken.' Astri Suhrke and Bruce Jones, 'Preventive Diplomacy in Rwanda: Failure to Act or Failure of Actions?' in Bruce W. Jentleson (ed.), *Opportunities Missed, Opportunities Seized: Preventive Diplomacy in the Post-Cold War World* (Lanham: Rowman & Littlefield Publishers, 2000), p. 242.

18 Scott R. Feil, *Preventing Genocide: How the Early Use of Force Might Have Succeeded in Rwanda. A Report to the Carnegie Commission on Preventing Deadly Conflict* (New York: Carnegie Corporation, 1998). This report concludes that an early show of force could have made a difference and saved hundreds of thousands of lives. It also acknowledges obstacles to mounting an effective, rapid intervention. Alan J. Kuperman, 'Rwanda in Retrospect', *Foreign Affairs*, Volume 79, Number 1 (January/February 2000) 94–118, argues that even a large force, immediately deployed, could not have saved 'even half' of those killed in the genocide. Although the assumptions he makes in the scenarios he analyses to reach this conclusion are not explicit, Kuperman seems to attribute greater operational capacity to the killers in the early stages than actually existed. His assertion (p. 112) that the killing began 'almost immediately in most of the country' is incorrect. It actually began in Kigali and a few other discrete population centers in northern Rwanda, only later spreading to the south.

19 Madeleine Albright, former Secretary of State who was the US Permanent Representative to the United Nations at the time the genocide began, cites 14 countries that were at the top of the State Department's agenda, noting that Rwanda was not among them. Madeleine Albright, *Madam Secretary: A Memoir* (New York: Miramax Books, 2003), p. 149.

20 Cohen, 2000, p. 223.

10
The Skopje Diplomatic Corps and the Macedonian Political Crisis of 2001

Paul Sharp

My purposes in this chapter are to chart the role of the Skopje diplomatic corps during Macedonia's political crisis in 2001, and to consider some possible explanations for its prominence in the efforts to reach a political settlement there. Diplomatic corps, in general, are not supposed to be very important to an understanding of what goes on in international relations. They are viewed as a second order institution concerned with defending the privileges and immunities of their members, maintaining professional standards and engaging in the residuals of state and court ceremony.[1] In the past, only a rare convergence of great power interest and local weakness has been said to permit the diplomatic corps to act collectively on policy and then only briefly.[2] It might be supposed that the Skopje diplomatic corps, in particular, would have confirmed these expectations. Even with its troubles, Macedonia remained on the periphery of the great powers' vision engendering neither conflict between them nor its corollary need to build a consensus. There were always bigger and more dangerous problems, both in its neighbourhood and elsewhere. Besides, its troubles, as these were generally understood, had a domestic character revolving around ethnic divides, albeit with transnational implications but scarcely the sort of thing in which a diplomatic corps, with its state-to-state emphasis and traditional conception of the distinction between internal and external affairs, might properly get mixed up. Indeed, since its independence in 1991, Macedonia had attracted an army of international agencies, offices, missions and, indeed, soldiers whose purpose in being there was to address these very problems as part of a broader multilateral effort to bring peace and prosperity in the Balkans by building market economies, political democracies and functioning civil societies.

Nevertheless, from the eruption of what appeared to be an armed rebellion by elements of its Albanian minority in February 2001 to the acceptance of a package of constitutional reforms linked to a NATO-supervised disarmament and amnesty the following August, the Skopje diplomatic corps played a critical, if little noticed, part in reaching what became known as the Framework Agreement. It did so by framing the nature of the crisis for foreigners, specifying the general outlines of a solution for Macedonians, and keeping talks going between the contending parties when they ran into difficulties. I shall argue that it was able to accomplish all this for both constitutive and circumstantial reasons. Constitutively, the diplomatic corps was greatly helped by the fact that nearly all the parties to the dispute accepted that it was about the terms on which Macedonia should be accepted as a member of the international society of states. The Skopje corps, therefore, provided a putative space for arguments, a real audience before whom they could be conducted and, on occasions, very material targets upon which they could vent their frustrations. Circumstantially, the Skopje corps was helped by the initial reluctance of external diplomatic actors to become involved, their difficulties when they finally did, and the fear that these difficulties created in internal parties that the dispute was passing beyond their control. Its success was incomplete, however, not least in the eyes of many Macedonians who came to realize that the corps' priorities were not theirs. And, although this is primarily of concern to academics, its successes were made possible by a degree of flexibility which casts some doubt upon the idea of the diplomatic corps in its narrow and formal sense as an actor. It is perhaps more accurate to say that the subject of this study is a group of diplomats based in Skopje whose membership shifted and which sometimes operated as the diplomatic corps, sometimes as the diplomatic community, and sometimes as diplomatic currents within the domestic political process.

The Skopje diplomatic corps and Macedonia's emergence as a sovereign state

The history of a people called the Macedonians stretches back to the time of Alexander the Great and beyond. Quite who Macedonians are, however, has long been, and remains, a matter of some controversy. The 19th century movement for independence from the Ottomans, definitively terrorist in some of its methods and intensity, was distinguished by its objective of integrating Macedonians with neighbouring

Bulgarians. When the Ottomans finally departed, it was as South Serbs that the people of Macedonia enjoyed their new freedoms in the Kingdom of the Serbs, Croats and Slovenes that was to become Yugoslavia.[3] By the time an independent sovereign republic of Macedonia emerged in 1991 from the collapse of Yugoslavia, its population consisted of a Slavic majority, some 65 percent, who regarded these various historical experiences as making them Macedonians, and a number of minorities among whom the Albanians, consisting of over 25 percent of the population, were the largest.[4]

Macedonia's secession from Yugoslavia was peaceful. This was widely credited, especially abroad, to the ability of the international community to learn from the disasters of Croatia's and Bosnia Herzegovina's experiences, and especially to the insertion of a small UN peacekeeping force comprised mainly of Americans to patrol Macedonia's borders with what remained of Yugoslavia. Indeed, and in contrast to its former presentation as the '...powder keg of the Balkans...,' Macedonia was often hailed as '...an oasis of peace...,' a multi-ethnic country which had made a successful transition to political independence and democracy.[5] It was initially governed by a 'left' political coalition between major Slav-Macedonian and Albanian parties and, after a third successful election in 1998, this coalition was replaced by one between a more nationalist or 'right' Slav-Macedonian party and a different Albanian party.

While Macedonia achieved its independence peacefully, however, it did not do so without a measure of controversy. Greece objected to its name, concerned that its use would have proprietary implications, both nominal and practical, for its own province of Macedonia.[6] As a consequence, the process by which the country attained full diplomatic recognition, and its confirmation by a full diplomatic corps in Skopje, was drawn out. While independence was claimed in 1991 and Yugoslav troops withdrew in 1992, the British embassy, for example, was not opened until the following year and the United States did not establish full diplomatic relations until 1995, following the signing of one of a number of agreements to disagree over the name issue between Macedonia and Greece. However, by 1999 and the NATO campaign against Yugoslavia over Kosovo, Macedonia could regard itself as a fully-networked member of the contemporary international society. A sense of what this means is provided by the diplomatic list at the time of writing. A country with an area of less than 10,000 square miles and a population of just over two million,[7] Macedonia has 24 resident embassies. Represented among these are the United States,

Russia, and China, four major European countries, all the countries bordering Macedonia and all the republics of the former Yugoslavia.[8] In addition, and befitting a country that has attracted a great deal of international attention, Skopje hosts the offices of over 20 international agencies and missions.[9]

From Macedonia's inception as an independent state, this diplomatic corps, together with the broader diplomatic community surrounding it, served to legitimize, normalize and confirm the country's international standing. It did so initially by arriving and establishing its system and society of embassies and missions. As in other states, the diplomatic corps served as a witness to major state occasions such as presidential addresses and the opening of parliamentary sessions. As in other small states, it also performed on occasions of less import. The attendance of members at the opening of a new business centre owned by a Slovenian drug company in 2000 is typical in this regard.[10] Unlike in other states, however, elements of the diplomatic corps were involved in aspects of Macedonia's core internal affairs from its very inception. Most obviously in this regard, the Organization for Security and Cooperation's (OSCE) 'Spillover Mission' was established in 1992 with an office in Skopje. The task of this mission was to make sure that troubles in the rest of the former Yugoslavia did not spread to Macedonia, but increasingly this was viewed as a process by which intercommunal relations in the country and public policy related to them could be monitored. Initially, this intrusive activity did not pose a problem. It was welcomed as confirming Macedonia's multi-ethnic virtue, a reputation which the international community sought to build up and to which its government and people sought to respond.[11] What is not clear, however, is the extent to which this intrusive activity by the 'internationals' was regarded as a source of help, as opposed to as a necessary evil which the government was prepared to tolerate as an earnest of Macedonia's goodwill towards the international community. Certainly, as conditions worsened, attitudes towards the 'internationals', as opposed to the diplomatic corps more traditionally defined, polarized along ethnic lines.

The crisis of 2001

Whatever the difficulties of its generally peaceful birthing, by February 2001 and the start of the crisis, Macedonian diplomatic life had manifested not only normalcy but also success. That month a multilateral summit on regional economic cooperation had been successfully hosted in Skopje, negotiations with the Greeks over the country's name had appeared to make progress, and a settlement of the border issues with Yugoslavia had been reached. The latter was matched by an agreement between the NATO forces in Kosovo (KFOR) and Yugoslavia about letting Serbian troops back into the Presovo area to drive out Albanian fighters who had established themselves there. As close observers noted, however, these successes masked long-term strains. A combination of external pressures and domestic economic collapse had steadily eroded the old terms on which the ethnic communities of the country had conducted their relations with one another. Indeed, domestic observers, especially, worried that the political successes with which Macedonia was credited abroad resulted from the manoeuvring of political forces which were, at best, incapable of resolving Macedonia's underlying problems and, at worst, direct beneficiaries of ethnic tensions and criminal activity. The Macedonian settlement, they argued, was far more fragile and far less attractive than was generally assumed.[12]

NATO's war on Serbia in 1999 confirmed this fragility. Its associated sanctions had already had a knock-on effect on Macedonia's economy, hurting legitimate business and encouraging smuggling. The war, itself boosted the military confidence and political ambitions of Albanian nationalists in both Kosovo and Macedonia. It burdened Macedonia, in the short term, with large numbers of Kosovar refugees who enjoyed much international sympathy but much less material support. Indeed, the Macedonian government's response to the influx of people was widely presented as grudging and hostile. And finally, the war permitted a great expansion of the international presence in Macedonia from the small UN force and an associated group of OSCE observers to a NATO army which was intended to fight its way into Kosovo. At the beginning of 2001, skirmishes between Kosovar fighters and Serbian forces in an Albanian-populated area of the now much-diminished Yugoslavia spilled over the adjacent border into Macedonia with attacks on local police units. The fighting escalated to a low-intensity contest over certain villages and vantage points close to major cities between an Albanian group calling itself the National Liberation Army (NLA) and the Macedonian government's police and army supported by certain irregular units. The former presented themselves as fighting for constitutional changes to improve the standing of the Albanian minority in the country. Many of them made it clear, however, that should concessions not be forthcoming they would fight for control of Albanian territory, as they termed it, in Macedonia.[13] The governing coalition said it was open to negotiating reforms with people not in arms against it and, though with less enthusiasm from its Albanian members, that it was committed to winning the war against rebels and terrorists.

The fighting precipitated two distinct but related negotiations and intensive diplomatic attempts to bring them to successful conclusions. The first concerned reaching agreement between the principal political parties on constitutional reforms.[14] The second negotiation involved getting the armed Albanians to stop fighting and surrender arms primarily by offering the reforms achieved by the first negotiation and by promising them amnesties. Since the armed Albanians were presented as using force illegitimately and unreasonably by virtually everyone until it became clear that costs of the government attempting a military victory would be prohibitive, the second negotiation initially remained in the background.[15] In response to the incursions and seizures, the Macedonian government called, in March, for a UN Security Council meeting to discuss setting up a buffer zone and appealed to Lord Robertson, the Secretary General of NATO, for a strengthening of KFOR border patrols. Trajkovski, the president, made a formal declaration to members of parliament and the assembled diplomatic corps that Macedonia had the resources to preserve its territorial integrity, and contacts were described as being conducted at all levels between the government, the diplomatic corps and the United Nations Interim Administration Mission in Kosovo (UNMIK) liaison office in Skopje.[16] International responses condemned the armed Albanians and supported a firm, if restrained, response by the government.[17] However, no buffer zone, of either UN or NATO provenance was forthcoming. Instead, NATO established a liaison office in Skopje for co-ordinating border operations and providing advice.[18]

By the end of March, the basic pattern of the crisis was established. Within a government which eventually contained all the principal parties, one element led by the prime minister and the interior minister sought a state of emergency and forceful military measures as the price of its continued participation in talks about constitutional change. Another element, around the Albanian parties wanted to keep military operations to a minimum and threatened to leave if civilian casualties occurred in any fighting. Military incidents would precipitate fierce arguments and result in appeals for diplomatic assistance made by the president, Trajkovski, to sanction some sort of military demonstration against the armed Albanians, or from the Albanian political leaders within the government for a direct NATO intervention.[19]

The Skopje diplomatic corps and the external response to Macedonia's crisis

The fighting and Macedonia's possible descent into civil war presented the members of the Skopje diplomatic corps with two sets of challenges. The first was managing the response of their governments, both individually and collectively, to what was going on. The second was providing what assistance they might make to the restoration of peace and normalcy in Macedonia. The external response was primarily collective in nature and most obviously manifested in a series of visits from senior figures within NATO and the European Union (EU), principally Robertson and Solana, but also Patton and Swedish foreign minister Lindh. These 'supranational impresarios', as Simon Jenkins somewhat unkindly called them, would arrive in Skopje when negotiations were stalled and threatening to break up and, by a combination of NATO threats, EU promises, and whatever personal persuasive powers they each possessed try to get talks moving again. Cancellations of planned visits, when the situation was exceptionally bad, also served the same purpose.[20]

The 'top down' view that it was the heroic shuttle diplomacy of senior statesmen which kept things moving rightly attracted a degree of scepticism both outside and within the country.[21] The 'bottom up' view, in contrast, namely that the Macedonians used both violent incidents and diplomatic interventions in finely calibrated manoeuvres to secure advantage over one another, enjoyed much wider credence. Both views captured a dimension to what was going on. On occasions, visitors provided critical momentum when talks were stalled.[22] And the local politicians certainly thought they were manipulating the process of talks, violence and the resulting suspensions of negotiations to their own advantage. However, neither the 'top down' nor the 'bottom up' view of what was going on captured the initial indeterminacy and the eventual structure of the situation in which the various parties pursued their strategies. It was in this regard that the Skopje diplomatic corps played its leading role. It did so in two ways. The first was in its collective support for the government's position that it need not and ought not to negotiate with armed Albanians until the latter stopped using force. The government, diplomatic sources noted, was well within its rights in seeking to re-establish control of its own territory.[23] Secondly, however, it also offered the collective judgement in the '...contacts at all levels...' referred to earlier, as well as in reports to international and regional organizations, that a military solution was beyond the government's ability. This view was based on the assessment by diplomatic observers of the initial encounters around Tetovo in March.[24] Left to itself, the government would lose, but improving the abilities of government forces would succeed only in driving the Albanian political parties out of negotiations and, hence, destroying Macedonia's multi-ethnic claim to international sympathy and help. Therefore, negotiations between all the constitutional parties to secure reforms which would remove the NLA's ostensible grounds for taking up arms represented the only way forward.

Beyond framing the situation in this way for protagonists and international visitors alike, the task of the Skopje diplomatic corps became one of establishing and facilitating the processes by which agreement might be achieved. This involved direct participation in consultations on the details of possible reforms to be negotiated between the party leaders and warnings, sometimes public, when the sins of commission or omission by either side were judged to threaten the process.[25] The complexities and ambiguities of its role in this regard are usefully illustrated by the events surrounding the NLA's occupation of Aracinovo in June. This was a village close to Skopje from which, it was claimed, they might be able to mortar the capital, its airport and refinery. This development coincided with new demands by the Albanian parties in the reform negotiations to have Albanians recognized as a founding people in the constitution rather than just to be given equality by the previously agreed citizenship formula. The Albanians were also requesting a vice-president with something close to veto powers over legislation. In response, the government ended a truce early and attacked the village with artillery and helicopter gunships with which they had recently been supplied by Ukraine. This move was widely condemned abroad, Robertson declaring it '...complete folly...' and Solana returning to Skopje to restore the ceasefire.[26] The details of the ceasefire, once authoritatively declared, were hurriedly worked out, principally by NATO officers in the field and with unfortunate consequences. The Albanian fighters were to be allowed to withdraw from the village with their arms and under NATO supervision, and the government's forces would not immediately replace them.[27] As it happened, the only NATO soldiers and the only transportation available at short order were both American. The spectacle of armed Albanian gunmen being driven off in American vehicles under American escort touched off demonstrations along the convoy's route and riots at the president's residence in Skopje in which Western journalists and others were threatened. Trajkovski's political survival was in doubt for several days.

The role of the diplomatic corps in the details of the improvised ceasefire is unclear. What is clear, however, is that members let it be known that they had regarded the Albanian constitutional proposals which had accompanied the military move with incredulity.[28] This damping of Albanian expectations was repeated on several occasions. It was also matched by the application of collective pressure on the prime minister and president when the former, in particular, sought to declare a state of emergency. This would have suspended elements of the existing constitution and allowed the government to mobilize more military and police reserves, developments which, the Albanian parties maintained, would spell an end to all discussions.[29] The most distinctive contribution of the diplomatic corps, however, involved the efforts of its members to keep nervous and angry politicians in the grand coalition government to which they had all agreed in May. Imer Imeri, leader of the Albanian Party for Democratic Prosperity (PDP), had to be talked back into the initial negotiations in May by several ambassadors after he had walked out in objection to prime minister Georgievski's, reference to the NLA as 'terrorists'. The following month, Ljube Boskovski, the interior minister, was persuaded back into the disarmament talks of an all-party security body by Peter Feith, NATO's special envoy, after he had walked out in protest at Albanian references to the Cyprus model as a solution to Macedonia's problems. And in July, the representatives of all the Albanian parties walked out when the prime minister accused the international community of trying to break up Macedonia. They maintained that the talks should now be transferred abroad and only with difficulty were persuaded to send their constitutional experts back to the negotiating table. Finally, in August, a day after agreement was reached at Ohrid, the delegates of Georgievski's Democratic Party for National Unity (VMRO) walked out after ten Macedonian soldiers were killed in an ambush, and had to be persuaded to return.[30]

The contribution of the diplomatic corps, or elements of it, was not always sure-footed. In particular, the so-called Prizren agreement negotiated in May between the Albanian parties and the NLA by the OSCE's representative in Skopje caused great difficulties. It promised amnesty and a part in negotiations in return for a cessation of violence. This violated the government's position, endorsed at that point by NATO and the EU, that there could be no negotiations with anyone seeking to advance their interests by force. Xhaferi, the leader of the major Albanian party, the Democratic Party of Albanians (DPA), called for NLA participation in the all party negotiations preceding the establishment of the grand coalition government, but NATO and the EU foreign ministers re-affirmed their support of the government's position at a meeting in Budapest, and senior members of the Skopje diplomatic corps were reported meeting in the US embassy to decide what to do about the OSCE's Ambassador Frowick and his initiative.[31]

It seems that the difficulties of the Prizren and Aracinovo episodes brought an end to the handling of the crisis by high profile visits between which the diplomatic corps attempted to hold the circle around negotiations. Instead two special envoys, former French defence minister, François Léotard, for the EU and former US special envoy to the Balkans, James Pardew, for NATO were appointed to preside over negotiations on the spot with a view to heading off a civil war.[32] The appointment of the two special envoys might be seen a compromise between the advantages of heroic diplomacy and the strengths of the diplomatic corps. The two men enjoyed a standing that the ambassadors and staffs of the resident missions did not. They may also have been able to muster a degree of focus on the negotiations which was beyond the ability of the major members of the diplomatic corps trying to work together. In addition, however, they possessed, if not the residential advantages exactly of the diplomatic corps, then at least the advantage of exerting the sort of sustained presence, initially in Skopje and then in Ohrid, which senior EU and NATO figures neither wished nor were able to manage.

The benefits were seen, not in the content of the negotiations, which remained substantially the same, but in the intensity with which they were conducted. As a result, two corollaries of the negotiation were made explicit. The first, of which everyone in Macedonia had been aware but which everyone, from their own point of view, had hoped might be avoided, was that the deployment of NATO troops depended on the grand coalition talks delivering an agreement on constitutional reform and, hence, a ceasefire. NATO had made it clear early in the crisis that the most to which it would agree was the deployment of a small force for a short period of time to collect weapons from the armed Albanians.[33] The parties clearly hoped that the deteriorating situation and the depredations, as they saw them, of their opponents would lead to an expansion of NATO's commitment on terms favourable to them, but the sequencing and focus of the Ohrid talks put an end to this aspiration. The prize would be 4,000 or so soldiers for 30 days. The only thing to be haggled over was whether a few of them would arrive early, before the cease-fire was firmly established, as a '...downpayment...,' as one diplomat put it, on NATO's commitment.[34]

The second corollary of the talks, however, was that at some point, someone would have to talk to the armed Albanians about the part laid out for them in the disarmament proposals which would be activated by a constitutional agreement. As the crisis precipitated by Frowick's Prizren agreement had demonstrated back in May, this was an intensely neuralgic issue for the Slav Macedonians. It was so for it gave substance to the complaint that their opponents were allowed to shoot, bomb and mine their way to political advantage while they, the legitimate government of a sovereign state, could not. This second corollary and its implications, however, had been present from the moment that the Skopje diplomatic corps had framed the conflict as one which the government could not win by force. Neither the senior international figures visiting from abroad nor the two special envoys ever seriously questioned this framing, resulting in what one military source referred to as '...the black limousine phenomenon...,' the process by which gunmen emerge from the hills and putatively fight their way up to respectability in the form of an invitation to the White House.[35] The external understanding of this framing and the diplomatic corps' part in it was that it was unfortunate, perhaps, but understandable and unremarkable. At times of political change, diplomats are nearly always faced with the double challenge of deciding whether advantage is to be gained by granting or withholding recognition to the purveyors of violence and, if granting, then how much and to whom. The internal implications, however, were another matter, especially for the diplomatic corps' role as representing and, indeed, constituting an expression of the international society of states within Macedonia itself. The process by which the armed Albanians were brought into the negotiations, albeit indirectly, exposed both the Macedonians' need for a relationship with the diplomatic corps and its troubling consequences for their respective senses of themselves.

The Skopje diplomatic corps and the domestic response to Macedonia's crisis

The most obvious consequence of this framing was the Slav-Macedonians' sense of grievance. Macedonia, they generally conceded, was not without its problems in terms of inter-ethnic relations, but it had been making a degree of progress which was, by the standards of the region, considerable. At the time of Yugoslavia's collapse in 1991–92, minority policies had been established as one of the criteria for international recognition, and only Macedonia and Slovenia of the six constituent republics had been judged to meet this criterion. By forcing the Macedonian government to negotiate, if not with the NLA, then under NLA pressure and about the NLA's terms, therefore, it was widely felt that the international community had given the sign that '... fighting pays.'[36] This sense of injustice shaded easily into suspicions that the international community (or parts of it – Germany and the United States especially) was biased towards the Albanians, and that Albanian demands for reform were but the first step in a program which sought the partition of Macedonia. As a result, at moments when the 'tilt' towards the Albanians appeared manifest, for example, during the Aracinovo episode or when meetings between diplomats and the NLA in the midst of further fighting around Tetovo were revealed, the diplomatic corps became the focus of the resulting political anger. Demonstrations, protests and, eventually physical attacks were mounted against the offices, vehicles, and personnel of Western embassies and the international organizations in Skopje.[37] Fighting might pay, but the problem for the more nationalist elements in the Macedonian government was they could not make it pay for them. The embassy protests, therefore, may have been an orchestrated attempt to use force against more vulnerable targets, either to signal the limits of Slav Macedonian patience or as pure intimidation. For the demonstrators themselves, however, they were an opportunity to act against what they believed to be the source of their frustration.

Violence against embassies, and the inability or unwillingness of host governments to secure the immunities and privileges of missions it implies, may presage a complete break in relations. This was not the case with the attacks on the Skopje embassies. The violent protests remained an aspect of a relationship in which the government, party leaders and the attentive Macedonian public alike all regarded the diplomatic corps as a combination of witness to their complaints, judge over their disputes and referee in their arguments with one another. The diplomatic corps responded accordingly. Its presence or absence from a public occasion, for example, would be taken as a moral judgement of the occasion's rightness and a political judgement of its success. At the end of 2001, with the Framework Agreement barely in place and the economy in great difficulties, the prime minister's wife hosted a New Year's ball which was televised nationally. '...Although invited....' a journalist noted, '...the absent diplomatic corps sounded its unequivocal message to the said elitist gathering of Macedonian upstarts...'[38] On another occasion, in contrast, a conference was organized by the 'Kiro Gligorov' foundation on the theme of

'Regional Crisis in Macedonia.'[39] President Trajkovski, many foreign experts and members of the diplomatic corps all attended, but it was noted that political leaders had declined their invitations to what was billed as an attempt to initiate '...political dialogue.'[40]

These expectations extended to the conduct of Macedonian politics. At the beginning of the year, a major scandal occurred when taps placed by the interior ministry and the intelligence services on the telephones of political opponents, diplomats and embassies were discovered. In this case, there was considerable disappointment that '...the diplomatic corps in Skopje, although otherwise it has opinions on everything, even in strictly internal affairs and developments, this time unanimously decided to keep quiet...' Individual diplomats, speaking off the record, stressed how the allegations, if proved true, would damage Macedonia's attempt to improve its standing with NATO and the EU but they stressed that this was a personal view '...rather than the official view of [the] embassy or, God forbid, agreed position of the western embassies in Macedonia...' The top priority was to demonstrate that all was well (this was a month before the crisis broke) and, thus '...the diplomatic corps in Macedonia failed to issue a single word of condemnation...'[41]

The diplomatic corps may have been regarded as a referee in Skopje but, as both the episode above and the violent protests at the embassies attest, it is the image of a referee at a football match, rather than as a respected international arbiter, which is more applicable. As at a football match, both 'players' and 'crowd' recognized the need for referees in general but did not like and doubted the fairness and competence of the one they actually got. Much of this was based on sheer frustration at the political consequences of the diplomatic corps' acceptance that the Albanians had legitimate grievances; that they were telling the truth when they said they wanted these addressed within a Macedonian framework; and that addressing them would have to precede the disarming of the NLA.

Among the media and the attentive public, however, there also existed a sense that the diplomats did not understand the situation and kept on getting things wrong. Before the crisis broke, this was sometimes explained as a function of diplomats in general, and the kind of diplomats who got appointed to places like the Balkans in particular. Prompted by the complaint by a former finance minister that members of the diplomatic corps had required bribes to secure investment and assistance, for example, Sam Vakin, the general manager of a consultancy firm, was moved to write an extended attack on what he called '...the Pettifogger Procurators.' He describes the local diplomats as '...paragons of indignant righteousness and hectoring morality...' who have taken on the '...imperial patina of Roman procurators...' because they have been '...emotionally injured...' as a result of being '...cast into the frigorific outer darkness of a ravaged continent...' They are career failures whose wives, '...bored to distraction in the impossibly catatonic societies of post-Communism...' impose their '...distaff voluntary urges and exiguous artistic talents...upon a reluctant and flummoxed population...' With the Cold War over, Vakin maintains these diplomats were only interested in advancing narrow commercial interests and their own reputations, although they employed the old methods of the Cold War, intelligence services posing as 'intrusive NGO's' engaging in '...shady acts and unscrupulous practices...' At the same time, however, he argues that the corrupting influences of the Balkans destroy whatever professionalism and virtue these diplomats have managed to retain. They all work under terrible pressure. Some try their best, but all succumb to mediocrity as a result of which '...they are nobody's favourites and everybody's scapegoats at one time or another...'[42]

I have quoted Vakin's article at length, not because it makes the generic and familiar case against diplomats entertainingly, but because it captures the tension involved in acknowledging that who they, the diplomats, are results in part from who we, the people of the Balkans, are. As the crisis developed, so too did the critique of diplomats. Complaints about the profession in general and its Western exponents in particular, gave way to analyses of how the external priorities of the diplomats were at odds with what was needed on the ground. That this was so was partly a matter of different interests, it was acknowledged. Increasingly, however, it was argued that 'they', the diplomats, could not provide the right sort of help because 'they' did not understand 'us' and, hence, misread the dynamics of local politics. This argument was expressed in a number of ways. Madzirov, for example, in his comments on the Framework Agreement, noted the difficulties societal change faces when it is '...initiated from outside...' Not the least of these, he argued, was the outsiders' assumption that Macedonia's minority problem consisted of a deficiency of legal and constitutional rights to be addressed by reforms. The real problem, in Madzirov's view, was the failure to implement existing laws and respect existing rights. Imposing a new set of laws and rights, therefore, would only widen the gap between the two communities in real life and make their relations worse.[43]

A second theme, familiar to students of Balkan politics, was that the diplomatic corps had accepted the framing of the Balkans' problems in terms of primordial ethnic hatreds or, at least, had not done enough to counter the weight of this conception in the calculations of its political masters. Whether or not it was true that the region was riven by ancient ethnic hatreds and violent nationalisms was not the issue, in this view. It was the consequences of allowing this assumption to shape attitudes and guide policy towards the region that was important. The principal practical consequence was that the diplomats would continue to talk to people who were '...at best, linked to the residual communist structures of power in the country...' with the resulting '...unintended empowering of political opportunists and irresponsible extremists...' Setting up negotiations between those who claimed to speak for the various ethnic groups simply reproduced ethnic divisions and rewarded those who benefited from them. The West, according to Isa Blumi, '...is so consumed by the myth of ethnic tensions...that it was impossible for their diplomatic corps to understand that patronizing party bosses does not work....'[44]

The mistakes that resulted from failing to understand the complex dynamics of local politics could be fundamental, according to the proponents of this argument. It was claimed, for example, that the initial fighting around Tanushevci, far from being the first phase of an NLA plan to advance pan-Albanian interests by military means, had resulted from an attempted rescue by the police of a reporter who, acting on a tip from the principal opposition party, had got himself kidnapped by local smugglers. There were also claims that the early phases of the fighting around Tetovo were highly scripted by both sides so that relatively harmless bombardments by the government would precede previously agreed withdrawals from positions in villages by the NLA. Without realizing that it was dealing with people who had a political and criminal stake in preserving the *status quo* of ethnic tensions, in this view, the Skopje diplomatic corps would not be able to serve even its political masters' short-term preoccupation with keeping Macedonia as calm as possible, as cheaply as possible, let alone advance a lasting solution. As with Vakin, however, these more pointed critiques of the Skopje diplomatic corps, and the myriad of 'internationals' which swirled around it, did not challenge the legitimacy or the potential usefulness of the internal role it was attempting to play. Rather, they asked that, instead of worrying so much about their own countries' interests and their own organizations' peace-building theories, '...Diplomats should...develop a greater appreciation for the internal, domestic dynamics of intercommunal conflict...'[45] Only then might they avoid such obvious mistakes as when, at the reception following the September election '...some members of the diplomatic corps commented that the best proof of Macedonia's...recovery was the presence of former UCK commanders (and now parliamentarians) at the reception...'[46]

Conclusion

These critiques of the operations of the Skopje diplomatic corps raise interesting questions about the nature of Macedonia's difficulties and throw into sharp relief the tension between internal and external assumptions about what needed to be done. It may well be, for example, that the diplomats would have made a better contribution to initiating lasting political change in the country if they had paid more attention to local conditions. How and why they might have done so, however, is not clear. The diplomats had interests and priorities of their own (as did those who criticized them). These entailed that they were looking for a solution that satisfied the interests of those they represented both individually and collectively, rather than some conception of the best solution for the people who lived in Macedonia. To achieve that end, they could not afford to ignore local people with official and actual power simply because they were, to various degrees, wicked, even if this entailed reproducing elements of the problem in the short term. However, the merits or otherwise of the case against the way the diplomatic corps operated are not the principal concern here. What is more important for our purposes is the way in which the Skopje diplomatic corps emerged as the focal point of both internal and external attention and maintained it throughout much of the 2001 crisis.

Within the country, mobs focused on the embassies – the corps' substantive expression. Politicians focused on what the diplomats were doing – its performative expression. And everyone, although commentators especially, constructed an implied diplomatic corps by their complaints about its inaction and their arguments about what it ought to be doing – its ideational expression. It might be objected that this is to belabour the obvious and without significantly increasing our understanding of what was going on. After all, on what alternative expression of the outside world might the Macedonians have focused and with what different consequences? In fact, posing the questions this way reveals that there were a number of other ways of identifying the outside world that were not customarily utilized. There were, for example, few open appeals to other countries on a bilateral basis, even though we know there was a great deal going on in these terms. Helicopter gunships and other aircraft were procured from Ukraine, tanks were obtained from Bulgaria, and requests went to the United States for troops (if only from KFOR). By and large, however, only hostility was openly bilaterally expressed (chiefly at the United States and Germany), and this on rare occasions. The Macedonian government, or elements in it, may well have sought the assistance of particular countries in terms of political or military alignments, but such efforts remained discreet. As the collapse of Yugoslavia had demonstrated, the game of Balkan politics was no longer to be played by acquiring overt great power patrons. Such support would be delivered only in the name of securing cosmopolitan values to which the international community as a whole was said to subscribe.

Despite the presence of both governmental and civil society manifestations of this new international community all over Skopje and, indeed, the country, however, it did not become the focus of appeals either. This might be regarded as surprising for a number of reasons, not least that the international community, as it presented itself to Macedonians, appeared to want to be worked with in this way on the issues which most concerned them – economic, political and military assistance. The World Bank, the International Monetary Fund, NATO and the UN in Kosovo, the OSCE and the EU, among others, all had their offices and representatives in Skopje. While they and their non-governmental counterparts were certainly worked with, however, they were rarely referred to collectively except by the term '...the internationals', with its connotation of dinner guests who had brought poor wine and then outstayed their welcome. A possible explanation of the neglect of broader conceptions of the international community in Skopje in favour of the diplomatic corps might be that the Macedonians realized where real power continued to lie. If you wanted soldiers or money, for example, it was with national governments and not their multilateral collaborative expressions that the final decision lay. The problem with this explanation, however, is that it was not always the case. The 4,000 strong NATO force that finally came to Macedonia to collect Albanian arms, for example, emerged from deliberations in Brussels and was sufficiently international that the contribution of no single state to it was clearly decisive. Besides, a sense that real power lay with national governments would lead one back to bilateralism, not to working with the diplomatic corps as the collective expression of those states on the ground.

A more plausible explanation might focus on state and civil society capacity in Macedonia. A recurrent theme during 2001 and since was that, as a new, small, poor and inexperienced country Macedonia was swamped by the level of international involvement in its affairs. Its people physically could not cope with all the agencies on their doorstep, cognitively did not know the appropriate agency to turn to when they required help or wanted to make a point, and emotionally were ill-prepared to come to terms with the agents of an international society to which their hard-purchased sovereign statehood seemed to mean so little. If this were so, then the Macedonians' focus on the diplomatic corps might be interpreted as an attempt to simplify or simply evade the new complex reality with which they were confronted. No doubt there were some difficulties of this order and, no doubt some state officials and party figures encountered the international world with assumptions about it that might best be termed archaic. However, and as many Macedonians quickly demonstrated, it is perfectly possible to become highly effective within complex networks without understanding any overarching organizing principle or purpose which they may have (not least because they may have neither). More importantly, state capacity explanations – material, cognitive or otherwise, do not account for the external focus on the diplomatic corps. Unless we concede, and this again is plausible, that everyone – not just the small, poor and peripheral – is struggling with the organizational complexity of transnational relations, then it is hard to explain why for outsiders too, the point of focus in relations with the Macedonians remained the Skopje diplomatic corps.

Two better arguments may be advanced to explain this centrality, the first constitutive and the second, following on from it, causal. In constitutive terms, it is worth recalling that the key issue presented by Macedonia for nearly everyone did not revolve around how to solve a particular problem or advance a particular policy, given the distribution of capacities and interests in and around Macedonia in 2001. If such instrumental considerations had prevailed, after all, it is by no means clear why Macedonia had been established as a sovereign state in the first place. It was too small, too poor, and too divided between a majority whose identity was sufficiently recent for its synthetic quality still to be apparent and a principal minority which looked to its kindred in adjacent territories, to please enough people in these terms. This, nevertheless, was how Macedonian had been established because it was hard to imagine, and remains hard to imagine, alternative arrangements which would result in fewer problems. No other country or entity wanted to take responsibility for the welfare of all the Macedonians, and even if they had, this would not have satisfied all the people of the country. Thus, while Macedonia might be a social construct, it was the only one its people had to work in, and it provided the setting in which multiple policies and multiple conceptions of what the problem was were advanced. Everyone, however, or nearly everyone, agreed that all these concerns played out against the same background, namely, the terms on which Macedonia's place within the international society of states should be re-stabilized.

This was a matter for states-talk, and the diplomatic corps provided an obvious setting for such talk. For the Macedonians, it provided an accessible site – between the foreign embassies in their own capital – and a reassuring medium – working with the diplomats of countries that recognized them as a country – in which such talk could take place. Even though the matters under discussion were usually internal and the way they were discussed deeply intrusive, to have such talks cantered on the diplomatic corps – rather than multilateral or non-government agencies or even under the auspices of a particular state – re-enforced Macedonia's standing in difficult circumstances as a state among states. This was also a consideration for those who negotiated with its people, for they regarded Macedonia's survival as a state as the premise of all they were attempting. Macedonia's failure would not only be a problem in itself but would undermine the state (and state-like) solutions established to settle the problems and advance the aspirations of other peoples in its neighbourhood.

To be sure, causal factors, the second string of the argument, also played their part. It is likely, for example, that the Skopje diplomatic corps was allowed its leading role because Macedonia was initially regarded as peripheral to the concerns of the great powers and successful, both as a multi-ethnic state and as a compliant recipient of international and transnational 'help' to the region. Once it became clear that this was not so, Macedonia quickly attracted attention at the highest level in terms of shuttle diplomacy by the great and good of NATO and the EU. The mixed results of such visits, however, left the initiative with members of the diplomatic corps. The special envoys represented a compromise between local and remote mediation, but the diplomatic corps continued to be involved and its original framing of the crisis was retained. It also became clearer during the crisis that, while most of the local parties to the dispute engaged in brinkmanship – threatening an end to negotiations and an escalation to civil war – their bluffs were repeatedly called when a breakdown looked likely.

They wanted a magic international circle in which negotiations could be conducted and guided and into which they could be talked back when they had talked themselves out of it. Governments, organizations, parties, insurgents, senior international figures and even diplomats all had interests and their respective understandings of the game in which they were advancing them during the events of 2001. The Skopje diplomatic corps, however, provided everyone with an accessible expression of the international society of states as a sort of meta-space within which their games could be played out.[47] The way that it did, and the eventual outcome provide *prima facie* evidence, at least, for the role of the diplomatic corps in giving expression to a bedrock aspect of the way in which people continue to think about international relations. And if this is so, then the Skopje experience may also suggest that the diplomatic corps ought to be used more often when other members of the international society of states struggle to maintain their part in the existing scheme of things.

Notes

1 For a useful history and list of functions see G. R. Berridge, 'Notes on the origins of the diplomatic corps: Constantinople in the 1620s' (unpublished paper) and Garrett Mattingly, *Renaissance Diplomacy* (Harmondsworth: Penguin, 1965). For a useful definition of the diplomatic corps see G. R. Berridge and Alan James, *A Dictionary of Diplomacy* (Houndmills: Palgrave, 2001) p. 65.

2 G. R. Berridge and Nadia Gallo, 'The Role of the Diplomatic Corps: the US-North Korea Talks in Beijing, 1988–94 in Jan Melissen (ed.), *Innovation in Diplomatic Practice* (Houndmills: Macmillan, 1999) pp. 214–30.

3 The use of 'enjoyed' might be contested by some.

4 'Macedonia', Country Profiles, Countries and Regions, *Foreign and Commonwealth Office (FCO)* web site. In this chapter, the majority will be termed Slav-Macedonians and the Albanian minority will be termed Albanians. There is no nomenclature which avoids political significance for one or both the main parties to the dispute. For example, calling the majority 'ethnic Macedonians' and the minority 'ethnic Albanians' both pose problems in the context of a country called Macedonia.

5 For commentary on this see Biljana Vankovska, 'Current Perspectives on Macedonia Part 1: the path from "Oasis of Peace" to "Powder Keg" of the Balkans', Heinrich Böll Foundation, undated.

6 Hence, the use of the inelegant Former Yugoslav Republic of Macedonia (FYROM) in all dealings with Greece or at meetings where the Greeks were present. While many other counties have now accepted its name as the Republic of Macedonia, difficulties with Greece persist and at the time of writing, Macedonia appears under T in the alphabetical listing of UN members (as in 'The Former Yugoslav Republic...'), http://www.un.org/Overview/unmember.html.

7 Thus slightly larger than Wales but with nearly a third less people.
8 The full list of resident missions is as follows: Albania; Austria; Bosnia Herzegovina; Bulgaria; China; Croatia; France; Germany; Greece; Hungary; Iran; Italy; Netherlands; Norway; Poland; Romania; Russia; Serbia and Montenegro; Slovenia; Ukraine; Switzerland; United Kingdom; United States. Thirty-three other ambassadors (not counting the Sovereign Military Order of Malta) based elsewhere are also accredited to Skopje.
9 The list includes: the Delegation of the European Commission; the Office of the United Nations Resident Coordinator; the United Nations Interim Administration Mission in Kosovo (UNMIK) Liaison Office; the United Nations Development Program (UNDP); the United Nations High Commissioner for Refugees (UNHCR); the United Nations Children's Fund (UNICEF); the International Organization for Migration; the United Nations International Criminal Tribunal for the Former Yugoslavia – Office of the Prosecutor; the NATO Civilian Liaison Office; the OSCE Spillover Monitoring Mission; the Office of the Special Representative of the European Union (EU); the European Union monitoring Mission; the International Centre for Migration Policy Development; the International Monetary Fund; the World Bank; the European Bank for Reconstruction and Development; the European Agency for Reconstruction; the International Management Group; the International Committee of the Red Cross; and the World Health Organization. During the September elections, Biljana Vankovska cites an estimate of 450 international and local NGOs involved in electoral training and support, 'Current Perspectives on Macedonia #2 Democracy and/or Peace? Macedonia's Dilemma', Heinrich Böll Foundation (undated).
10 Leks Drug press release, May, 2000, http://www.lek.si/eng/media-room/press-releases/2590/
11 'Vankovska', p. 3.
12 'Vankovska'.
13 The Albanian acronym for the NLA, UÇÇK was the same as that for the Kosovo Liberation Army, Eleanor Pritchard, *Central European Review (CER)*, 3, 4, January 29, 2001. For discussion of NLA objectives see *Times*, August 20, 2001.
14 The Framework Agreement reached at Ohrid in August promised constitutional changes in the basic standing of minorities by redefining nationals by citizenship rather than ethnicity. It gave minority languages official standing when certain local conditions were fulfilled, and it committed the government to increasing minority employment in state sectors, especially the police. The agreement was coupled to measures for an amnesty, a cease-fire, and a disarmament process supervised by NATO troops.
15 The Macedonians used the term 'terrorist' freely, but members of the international community avoided the term to begin with to avoid legal implications, former Skopje diplomatic source.
16 Pritchard, *CER*, 3, 10, March 2001.
17 Condemnation of the Albanians and support for the government's position of not negotiating with terrorists was secured from Lord Robertson, NATO's Secretary General, Javier Solana – the EU's foreign and security representative, James Pardew – the US special envoy to the Balkans at that time, and the US ambassador to Albania, among others.

18   *New York Times*, March 19, 2001.
19   Ljbuco Georgievski, the Prime Minister, and Ljube Boskovski, the Interior Minister, were both Macedonian Slavs with strong nationalist reputations. Arbëën Xhaferi and Imer Imeri were the leaders of the two principal Albanian parties. Everyone agreed that the NLA and its political allies should not be involved in negotiations about anything but their own disarmament.
20   It is estimated that by mid-May, Solana had made seven trips to Skopje and Robertson four in a six-week period, *New York Times*, 21 May, 2001. Patton represented the EU Commission and Lindh the Swedish presidency of the EU and, thus, EU foreign ministers.
21   In addition to Jenkins (August 22, 2001) see also Jenkins, *Times*, March 21 where he speaks of Solana and company '...lurching from photo op. to photo op....' and Misha Glenny, *Times*, June 27, 2001, speaking of Solana's '...dropping in and out like a yo yo...' and the doubts of other diplomats regarding '...the parachute approach...'
22   For example, Solana was present during the final negotiations for the Government of National Unity and he played an important part in ending the deadlock resulting from the Frowick revelations. Local diplomats acknowledged that these visitors could accomplish more than they when things were really stalled, former Skopje diplomatic source.
23   *New York Times*, May 26, 2001.
24   *New York Times*, March 26, 2001.
25   *New York Times*, June 20, 2001.
26   *New York Times*, June 23 and *Times*, June 25, 2001.
27   Macedonian sources maintained that the armed Albanians in Aracinovo, under pressure from Macedonian forces, had requested a ceasefire through '...foreign envoys.' Whether these were diplomats is not clear, *New York Times*, January 25, 2001.
28   Eleanor Pritchard, *CER*, 3, 23, 25, June, 2001.
29   A two-thirds majority of the legislature would have been required for this, and so legislators, as well as the authors of the proposed measures, were the targets of this diplomatic pressure, *Times*, June 7, 2001.
30   Eleanor Pritchard, *CER*, 3, 18, May 21, 2001, *Times*, June 22, July 21, and August 9, 2001. The task of talking people back into the process persisted into the implementation period. Léotard and US ambassador, Mike Hoenick, were reported as meeting with the Party for Democratic Prosperity (PDP) legislators after their abstentions in parliament left President Trajkovski in a vulnerable position, Zelijo Bajic, 'A Week of Resounding Silence', *Aim Skopje* October 21 (15) 2001.
31   *New York Times*, May 21, 2001 and Michel Chossudovsky, 'Proxy War in Macedonia: US uses private military connections to play both sides in growing conflict', in *Toward Freedom: online magazine* June/July 2001. Also, 'Pritchard' *CER*, 3, 19, May 28, 2001, notes the role of diplomats in resolving the resulting crisis between Albanian and Macedonian political leaders from the new governing coalition. Solana eventually returned to get the Albanian leaders, Xhaferi and Imeri, to repudiate the Prizren accord, 'Pritchard', *CER*, 3, 20, June 4, 2001.
32   *New York Times*, July 5, 2001.

33 *New York Times*, June 16, 2001.
34 *New York Times*, August 16, 2001. A follow-up force was eventually agreed to escort OSCE observers after the 30-day mission was over but, again, its size made it clear that it would be in no position to enforce the agreement, the peace, or the aspirations of any of the protagonists.
35 *Times*, August 18, 2001.
36 Pavle Madzirov, 'Conclusions from Macedonian Conflict of 2001 and Future Prospects' http://www.realitymacedonia.org.mk/web/news_page.asp?nid=2392
37 The US, British and German embassies, together with the OSCE offices were targets of violent protests (although so was a McDonald's hamburger restaurant), *Times* and *New York Times*, July 24–6.
38 Branka Nanevska, 'Ball Extravaganza, Soup Kitches and Garbage Containers', *AIM*, January 25, 2002.
39 Gligorov was the first president of the independent Macedonia and widely credited for his contribution to its peaceful session and initial development.
40 Balkan Human Rights List from Greek Helsinki Monitor, April 24, 2001.
41 NM, 'Tacit Support for Big Brother', Skopje January 26, 2001. There was a domestic complication to this episode in that all wiretapping was against the law in Macedonia (unlike most countries), and that the authority for the wiretapping came from faction controlling the relevant part of the Ministry of the Interior. Diplomats would not have been particularly surprised at wiretapping *per se* according to one diplomatic source there at the time.
42 Sam Vakin, 'The Pettifogger Procurators', *CER*, 3, 1, January 2001.
43 'Madzirov'.
44 Isa Blumi, 'Making Drizzle in a Rain Storm: lessons to be learned from the conflict in Macedonia', *East European Studies*, summary of talk at Woodrow Wilson Centre, November 14, 2001.
45 'Blumi' and Biljana Vankovska, 'Current Perspectives on Macedonia: No. 1 the path from "Oasis of Peace" to "Poweder Keg" of the Balkans', Heinrich Böll Foundation (undated).
46 This refers to election of Ali Ahmeti, who came to the fore as the leader of the NLA (UCK/UÇÇK are the initials in Abanian) and then parlayed his success into leadership of the largest Albanian party in the Macedonian parliament. He was, in this view, the most spectacular beneficiary of the gangster politics rather than a nationalist hero persuaded of the merits of the constitutional route. Biljana Vankovska, 'Current Perspectives on Macedonia: No. 3 International Mediation of the Macedonian Conflict: capabilities and limitations', Heinrich Böll Foundation (undated).
47 Accessibility in Skopje's case was facilitated by the intimacy of a small city in which members of the political class and the diplomatic corps might run into each other in places like the local supermarket. One former diplomatic source suggested that this accessibility might have led locals to over-estimate the importance of the views of the diplomats among them in shaping political events.

Part V

The Future of the Diplomatic Corps

11
A European Epistemic Community of Diplomats

Mai'a Keapuolani Davis Cross

With the 2004 and 2007 enlargements of the European Union (EU), as well as divisive debates over the transatlantic alliance, ratification of the EU Constitution, and Turkish accession, an important question today is whether continued European political integration can occur or whether a critical insurmountable gridlock has been reached. To shed light on future EU prospects, this chapter examines the role of diplomats in Europe in fostering cooperation or non-cooperation among member-states of the EU.

The focus here is on a particular group of diplomats, the Committee of Permanent Representatives, known as Coreper, as they are at the centre of the process of political integration in the EU. The members of the combined foreign services of the 27 member-states (including Romania and Bulgaria) are diverse, and can be thought of as comprising four distinct categories. First, diplomats in Europe serve in traditional, bilateral embassies between member-states, which are decreasing in importance. Second, diplomats represent individual member-states to third-countries and international organizations. This domain is shared with the third category, the European Commission's common representation to third parties under the community method, especially in the area of economic policy where the EU speaks with one voice. Indeed, if the Constitution Draft Treaty had been passed, this area would have undergone significant re-structuring with the creation of a common EU diplomatic service and the post of Foreign Minister. Finally, the most distinctive and influential fragment of this wide-ranging, multi-level system of representation, is the fourth category, Coreper, which provides multilateral representation of the member-states to each other in Brussels.

Critically, it is the fourth category, not the first, which really represents the latest step in the evolution of the practice of diplomacy in

Europe. Traditionally, a 'diplomatic corps' is defined as 'the body of diplomats of all states, including attachés, who are resident at one post'.[1] Coreper can be thought of as a fragment of a traditional diplomatic corps because its members reside together in Brussels, hold the rank of ambassador, follow traditional norms of protocol and procedure, and deal with policy areas that have concerned professional diplomats for centuries. But in an integrated, institutionalized Europe, this elite group is confined to only diplomatic representatives of EU member-states, it is assigned institutional space in the Council of the EU directly under the Council of Ministers, and its policy role extends well beyond the traditional domain. Its duties include: (1) dealing with day-to-day technical issues critical to the internal operation of the EU (2) managing its jurisdiction over the Common Foreign and Security Policy, and (3) preparing in advance all decisions pertaining to treaty revision. Naturally, there are many other individuals in Brussels who are part of a wider, more inclusive diplomatic corps and not part of Coreper, i.e., representatives of bilateral embassies to Belgium and third-country embassies to the EU.

This wider diplomatic corps, including Coreper, is transnational because its members represent multiple states with varied interests, and whose interaction results in a loosening of borders. To an extent, diplomacy as a professional activity has always contributed to the process of growing transnationalism. Coreper, however, is more complex than this as it holds a structural position in the EU bureaucratic apparatus, and a very high status relative to other individuals in the diplomatic corps. As a high-level committee in the Council, Coreper was intended to provide intergovernmental representation, but in practice Coreper has developed many supranational elements by virtue of its transnational diplomatic underpinnings. To clarify, while intergovernmental approaches to EU policy preserve member-state control over issue areas, and require member-state approval, supranational approaches involve decisionmaking above the level of the states. As will be shown, the work of Coreper often does not involve member-state approval and essentially symbolizes, and in large part enables, the idea of 'Europe' to exist. Thus, I refer to Coreper as the European diplomatic corps, even though it is understood that they are only one fragment of a vast, multi-layered system.

In this chapter, I argue that the strength and shared expertise of the European diplomatic corps is so significant that these influential actors constitute an epistemic community of experts who often exercise their own agency separate from member-state preferences. An epistemic community, according to the definition offered by Peter Haas, is 'a network of professionals with recognized expertise and competence in a particular domain and an authoritative claim to policy-relevant knowledge within that domain or issue area.'[2]

Epistemic communities are fundamental to the concept of international society employed by many of the chapters in this book. Many actors comprising international society can be viewed as epistemic communities, and like other actors, epistemic communities play a moderating role in what might otherwise be a system governed by *realpolitik*. Hedley Bull and Adam Watson, proponents of the English school, argue that international society exists when 'states... have established by dialogue and consent common rules and institutions for the conduct of their relations, and recognize their common interest in maintaining these arrangements.'[3] In Bull's earlier work, *The Anarchical Society*, he argues that diplomats are representative and symbolic of the existence of international society. Without diplomatic corps, it would be difficult for states to communicate, and to demonstrate to each other that they are 'bound by a common set of rules...and share in the working of common institutions'.[4] Alan James, however, argues that some kind of diplomatic machinery is necessary even for an international system to function because without a means of peaceful communication the only form of interaction would be war.[5] The English school definition of international system does assume regular contact among states which establishes order even if they do not feel bound by common rules and mutual understandings. If diplomacy is not necessarily exclusive to international society, where then does the role of diplomatic corps fall in the distinction between system and society? As James suggests, perhaps it is a matter of degree of institutionalization of the diplomatic profession. This, in turn, is best understood if the distinction between international system and society is conceived of as a continuum instead of separate building blocks. Indeed, Barry Buzan argues that the institution of diplomacy can set the rules of co-existence, but it can also lead to thicker, solidarism in the form of greater institutionalization of rules, as we observe in the EU.[6] It is clear that purposeful relationship-building among diplomats advances the 'dialogue and consent' among political communities, leading to a stronger international society. Thus, I argue that the level of cohesion of diplomats' epistemic community determines their contribution to international society.

The concept of epistemic community has traditionally been reserved for scientific or technical groups,[7] and has thus far not been applied to diplomats. However, there are numerous reasons why expanding the concept to incorporate diplomats is appropriate.[8] Diplomats are typically considered generalists rather than experts, and extensions of governments rather than actors in their own right. In reality, diplomats may begin as generalists, and do represent governments, but they certainly become experts relatively quickly (e.g., trade, arms control, the EU budget) and, as such, contribute independently to the outcome of diplomatic efforts. They are in a unique position to understand the complexities of international relations, both in minor and grand-scale matters, and they are ongoing experts at negotiation procedure, relationship-building among nations, and the art of compromise. The key purpose of epistemic communities, as transnational groups of experts, is to resolve conditions of uncertainty, situations that political leaders may not be able to address because of lack of information. Diplomats are a part of this category in the realm of international cooperation, and help define state interests by virtue of their expertise. Most importantly, epistemic communities may actually be a part of the policy process, rather than just tangential to it. This does not mean that they are synonymous with governments, but rather, they are actors in their own right.

Besides the classification of diplomats as an epistemic community, I also advocate a refinement of the concept itself which assumes that conditions of uncertainty are obvious, and that epistemic communities either exist or do not exist. First, through a historical survey of diplomats in Europe, it becomes evident that it is not always clear when conditions of uncertainty exist or whether they will be recognized as such. For example, in a case of international negotiation, a political leader may feel certain about the climate among other nations, but it might require the expertise of a diplomat to really gauge what other countries are willing to accept or not at that point in time. This involves more than a bilateral understanding, but an ability to put all the pieces of a multinational negotiation together. These preferences may not be reflected in a simple model of self-interest.

Second, an epistemic community does not simply exist or not exist by virtue of a particular kind and level of knowledge, but is characterized as strong or weak. This is correlated with its capacity to have an effect. A strong epistemic community is characterized as one that is cohesive and influential, i.e., its members have strong professional norms, high status, and homogeneity. A weak epistemic community is one that has overall low status, weak norms, and heterogeneity among its members. Besides shared norms, the issue of cohesiveness is largely determined by the social background, selection, and training of an epistemic community's members. The strength of an epistemic community may also change over time depending on how often the members hold meetings, and interact to reinforce their cohesiveness. In addition, the membership of an epistemic community can be contained with few involved, or wide-ranging with thousands of people contributing to outcomes.

In this chapter, I begin with an overview of the literature that is relevant to diplomatic negotiations focusing on the major alternative argument, bargaining theory.[9] I then discuss the role of the epistemic community of diplomats in the EU setting. Although there are many diplomats in Europe, Coreper is unique in that it is an elite fragment of the traditional diplomatic corps, but is also allotted bureaucratic space, giving it direct internal access to decisionmaking processes. Over time, Coreper has become an agent in its own right, bringing supranationalism into a largely intergovernmental institution. I argue that there are many cases in which Coreper has contributed to international society in Europe beyond what bargaining theory or rationalist approaches would predict. This has important bearing for the role of diplomats today, and for the future potential of EU integration, particularly in the political and security realms.

Transmission belts or agents of cooperation?

Bargaining theory is arguably the most directly opposed to the notion that epistemic communities have a real impact on outcomes of international cooperation in the EU setting. A key premise of bargaining theory to which I refer is that state leaders act autonomously according to national preferences, which they rank at the beginning of negotiations. Andrew Moravcsik leads the wave of scholarship that seeks to advance qualitative bargaining theories to explain European integration. The theory most associated with Moravcsik is liberal intergovernmentalism, which argues that national civil servants and supranational actors have a negligible role in EU decisionmaking. Although liberal intergovernmentalism is a theory that incorporates domestic level interests, Moravcsik's intergovernmental bargaining approach explicitly ignores factors other than state leaders' preferences and autonomy.[10]

In an article in the *Journal of Common Market Studies*, Moravcsik and Nicolaïdis look specifically at the 1997 Amsterdam Treaty negotiation processes.[11] According to their analysis, national governments were constrained by their relative interdependence, understood their preferences during negotiations, and ranked them accordingly. Although diplomats and supranational actors were involved in the negotiations, Moravcsik and Nicolaïdis argue that these actors did not alter outcomes beyond the rational weighing of national preferences. Thus, they conclude that bargaining theory can predict outcomes by knowing the pre-existing fixed preferences of national governments.

The major weaknesses of this approach are that (1) it does not distinguish between autonomy and agency, thereby ignoring an important subtlety that characterizes the role of diplomats (2) it does not recognize the importance of continued interaction among diplomats over time, and (3) it fails to appreciate the empirical evidence that state preferences are variable over time. First, it is important to distinguish between autonomy and agency. I define autonomy in terms of the room diplomats have to act within the structure that constrains them. Structure can come in many forms, but it finds its expression in the instructions received by diplomats and the rules established within bureaucracies. In other words, autonomy is dictated by the explicit rules of the game specifying the context under which diplomats should operate. Autonomy is the permitted space for action. I define agency, by contrast, as what diplomats do with their autonomy. In more extreme cases, a strong epistemic community of diplomats may exercise agency beyond the explicit boundaries of their autonomy, i.e., by defying their instructions or pushing the flexibility of bureaucratic rules.

Second, I argue that increased interaction among diplomats over time, as both transnational actors and as national representatives, creates a shared culture and common language which enables them to reach consensus with relative ease. Diplomats not only engage in negotiation during the lead-up to major intergovernmental conferences, but also as a part of their daily activities in Coreper. They are highly trained at reaching consensus and have familiarity with their counterparts from other countries. In effect, they comprise an important and influential epistemic community with shared professional norms and a common background. Bargaining theory does not account for these relationships.

Third, I argue that it is wrong to assume *a priori* that state interests are fixed over time. Empirically, state leaders do not spend much time negotiating treaties, nor do they maintain fixed preferences during periods of negotiation.[12] For example, during the lead-up to the Maastricht Treaty negotiations, to the extent that statesmen or ministers did meet, diplomats provided all the documentation and draft treaties negotiated ahead of time for state leaders to use as a starting basis. It is only through a methodology of historical process-tracing examining the inter-delegation memos, working and non-working papers, and secretariat summaries that it is possible to observe the strong role diplomats played behind the scenes, and the extent to which agreement would not have been possible had statesmen only bargained amongst themselves (or used diplomats as transmission belts). Moreover, it is difficult, if not impossible, to determine what outcome statesmen would have reached had they performed the negotiations without the aid of their diplomatic personal representatives unless one assumes that their preferences remain fixed.[13] Therefore, although rationalist arguments are theoretically parsimonious, the trade-off is that they often get it wrong.

A principal–agent approach comes closer to the argument advanced here, but tends not to be fully articulated by its proponents. According to this approach, the principals or political leaders delegate authority to the diplomats or agents to negotiate on their behalf as this makes the transactions costs lower than if the principals had performed the negotiation themselves. Since the diplomat-agents are at the negotiating table, they can exercise agency in their own decision-making even if they have instructions. Proponents of principal–agent theory assume that to the extent that diplomats stray from their instructions, it is necessarily opportunistic behaviour that disadvantages principals. The reason for this rather pessimistic outlook is that principal–agent theory rests on rationalist assumptions about human nature, i.e., the world is a zero-sum environment, and even at the individual level one person's gain is another's loss. Although this approach recognizes the distinction between autonomy and agency, it actually considers agency to be a cost that principals must bear rather than the main point of delegation. Despite this, principals continue to delegate to agents, because they simply cannot afford to do all of the negotiations themselves.[14]

Both principal–agent and bargaining theory's methodology of comparing initial state preferences to final outcomes misses the critical processes that occur in between. The area beyond the autonomy statesmen grant diplomats is what is really interesting in an analysis of the processes of international cooperation. These processes reveal first the ability of diplomats to reach consensus amongst each other, and second the extent to which they are able to persuade statesmen to accept outcomes that are different from initial expectations or preferences. I argue that their ability to do this rests on their strength as an epistemic community. If this is true then it holds important implications for the future of cooperation in the EU, and by extension, what has become known as the democratic deficit. Although an argument can be made that by defying the instructions of democratically elected political leaders, diplomats are diminishing democratic participation, I will actually argue that this is not the case in practice. Before dealing with these implications, I turn to an analysis of the European diplomatic corps today.

An epistemic community of diplomats: Coreper

The strength of this particular epistemic community of diplomats can be measured through an evaluation of their collective (1) social background (2) professional status (3) meeting frequency, and (4) training.[15] Diplomats of similar social background, whether class-based or education-based, are more easily able to share and appreciate each other's worldviews, and this facilitates action as a collective group. Although a homogeneous social background is not ideal in terms of representing citizens' diversity, the end result is that the epistemic community is more cohesive. Increasingly, similar social background is reflected in the fact that from the early 20th century, many diplomats in Europe have attended the same universities and undergone a similar selection process. Universities, in turn, are accepting a greater diversity of students, which helps reduce the tendency for diplomats to be white males of upper-middle class origins. However, this greater diversity will unlikely detract from the homogeneity of future diplomatic corps as early socialization will still occur during the course of a university education. Universities are the primary locations of the initial shaping of norms within the future diplomatic corps, and can thus account for and incorporate cultural, social, racial, and gender diversity early on. As diversity continues to trickle up from educational institutions to elite bureaucratic positions, this will likely mean that the diplomatic corps will be increasingly respectful of such differences, rather than emphasizing them.

The professional status of diplomats not only impacts the ability for them to gain autonomy and trust from statesmen, but also affects recruitment and self-selection into the corps. Meeting frequency gives diplomats face-to-face time to create norms of understanding, and to develop working and personal relationships. Training for diplomats occurs both during university, and on-the-job. It is a continuation of earlier education, and reinforces professionalism. The tradition of diplomacy is centuries-long in Europe, and over time various countries' foreign services have developed standard practices and protocol. Thus, training tends to reinforce and add to the cohesiveness of the European corps.

These four variables also contribute to overarching shared professional norms, which include protocol, procedure, and norms of consensus that diplomats share in common. These norms give diplomats a common starting point or basis of understanding from which to begin negotiations. They provide a roadmap for how the practice of diplomacy plays out, from the shape of the negotiating table to the shared desire to reach consensus in the face of divergent member-state interests. While it is typical to characterize the profession of diplomacy in general as consensus-friendly, in the EU norms of consensus naturally converge with pro-integration norms. Increasingly, the issues on the table deal with questions about future EU prerogatives, and reaching consensus tends to mean solidifying the integration process. However, these shared professional norms are distinctive from shared worldviews or substantive causal values that diplomats have about international relations, even though the former certainly shapes the latter.

Overall, in Europe today, the four variables of social background, professional status, meeting frequency, and training lead to strong professional norms. Because the epistemic community is strong, diplomats are more likely to exercise agency, and there are many examples of this.[16] However, these variables have emerged over time, and have not always been strong.[17] Of the four variables, similarity in social background has been relatively constant among the epistemic community of diplomats in Europe well before the 1958 Treaties of Rome, establishing the pre-cursors to the EU. But other variables have not. For example, during the interwar period, the status of diplomacy as a profession fell drastically as diplomats were blamed for the failure of past alliances and the outbreak of war in 1914. As these variables changed over time, they reinforced or detracted from the cohesion of the epistemic community of diplomats, and the norms they shared.

The most influential group of diplomats in today's EU setting is Coreper. The Council of the EU is the umbrella under which Coreper operates and these diplomats serve directly under the Council of Ministers. For each of the member-states there is a deputy ambassador (Coreper I) who deals primarily with social and economic issues, and an ambassador (Coreper II) who manages political and foreign policy issues. The ambassadors have a more traditional diplomatic role, negotiating political relationships among states while the deputy-ambassadors focus on internal EU matters, which requires a detailed knowledge of the inner-workings of the EU bureaucratic apparatus and legal system. On its own, Coreper comes to a decision on 70–90 percent (labelled 'A') of the policies addressed to the Council, and the remaining areas (labelled 'B') are passed to the ministers for debate.[18]

Since the ministers do not reside in Brussels as Coreper does, diplomats must take on the responsibility of day-to-day interactions. However, mutual understanding is a near constant because of shared backgrounds, knowledge, expertise, norms, and continual interaction. Indeed, it is this mutual understanding that makes Coreper an actor in its own right. Even the 'B' issues are more often than not passed back from the ministers to the diplomats for re-negotiation. French Ambassador Christian Masset, a member of Coreper, said:

> Coreper's added value is compromise-making because given that we see all dossiers we are able to arbitrate between different dossiers and over a period of time. For example, I will say to another Coreper member that a certain issue is important for me, but I know it is more important for him. I will give it to him this time, but next time it will be my turn. There the bonding effect is improved because we have to trust each other. I believe him and he knows next time I'll get something in return.[19]

Importantly, even though the Council is an intergovernmental institution, diplomats make it more than that. The Commission is the main supranational institution with commissioners swearing an oath of loyalty to put the Union above any individual state's interests. Diplomats do not swear such an oath, but the strength of their epistemic community makes this unnecessary.[20] Irish Ambassador Anne Anderson, a member of Coreper in 2004, said, 'It is our job to achieve the general EU interests. It is a dual job. We are not just here to articulate national positions. We are here to find a shared outcome in which national positions are reflected.'[21]

Besides having a similar social background (Ambassador Anderson was the first female member of Coreper), the permanent representatives meet frequently, spending an average of 119 days per year in meetings together.[22] Their weekly interactions and informal 'working lunches' or 'working coffees' represent a much higher level of interaction than in traditional, bilateral embassies. The opportunity to meet in an informal way, in addition to formal meetings, allows diplomats to discuss sensitive issues openly before the official discussions begin. Irish Ambassador Peter Gunning, a member of Coreper, said:

> It is common to discuss gridlocked issues and longer-term issues in informal settings. There are big things that are not yet out there and haven't been tabled, but are influencing peoples' approach. For example, the Turkish issue. It affects all policies of the Union and you can't conduct business without being aware that other parts of the administration are taking a position.

It is not unusual for scholars to describe the more general norm of collegiality in Coreper. For example, Jeffrey Lewis, argues that permanent representatives share a *vue d'ensemble*. He demonstrates that diplomats work under multiple, cross-cutting pressures: the shadow of the future (knowledge that negotiation will happen again), the ongoing goal to make the Council a strong EU institution, and the desire to report success back to their home governments. Because Coreper negotiations are essentially never-ending, the overarching norm of collegiality is stronger than it has been among European diplomats in the past. Ambassador Anderson said:

> The capital relies very much on the accuracy of the account that comes from Coreper. There is a kind of spirit of Coreper that people are conscious of and is often quoted. We have to make judgments individually, but really it is the whole skill of running Coreper, in making the best possible decisions about which issues need to go to the political level. We clear away the undergrowth and isolate the key points. It is our service to our political bosses to reduce the list of issues. There is a lot of trust in Coreper by authorities and this does play a key role. We have to keep the pyramid working so we aren't constantly referring upwards. We have to be efficient and productive.

The need for continuous negotiations among EU member-states means that the permanence of Coreper provides coherence even as issues change. To accomplish this, Coreper also relies on a wide array of around 250 'working groups', consisting of diplomats, scientists, and other experts. In terms of reaching cooperative outcomes, the permanent representatives are better able to anticipate their ability to push the boundaries of their autonomy and persuade statesmen of their collective preferences.

The ability to persuade also rests on a high collective status. Diplomats in Europe have a relatively lofty status compared to diplomats from other regions or countries. In the US, for example, elite university students tend to work in business, academia, or politics, not the government's bureaucracy. In most EU member-states, government jobs are reserved for only the top graduates from the most competitive universities. Moreover, a job in the Foreign Service is the most competitive of the government jobs. In France, the top quarter of graduates from the Ecole Nationale d'Administration, a highly selective public administration school, choose the Foreign Service. In Britain, diplomats are typically graduates of Oxford or Cambridge. Once an individual embarks on a diplomatic career, the rank of ambassador is the highest he or she can obtain, and a post in a multilateral organization is often considered more prestigious than a bilateral embassy.[23] For European diplomats, the top choice among all multilateral posts is Coreper, although a post at the United Nations in New York City would certainly be a favourite in all foreign services.[24] Coreper, however, is truly the crème de la crème of European Foreign Service postings. An ambassador is appointed to Coreper only after years of experience in other multilateral settings. A Coreper appointment typically lasts for five to seven years, but is often renewed several times throughout a career.

Overall, in today's EU, Coreper diplomats exercise a high level of agency, and enjoy some degree of individual and collective autonomy from their state leaders. The next section deals with the ways in which Coreper has had an impact on recent EU policies.

The impact of the European diplomatic corps

With the recent rejection of the 'Treaty Establishing a Constitution for Europe', it is easy to assume that the EU has reached the limits of its capacity for integration. But a deeper reflection on the path of integration suggests otherwise. The EU has suffered many set-backs in the past 50 years, and few have proven to be lasting obstacles to the recovery of its momentum. This section focuses specifically on political and security integration, which are the most controversial areas for the creation of common policies. While statesmen may publicly disagree, diplomats are often behind the scenes pushing consensus forward. The 1992 Maastricht Treaty, arguably the most significant EU Treaty since the founding Treaty of Rome, was largely the result of diplomatic initiative.

In the lead up to the Maastricht Intergovernmental Conference (IGC), several factors led to efforts among EU officials and statesmen to create a political union alongside the economic agreements that were already in place. The economic downturn, fall of the Berlin Wall, and political crises in Iraq, Kuwait, the Soviet Union, and Yugoslavia made the 1980s a period of great transformation alongside growing uncertainty about the future of Europe. With German reunification, both French and German political leaders sought to emphasize their continued commitment to the EU. The founding of a political union would serve as a solid gesture towards this end. On 28 April 1990, the European Council in Dublin launched the planning and preparation for an IGC, a core component of which would be the political union, and the Council of Ministers approved such a meeting two months later.[25]

The Maastricht summit was a 21-hour meeting on 11 and 12 December 1991, but it is important to remember that this was only the culmination of years of prior diplomatic negotiations.[26] The ministers had invited EU ambassadors to define a European Defence Concept,[27] and for two years before the Maastricht summit convened these diplomats negotiated the terms of a political union as well as a possible Common Foreign and Security Policy (CFSP). The ambassadors involved were largely Coreper or former Coreper ambassadors, but they wore different hats. Coreper is not officially responsible for IGC negotiations, but its members are frequently appointed as personal representatives of political leaders and ministers, and thus take on a dual role. For this reason, it is important to have a clear picture of Coreper as an actor, including its composition and level of cohesion, to be able to understand its role in a different context. A close examination of the two years of negotiation leading to the Maastricht summit demonstrates that the cohesion and expertise of the diplomatic corps in their primary role as members of Coreper carried over into their secondary role as personal representatives. By the time the Maastricht summit convened, statesmen were given a full draft of the treaty, for which the personal representatives were responsible. In the lead-up to the summit, the Ministers met once per month, while the ambassadors met at least every week, and even more often as the IGC drew near.

What were these diplomats trying to achieve? How did CFSP differ from the system already in place?[28] The previous system, European Political Cooperation (EPC), had an intergovernmental method of cooperation, while CFSP would have a common method (i.e., one based on consensus).[29] EPC involved the European Parliament to a greater extent, whereas CFSP would mainly just inform Parliament rather than involving members of parliament in the process. EPC was based on a moral obligation while CFSP was binding with unified execution – i.e., a single, combined military effort. EPC did not require a transfer of powers from the member-states to the EU, while CFSP did, but decisions would still be made on a case-by-case basis.

CFSP went significantly beyond the previous system in place, representing an unprecedented level of political integration, but it did not result in a fully federalist agenda even though some member-states, like Italy, France, Germany, and Belgium, might have preferred this. At the same time, other countries, primarily Great Britain and Denmark and to a lesser extent Ireland, Greece, and Portugal wanted to preserve EPC, and avoid common policies which might alienate NATO and the US. For example, the Danish only wanted political union in so far as it was necessary to achieve economic union.[30] Thus, the compromise struck between those who did not want CFSP at all, and those who wanted to go as far as federalism was a significant step forward in political and security integration. Moreover, it paved the way for future integration, albeit gradual. The years of negotiation leading to the Maastricht Treaty required that diplomats overcome a large divide among member-states, and reach an entirely new European consensus. Documentation of the diplomatic dialogue during the time clearly demonstrates the process of gradual consensus led by the diplomats.

Critically, the Maastricht Treaty actually increased the power of Coreper, making the diplomats responsible for all of the preparatory and follow-up work involving CFSP. Coreper elevated its own status by making itself indispensable, and the treaty itself embodied an unprecedented level of community method plus 'common' method instead of intergovernmental cooperation. The transition from EPC to CFSP led to the creation of the post of High Representative of CFSP (now occupied by Javier Solana) charged with conducting EU foreign policy with outside parties. It also gave the Council of Ministers (usually Coreper) the authority to adopt joint positions on specific cases in which the EU might act, and common positions outlining general rules about EU conduct. This case demonstrates the importance of the ambassadors before, during, and after the summit. Remarkably, the diplomats were able to produce a Treaty that was tenable for the member-states. They acted even beyond their delegated autonomy going against the lowest-common denominator outcome (i.e., no political integration) that rationalist bargaining theory would have predicted.

Why? Bargaining theory relies on state preferences being set at the onset and remaining the same throughout the negotiation. As Paul Pierson argues, it is essentially a 'snap-shot' approach, which assumes there are no long-term or unintended consequences, and that every state seeks to increase its sovereignty (i.e., government control over domestic politics) with every bargain.[31] Outcomes are determined through rationalist weighing of preferences, and deal-striking. In the end, every agreement would have been acceptable to all actors at the outset because of its instrumental benefit, such as reducing transaction costs. According to the theory, supranational, transnational, non-state actors should not have any role in changing preferences through deliberation, learning, or persuasion, and thus the universe of outcomes is predictable.

However, the lead up to CFSP clearly shows that there were major disagreements among political leaders, which were later resolved by diplomats in a way that did not reflect a lowest-common denominator bargain. French President François Mitterrand, German Chancellor Helmut Kohl, and British Prime Minister John Major, in particular, were the most outspoken about their states' preferences. They all ultimately signed onto a treaty that they could not have anticipated at the beginning. Major was adamantly opposed to any significant step toward political cooperation, particularly one that entailed security integration. Mitterrand and Kohl shared a strong vision for federalism in the EU. The final treaty contained no mention of the word federalism. It was because the diplomats reached compromise when the statesmen could not that the outcome was so different from what bargaining theory would have predicted.

Why did the statesmen ultimately agree to the treaty during the Maastricht summit? First, they agreed to it because their diplomats were able to persuade them to change their preferences, and had anticipated in advance what was possible. The diplomats' confidence about their ability to persuade was borne out of the strength of an epistemic community that defined the reasonable and achievable. Second, the statesmen were not accustomed to participating in a complex, multilateral negotiation, and did not have the same close relationships as the diplomats did among each other. Diplomats defined success as a compromise agreement, and this trumped pure appeasement of state preferences.

The role of Coreper has been significant in many other cases and continues to be so, particularly since diplomats are much closer to the issues than are statesmen who must also occupy themselves with domestic governance. A member of Coreper said,

> In past IGCs, it was thought so important that [member-states] sent the secretary of state from each capital, but they ended up not being

negotiators because they couldn't. You need the technical insight which a politician does not always have. I have seen how they have flown in ministers or deputy ministers and they did not show up for meetings and their permanent representative went for them. This was true in Amsterdam for the French and British.

Besides the Amsterdam Treaty, European diplomats played a strong role in the enlargement negotiations of February 1994. The former Head of Division in the Directorate General Agriculture of the European Commission Ejner Stevdedad commented on the nature of the diplomatic epistemic community during these particular negotiations, three years following Maastricht.[32] He writes,

> In principle it was a conference between the governments of the then existing EU and the then candidate countries, Austria, Finland, Norway and Sweden. In practice ministers were supported by diplomats on all levels, and all worked around the clock in order to solve all the outstanding questions before a given deadline. In this process the diplomats had to work very independently, and they had to take a lot of risks, but it was surprisingly few cases, where the ministers overruled them. In fact I recall only one real case, where a member state – a big country – did not accept the result of diplomats' carefully established compromise. It caused embarrassment for all diplomats concerned, and in particular for the candidate country, but this was in a way the price to pay for, in general, a very effective negotiation culture, which secured that the deadline was met.

The role of diplomatic epistemic community is not confined to the way they reach consensus in controversial negotiations, but also in the continuity they provide. Referring to the 2004 enlargement, Danish Ambassador Jeppe Tranholm-Mikkelsen, a member of Coreper, said,

> In Coreper, the enlargement has taken place and has been carried through, but in most parts of the union it is not a reality. In Coreper, the new members have become fully integrated. There are no language barriers, these are professional diplomats.

Thus, European diplomats not only create new paths for accomplishing compromise over controversial issues, they also see treaties through to fruition. With every enlargement, existing EU diplomats welcome new diplomats into their ranks almost seamlessly, and the processes of deliberation do not falter. In the case of CFSP, the diplomats carved out for themselves a new capacity to make decisions about execution of the policy, and continued to refine it in their daily work, and in subsequent IGCs. When they are not wearing the hats of personal representatives, Coreper continues working through a wide-array of policies on a day-to-day basis. The question remains whether Coreper is still an elite fragment of a regional diplomatic corps or whether it is becoming an entirely new kind of agent for an emerging world player.

Conclusion and implications

Constructivists use norms and ideas to explain how and why states or individuals make decisions in a world of social interaction, not simply a kind of billiard game in which they are blind to each other's identities, values, and motivations. Theories that do not appreciate the role of norms and identity fail to explain many historical outcomes. Bargaining theory, in particular, casts aside the role of identity, historical experience, visionary leadership, and trust among actors. Epistemic communities, as knowledge-based, transnational networks of professionals who share beliefs and values, are best analysed through a constructivist methodology that considers underlying processes and human agency. To that end, it is useful to conclude by highlighting a future challenge for EU integration, and an implication for the European diplomatic corps as described in this chapter.

A particular challenge for the rationalist-constructivist debate is European security integration. The latest political and security issue on the EU agenda has been how to deal with the growing threat of terrorism. But if political integration more broadly was not anticipated, security integration poses an even greater puzzle. The classic concept of state sovereignty includes a monopoly over the legitimate use of force. Security is the central concern of governments, and is at the heart of sovereignty. And yet security is starting to become a central issue of concern for the EU as a whole. At a minimum, the EU constitutes what Adler and Barnett label a 'security community', 'a transnational region comprised of sovereign states whose people maintain dependable expectations of peaceful change'.[33] But the EU is more than that because member-states currently do not worry about war with each other. Now, the security threat is a shared concern that comes from the outside. Member-states are looking outward, and continuously redefining themselves as an increasingly coherent whole. The EU is perhaps more accurately what Adler and Barnett describe as a 'tightly coupled security community'. Member-states provide mutual aid, and there is a system of rules representing pooled sovereignty which is maintained through supranational, transnational, and international interactions.

In today's security environment, pressing terrorist threats may provide the impetus for strong epistemic communities, like diplomats, to push for security integration beyond the system created under Maastricht. However, because relinquishing sovereignty in the security realm will meet with resistance from member-states, the key actors who are most likely to have the ability and capacity to accomplish security integration are particular civilian, military, and diplomatic epistemic communities. The cost from the point of view of member-states is further erosion of traditional state-cantered sovereignty.[34] It remains to be seen how successful these members of international society will ultimately be.

An implication of the strong role of the European epistemic community of diplomats is the question of whether exercising a high level of agency contributes to the so-called democratic deficit in the EU. The European diplomatic corps in Brussels has an elite status, which may be cause for concern when examined in the context of calls for increased transparency and accountability of EU institutions. Because decisions are made behind closed doors with much of the documentation relating to the meetings remaining classified, citizens are not able to participate as they would if the decisionmaking had remained at the domestic level.

The issue of the democratic deficit is complex, wide-ranging, and may involve all of the institutions of the EU as well as the way in which society participates in EU processes. I would argue that diplomats do not contribute to a potential democratic deficit. First, democratic governments have always required a degree of delegation.[35] Elected leaders cannot take on all of the tasks of governing themselves, and ideally, they appoint qualified experts to make decisions in their stead. A parallel example of this would be the US Supreme Court Justices. Generally, they are delegated much authority in deciding judicial precedence, and interpreting the constitution.

Second, if anything, epistemic communities tend to fill what would otherwise be a 'democracy-gap'. Rather than taking participation away from regular citizens, they actually add a dimension of deliberation that would not otherwise exist. Citizens cannot be expected to stay abreast of all the various issues their country is involved in on the domestic and international levels, and diplomats can strive to make the process democratic and pluralistic. It is also important to remember that diplomats and other groups in international society are citizens themselves. Third, the European diplomatic corps itself embodies certain norms of democracy. Modern diplomats do not generally have a propensity to obstruct democracy in the treaties they write. Rather, they tend to be conduits of democracy. Fundamental to the diplomatic profession is a belief in the value of true deliberation, compromise-seeking, and a respect for pluralism.

In today's EU, the epistemic community of diplomats is influential and cohesive. The members of the diplomatic corps have a high status, and they are relatively homogenous in terms of their training and social background. Because of their frequent meetings, they not only share historic norms of diplomacy and protocol, but are developing new norms of their own. This bodes well for the future of EU integration, even in areas that are traditionally divisive, such as the political and security realms. It is only through due consideration of this elite stratum of international society that the EU's progress and setbacks can be fully understood. At the same time, policy practitioners can impact the future course of EU integration through a proper understanding of the diplomatic role. Although the European diplomatic corps is relatively strong now, this has not always been the case. In a world in which the bonds of international society hang in the balance, it is important to foster a diplomatic dialogue and culture of compromise, whichever direction integration takes.

Notes

1 Berridge, Geoff and Alan James, 'Diplomatic Corps', in *A Dictionary of Diplomacy* (Houndmills: Palgrave Macmillan), 2001.
2 Haas, Peter M., 'Introduction: Epistemic Communities and International Policy Coordination', *International Organization* 46, no. 1 (1992): p. 3.
3 Bull, Hedley, and Adam Watson, 'Introduction', in *Expansion of International Society*, edited by Hedley Bull and Adam Watson (Oxford: Clarendon Press, 1984), p. 1.
4 Bull, Hedley, *The Anarchical Society. A Study of Order in World Politics* (New York: Columbia University Press, 1977).
5 James, Alan, 'System or Society?' *Review of International Studies* 19, no. 3 (1993) 269–88.
6 Buzan defines solidarism as 'the extent and degree of institutionalization of shared interests and values in systems of agreed rules of conduct.' (p. 61)
7 Examples of epistemic communities are environmentalists, lawyers, judges, human rights advocates, health networks like the Red Cross, and other scientists. Many of these groups rely on diplomats to help achieve their goals at the policy level.

8 For more on this see Cross, Mai'a K. Davis, *The European Diplomatic Corps: Diplomats and International Cooperation from Westphalia to Maastricht* (Houndmills: Palgrave, 2007).

9 There are many strains of bargaining theory, but the one most associated with theories of EU integration is Andrew Moravcsik's liberal intergovernmentalism, which is rationalist and qualitative, but still considers domestic-level preferences.

10 Moravcsik, Andrew, 'Preferences and power in the European Community: a liberal intergovernmental approach', *Journal of Common Market Studies* 31, no. 4 (1993) 473–524.

11 Moravcsik, Andrew, and Kalypso Nicolaïdis, 'Explaining the Treaty of Amsterdam: Interests, Influence, Institutions', *Journal of Common Market Studies* 37, no. 1 (1999) 59–85.

12 In an earlier work Moravcsik (1991) argues that changes in national preferences are a key component of institutional intergovernmentalism. In a more recent article (Moravcsik and Nicolaïdis 1999) he argues that initial state preferences remain stable throughout the negotiations.

13 For a more detailed analysis, see Cross, *The European Diplomatic Corps.*

14 Kassim, Hussein, and Anand Menon, 'The Principal–Agent Approach and the Study of the European Union: Promise Unfulfilled?', *Journal of European Public Policy* 10, no. 1 (2003) 121–39.

15 See Cross, *The European Diplomatic Corps.*

16 Ibid.

17 For cases that demonstrate variance over time see Cross, *The European Diplomatic Corps.*

18 Hayes-Renshaw, Fiona and Helen Wallace, *The Council of Ministers* (London: Macmillan Press 1997).

19 Personal Interview 10/2004.

20 Future research is necessary to determine the extent to which Coreper's interests are consistently in line with the common EU interest over time. I advance the preliminary argument here that this is the case.

21 Personal Interview 10/2004.

22 Sherrington, Philippa, *The Council of Ministers: Political Authority in the European Union* (London: Pinter, 2000) p. 46

23 Possible exceptions might be bilateral posts in cities like Washington D.C. or Paris.

24 European ambassadors who have been appointed to the UN would make an easy transition to Coreper.

25 European Documents 9431/90.

26 For a full analysis of this case study see, Cross, *The European Diplomatic Corps,* Ch. 6.

27 Mortimer, Edward, 'European Union Advocated.' *Financial Times*, 16 January 1989, 3.

28 Summary of the proposed changes to create CFSP, provided by the Spanish Delegation (EU Documents 10356/90 ADD1, Annex 31990: 5).

29 The issue of what actually constitutes CFSP is still a work in progress in the EU, however decisionmaking is intended to be more consensus or community-oriented among a quasi-federal group of states rather than an international bargain among European countries.

30 EU Documents 6356/90. From Denmark to Secretary General of the Council, 11 May 1990.
31 Paul Pierson, 'The Path to European Integration: A Historical Institutionalist Analysis', *Comparative Political Studies* 29, no. 2 (April 1996) 123–63.
32 Personal Correspondence 2004.
33 Adler, Emanuel and Michael Barnett, *Security Communities* (Cambridge: Cambridge University Press, 1998), p. 30.
34 As Keohane argues, it may be necessary to redefine the concept of sovereignty. He writes, 'Sovereignty is a variable not a constant.' The EU restricts external and absolute sovereignty, but it is still rule-based. Treaty-based rules about sovereignty may not weaken sovereignty, but transform it. See 'Political Authority After Intervention'.
35 Thomas Zweifel provides evidence that the EU compares favourably to federal systems like the United States and Switzerland. However, the unique European context of democracy alongside supranational integration means that citizens and politicians must be constantly aware of how democracy is being transferred to the supranational level, and ensure that democratic participation is preserved. This is not something that will naturally happen without close attention. Resolving the democratic deficit may require some re-structuring of EU institutions, especially the European Parliament which is the only elected body.

References

Adler, Emanuel and Michael Barnett, *Security Communities,* Cambridge Studies in International Relations, Cambridge University Press, 1998.
Adler, Emanuel, and Peter M. Haas, 'Conclusion: Epistemic Communities, World Order, and the Creation of a Reflective Research Program', *International Organization* 46, no. 1 (1992): 367–90.
Antoniades, Andreas, 'Epistemic Communities, Epistemes and the Construction of (World) Politics', *Global Society* 17, no. 1 (2003): 21–38.
Berridge, Geoff and Alan James, 'Diplomatic Corps', in *A Dictionary of Diplomacy,* Houndmills: Palgrave Macmillan, 2001.
Buchan, David, 'Pugnacious Major Outshines His Counterparts – the UK Prime Minister Impressed, the Italian One Slept, the French President "Was Just Plain out of It",' *Financial Times*, December 12, 1991.
Bull, H. and A. Watson, Introduction, *Expansion of International Society*, Oxford: Clarendon Press, 1984.
Bull, Hedley, *The Anarchical Society. A Study of Order in World Politics*, Basingstoke: Columbia University Press, 1977.
Bull, Hedley and Adam Watson (eds), *Expansion of International Society*, Oxford: Clarendon Press, 1984.
Burley, Anne-Marie, and Walter Mattli, 'Europe before the Court: A Political Theory of Legal Integration', *International Organization* 47, no. 1 (1993): 41–76.
Cross, Mai'a K. Davis, *The European Diplomatic Corps: Diplomats and International Cooperation from Westphalia to Maastricht*, Houndmills: Palgrave, 2007.
Duff, Andrew, John Pinder, and Roy Pryce (eds), *Maastricht and Beyond*, London: Routledge, 1994.

'European Community; Thunder Off', *The Economist*, 12 September 1992, 48.

Eisenhammer, John, 'Germany's True Believer Who Will Not Be Fobbed Off', *The Independent*, 28 June 1991, 10.

EU Documents. (1990–92) Courtesy of the Council of the European Union.

'European Defence: Initial Rapprochement among the Twelve', *European Information Service*, 28 March 1991, 5.

Fligstein, Neil, and Iona Mara-Drita, 'How to Make a Market: Reflections on the Attempt to Create a Single Market in the European Union', *The American Journal of Sociology* 102, no. 1 (1996): 1–33.

Flynn, Sean, 'Windfall in structural funds now under threat', *The Irish Times*, 23 September 1992, City Edition, 8.

Fonblanque, J.R. de, Letter, 25 September 1990.

Haas, Peter M., 'Introduction: Epistemic Communities and International Policy Coordination', *International Organization* 46, no. 1 (1992): 1–35.

Hayes-Renshaw, Fiona and Helen Wallace, *The Council of Ministers*, London: Macmillan Press Ltd., 1997.

James, Alan, 'System or Society?' *Review of International Studies* 19, no. 3 (1993): 269–88.

Kassim, Hussein, and Anand Menon, 'The Principal–Agent Approach and the Study of the European Union: Promise Unfulfilled?', *Journal of European Public Policy* 10, no. 1 (2003): 121–39.

Keck, Margaret, and Kathryn Sikkink, *Activists Beyond Borders*, Ithaca, N.Y.: Cornell University Press, 1998.

Keohane, Robert O., 'Political Authority After Intervention' in Keohane and Holzgrefe (eds). *Humanitarian Intervention*. Cambridge: Cambridge University Press, 2003.

Laursen, Finn, and Sophie Vanhoonacker (eds), *The Intergovernmental Conference on Political Union: Institutional Reforms, New Policies and International Identity of the European Community*, European Institute of Public Administration. Leiden, The Netherlands: Martinus Nijhoff Publishers, 1992.

Lewis, Jeffrey, 'Is the "Hard Bargaining" Image of the Council Misleading? The Committee of Permanent Representatives and the Local Elections Directive', *Journal of Common Market Studies* 36, no. 4 (1998): 479–504.

———, 'The Methods of Community in EU Decision-Making and Administrative Rivalry in the Council's Infrastructure', *Journal of European Public Policy* 7, no. 2 (2000): 261–89.

Lhuillery, Jacques, '"Federal" Row Revives Doubts over Dutch Tenure of EC Presidency', *Agence France Presse*, 4 December 1991.

Mazzucelli, Colette, *France and Germany at Maastricht: Politics and Negotiations to Create the European Union*. New York: Garland Publishing, Inc., 1997.

Moravcsik, Andrew, 'Negotiating the Single European Act: National Interests and Conventional Statecraft in the European Community', *International Organization* 45, no. 1 (1991): 19–56.

———, 'Preferences and power in the European Community: A Liberal Intergovernmental Approach', *Journal of Common Market Studies* 31(4) (1993): 473–524.

Moravcsik, Andrew, and Kalypso Nicolaïdis, 'Explaining the Treaty of Amsterdam: Interests, Influence, Institutions', *Journal of Common Market Studies* 37, no. 1 (1999): 59–85.

Palmer, John, 'Federalists Set to Leave Britain in Cold', *The Guardian*, 19 November 1991.

———, 'The Road to Maastricht: The Dapper Scot with a Firm Hand on the Minister's Elbow – Key Player: Sir John Kerr', *The Guardian*, 2 December 1991.

'Political Union: A Week before Maastricht, Compromise Begins to Emerge', *European Information Service*, 30 November 1991, 4.

'Political Union: Ministers Move Ahead Inch by Inch', *Europe Information Service*, 26 November 1991.

'Political Union: UK Proposes Taking Foreign Policy Decisions on a Case-by-Case Basis', *Europe Information Service*, 20 July 1991, 2.

Pond, Elizabeth, *The Rebirth of Europe*, Washington, D.C.: Brookings Institution Press, 1999.

Sherrington, Philippa, *The Council of Ministers: Political Authority in the European Union*, London: Pinter, 2000.

Slaughter, Anne-Marie, *A New World Order*, Princeton, N.J.: Princeton University Press, 2004.

Zweifel, Thomas, 'The EU's democratic deficit in comparison', *Journal of European Public Policy* 9, no. 5 (October 2002): 812–40.

12
Esprit de Corps: Sketches of Diplomatic Life in Stockholm, Hanoi, and New York

Geoffrey Wiseman[1]

This chapter uses evidence from the diplomatic corps in Stockholm, in Hanoi, and at the United Nations (UN) in New York to explore the relationship between the diplomatic corps and international society. I argue that any generalization made about the world's more than 190 diplomatic corps must be sensitive to the differences that exist among these three and all other diplomatic corps. I also argue that the generalizations that can be made suggest that the diplomatic corps is an institution whose socializing and constitutive force in international relations and in diplomatic culture has been underestimated.

The more perspicacious of the diplomatic writings include the idea that diplomats might act not only in the national interests of their own countries, but also in deference to the preferences and norms of their professional colleagues and host country and to international society as a whole. In *Esprit de Corps*, Lawrence Durrell treats this theme with humour, giving us a fictional account of the Belgrade diplomatic corps in Tito's communist Yugoslavia of the early 1950s.[2] Geoffrey Berridge and Garrett Mattingly also deal with this theme in their accounts of, respectively, the diplomatic corps in Istanbul and Rome, but they take a strictly historical, serious approach.[3]

My approach is somewhere between humour and serious diplomatic history. I offer my observations on diplomatic life in Stockholm and Hanoi and at the UN in New York for any insight they may provide on the diplomatic corps as an institution of diplomacy and international society. My approach is eclectic, calling on autobiographical 'field' evidence – experiences, observations, anecdotes, conversations, recollections – from two of my three diplomatic postings with the Australian Foreign Service and a stint at the UN in 2006–07. Arguably, I am approximating Robert Jackson's theorist 'who enters into the subject and interprets it from the inside' and therefore am flirting with this approach's attendant risks and benefits.[4] With those limitations in mind, I propose to examine the extent to which the diplomatic corps is indeed an important – even if neglected – manifestation of a diplomatic culture, a culture that underpins and helps constitute the international society of states.[5]

As my definitional starting point, I take diplomatic corps to mean the body of diplomats of all states posted in the same capital city. The idea of the diplomatic corps having, as Berridge and Alan James put it, a distinct, 'corporate existence' is found in several authoritative texts and manuals of diplomacy.[6] Kishan S. Rana, a former Indian diplomat and contributor to this volume, elsewhere describes the corps as 'virtually an association, even a brotherhood, with its own code of behaviour and rites'.[7] As for the corps' theoretical significance, Hedley Bull sees the diplomatic profession as 'a custodian of the idea of international society, with a stake in preserving and strengthening it'. In Bull's formulation,

> diplomacy fulfils the function of symbolising the existence of the society of states. Diplomatists, even in the pristine form of messengers, are visible expressions of the existence of rules to which states and other entities in the international system pay some allegiance. *In the developed form of the diplomatic corps that exists in every capital city they are tangible evidence of international society as a factor at work in international relations.*[8] (Emphasis added.)

Bull's colleague, the former British diplomat Adam Watson, who wrote extensively on diplomacy, summarized the diplomatic corps as follows:

> [T]he diplomatic corps in each capital, that is the diplomatic missions taken together, acts as a multilateral network of diplomatic brokerage.... [A]mbassadors accredited to a capital often need to *coordinate* their actions and their reports with colleagues. These exchanges extend to most other diplomats in the capital, at various levels of seniority. There is a constant dialogue, and much mutual *adjustment* of the various embassies' assessments of the host government's policies and intentions. There can be no resident diplomat abroad who has not had the experience of having his understanding of some aspect of the host government's policy *corrected* and *amplified* by a member of another embassy which happened to be better informed on that issue.[9] (Emphasis added.)

In Watson's account, diplomats in the corps adjust policy assessments based on interactions with other diplomats, but he does not address how far these adjustments go, which is a main interest of mine. Bull and Watson's thesis on the expansion of international society relies heavily on the belief that Western diplomatic ideas and practices have been spread *via* the diplomatic corps established in post-colonial states (although historical expansion had, of course, started much earlier, as other chapters in this volume show).[10] From Kigali to Kathmandu, the diplomatic corps remains recognizable as an 'institution' of diplomacy.

The illustrations I use in making my argument focus not on crises, but on the 'normal' way of life, or *modus operandi*, of the diplomatic corps in Stockholm and Hanoi and at the UN. Based on a small sample, comprising two bilateral cases and one multilateral case, my argument challenges the traditional view – that of the Realists in International Relations theory – which sees the corps in narrow terms: diplomats at embassies are there to represent, promote, and defend the national interests of their sending countries. Under this view, any cooperation between embassies serves merely one restricted, instrumental purpose: to protect the position and privileges of a corpus of self-interested units. And by extension, the behaviour of the individual diplomat is seen as highly predictable. My goal is to explore whether the diplomatic corps is a more complex social construction than this, one in which there is evidence to support a multilayered diplomat and a related (broader) range of normative obligations alongside national interest.

Stockholm

In the early and mid-1970s, two 'episodes' occurred within the normally quiet Stockholm diplomatic corps that clashed with the norms of diplomacy. The first episode was the war in Vietnam. Swedish opposition to the US intervention in Vietnam led to serious friction in US–Sweden relations. In 1968, Olof Palme, an outspoken education minister, marched with the North Vietnamese ambassador to the Soviet Union in a Stockholm street protest against the war. Subsequently, in 1970, Palme visited the US as Sweden's prime minister without having been invited to meet the US president. Bilateral relations deteriorated so badly that the US withdrew its ambassador from Stockholm in 1972 and declined to accept a Swedish ambassador in Washington for over a year.[11]

The second episode took place in April 1975. In this case, members of the Baader-Meinhof terrorist group carried out a violent seizure of the West German embassy in which the embassy's top floor was blown off and two embassy officials were killed, including the military attaché. This attack occurred just a few months before I arrived on my first diplomatic posting.

These two legacies were a conspicuous part of the Stockholm diplomatic corps' own narrative. However, even I, a third secretary at the time, appreciated that Stockholm was not 'the diplomatic centre of the world'.[12] My first impressions of the Stockholm corps differed greatly from Durrell's 'first impressions' of the Belgrade corps, as captured in his *Esprit de Corps*. This is an interesting, and perhaps ironic, point given that Sweden and Yugoslavia were often compared for their similarities in some foreign and defence policy matters.[13] By the 1970s, Sweden had established a reputation as a tolerant, prosperous (though high taxing), 'neutral' European state that supported multilateral institutions and gave generously to developing countries.

The Stockholm corps was influenced by Sweden's famously egalitarian and open democracy. As I argue below, the ministry of foreign affairs (MFA) did not serve as what Brian Hocking calls the gatekeeper – that is, the manager of all relations between the government and embassies – as can be the case in other capitals.[14] The MFA's Protocol Department is responsible for formal contacts with embassies and international organizations in Sweden and handles safety and security issues; it also arranges *agrément* for and accreditation of ambassadors.[15] Except for the impressive ceremony for presentation of credentials and the annual celebration of national day, protocol in Stockholm was observed without anachronism (although the diplomats from the other Nordic countries did joke about official Sweden's more formal ways).

Unlike the many embassies that are housed in an up-scale diplomatic area not far from the city centre, the Australian embassy occupied two levels of a high-rise building in the heart of the city's downtown. In consequence, there was no architecturally identifiable building to serve as a distinct Australian physical presence. The Australian ambassador, Lance Barnard, was a political appointee (and thus a member of a group that traditionally represents a very small percentage of the Australian foreign service). He had been a deputy prime minister and defence minister under Labour prime minister Gough Whitlam. Barnard's appointment was seen by some as a deft move given Sweden's history of social democratic governments. However, following a budget crisis in late 1975, the Australian governor-general dismissed Whitlam as prime minister. In subsequent elections, Whitlam's Labour party was defeated, and Malcolm Fraser became prime minister as leader of a conservative coalition government. The change of government caused the embassy staff (and, indeed, the Australian press) to speculate about the ambassador's withdrawal. However, the new prime minister decided to keep Barnard as ambassador in Sweden (he was also accredited to Norway and Finland).[16] Ironically, Sweden elected a conservative coalition the following year. This election of conservative governments in both countries seemed to undermine the rationale for appointing a former Labour minister to Sweden in the first place.

Under these unexpectedly controversial political circumstances, I made my initial calls, starting with junior colleagues at other embassies. Professional socialization started within the corps. At first I relied on more experienced colleagues at my level (e.g., at the British, Portuguese, Irish, and Pakistani embassies) for information and advice; but they became less important as I developed a network of professional Swedish contacts, including journalists, trade unionists, bureaucrats, researchers, and students. Moreover, government departments, political parties, and the major trade unions generally had well-staffed international departments, and it was very common for diplomats to deal with them directly. While I did keep in close contact with the MFA desk officer who covered Australia, Stockholm was not socializing me as a traditional diplomat. Rather, Stockholm was foreshadowing diplomacy's future.

In short, Sweden, like other open societies, limits the host MFA's role as gatekeeper, and the diplomatic corps becomes less important as a site of diplomatic activity. Such societies allow diplomatic agents to interact extensively with the country's people and institutions. This weakens the traditional diplomatic corps as a discrete entity and shifts diplomatic culture from a system of one-state-to-another to an international system of multiple actors.

Hanoi

In the early 1980s, Vietnam still showed the signs of a war-ravaged economy (the US war ended in 1975). Compared with Sweden, which was known for its post-Napoleonic historical capacity to stay out of wars, Vietnam had a two-millennia history of being unable to avoid them. And whereas Sweden was one of the most open and prosperous countries in the world, Vietnam was closed and one of the poorest. These basic historical, political, and social conditions hugely affected the nature of the diplomatic corps in Hanoi.[17]

In many ways, Vietnam's isolation in the years following the war was self-induced, the result of a post-war mentality of distrust and the country's highly centralized communist system. Bad Vietnamese policy choices on refugees and Cambodia compounded the problem, especially in terms of relations with the US and the countries of the Association of Southeast Asian Nations (ASEAN). By the early 1980s, Vietnam was isolated diplomatically from all but the Soviet Union and its allies, Laos, non-aligned countries such as India, and outlier Western donor countries such as Sweden.

The small diplomatic corps in Hanoi reflected Vietnam's international circumstances: it was polarized by the Soviet and East European missions, on the one hand, and by the 'Rest' (including the West), on the other. The centrally located, colonial-style French embassy was prominent, as was the modern Swedish embassy compound that lay outside the city and was the envy of every diplomat in town. The UK and West German missions were small but active. The other European missions (e.g., those of the Netherlands, Belgium, and Denmark) were staffed minimally and headed at the *chargé d'affaires* level, primarily to protest Vietnam's post-unification policies, notably those on refugees and Cambodia. The Japanese kept a relatively low profile. The Indian embassy, in contrast, was well connected with both the Eastern and the Western missions, reflecting India's strong relations with Vietnam and India's non-alignment policy.[18] The Chinese, who had a large and impressively maintained embassy, were active in cultivating contacts and trading information with the Western missions but were less at ease with Soviet bloc counterparts and Vietnamese officials.

Within the corps, there were distinct sub-groupings. The Soviet bloc was the largest of these because of its political support and extensive aid programs. Of the Soviet bloc embassies, only the Hungarian embassy interacted comfortably with the Western missions, although the Yugoslav and Albanian missions kept up informal contacts with Western diplomats as befit their independent status within the communist bloc. There were also sub-groupings based on region, two of which were noteworthy: the diplomats representing the European Community (EC) and the diplomats representing the ASEAN countries. Both of these groupings were active in the corps because of the Cambodian and refugee issues, and both emerged as information-sharing groupings that sometimes held joint meetings with the Vietnamese authorities.

In the case of Australia, Malcolm Fraser's conservative government withdrew support for a small aid program after the Vietnamese invaded Cambodia, but he eventually decided to keep the embassy's diplomatic representation at the ambassadorial level (Ambassador John McCarthy was a rising star in the Australian Foreign Service), albeit with a slightly reduced political staff.[19] Canada had no mission in Hanoi, and neither did New Zealand. But the main missing link in the diplomatic corps was the US. The absence of a US embassy in Hanoi was a constantly discussed subject in the diplomatic corps, and one to which I return below.[20]

During this early post-war period, the Vietnamese authorities defended their policies publicly in ideological terms. The challenge was to penetrate and decipher the language. The 'consensus' among the Western and ASEAN missions was that the Vietnamese would be willing to make concessions to win wide international respectability and closer diplomatic contacts with the world, especially with Washington. But Hanoi's perceived inflexibility on Cambodia was a particular sticking point, although some compromises were reached – for example, those on the orderly departure of refugees. The Vietnamese welcomed the presence of the UN, which was led by the UN Development Programme and included such agencies as the UN children's fund, UNICEF. The International Committee of the Red Cross also maintained a small office. The aid agencies were important not only for Vietnam's respectability as a new UN member, but also because they allowed Western states to funnel aid to Vietnam through multilateral rather than bilateral channels. These agencies were well informed about Vietnam's local socio-economic conditions, and their presence added a vague sense of normalcy to the otherwise isolated diplomatic community in Hanoi.

Government restrictions kept the corps' contacts with ordinary Vietnamese citizens extremely limited except in Saigon, the much larger, free-wheeling old capital of South Vietnam that was renamed Ho Chi Minh City after the war. Consequently, enterprising Hanoi-based diplomats travelled as much as they could to Ho Chi Minh City and the south in general to assess political and social developments. They also went to assess attitudes towards Cambodia and to look for possible trends in the refugee outflow.

In contrast to the open and almost decentralized diplomatic corps in Stockholm, the corps in Hanoi was concentrated and interdependent. It came together twice a year for state occasions (Independence Day, on 2 September, and Tet, the Vietnamese New Year), and it came together for other functions as well, including national day receptions and frequent embassy dinners. However, the Soviet ambassador, who was the dean of the corps and represented Vietnam's most important political backer, rarely if ever called on the support of the corps as a whole.[21] Another variation in Hanoi was that the diplomatic hierarchy was flatter than usual.

Since the corps was small and intimate, embassies often invited diplomats of all levels, rather than just heads of missions, to receptions and other functions, including the frequent embassy dinners. These events were important for exchanging and gathering information about Vietnam, and they engendered an intimacy that would not have been found in most Western capitals. Additionally, the regular courier runs to Bangkok for deliveries and to procure basic supplies led embassies to informally share many services, including the delivery of diplomatic pouches to embassies and UN agencies in Bangkok.

Overall, the degree of diplomatic collaboration and socialization in Hanoi was far greater than in Stockholm. As the only political officer at the Australian embassy besides the ambassador, I served as *chargé d'affaires* during his brief absences from Hanoi. As any junior diplomat knows, such periods provide one with opportunities to meet with ambassadors and senior governmental officials. In my case, this included Vietnamese foreign minister Nguyen Co Thach.

The prevailing corps consensus in Hanoi was that it was better to engage and negotiate with the Vietnamese – especially over the occupation of Cambodia – than to isolate and punish them. This view reflected a strong preference for the diplomatic norms of engagement and negotiation, a preference also manifest in the widely held corps view that the Americans were mistaken in refusing to move towards normalization with the Vietnamese to help resolve the Cambodia problem. In contrast, the diplomatic corps in Bangkok tended to adopt a hard-line anti-Vietnamese view. Arguably, some embassies in Hanoi did not fully consider the domestic political pressures that US policymakers were under not to normalize, especially from groups representing Americans missing-in-action (MIAs).[22] And the corps consensus may have been based on over-commitment to the idea that formal diplomatic relations are necessarily a good thing, as distinct from, say, an informal system of contact.[23] Still, can it be said that the Hanoi corps was suffering from a form of collective localitis, a condition that has been defined as the 'adoption by diplomats of the point of view of the government of the receiving state, traditionally assumed to be the result of being posted for too long in the same state'?[24] I view localitis, focused as it is on the rare individual who 'goes native', as too narrow and distracting a concept for understanding the wider socializing dynamic of the corps as a whole. No one went native in Hanoi. Indeed, some diplomats there openly expressed hostility towards Vietnam.

In Hanoi, one became a diplomat in the traditional sense because of the closeness of the Hanoi diplomatic corps.[25] This was a small, isolated, and yet consequential posting offering a palpable *esprit de corps*. Part of this esprit came from our shared deprivation of creature comforts; part of it resulted from our exasperation in the face of the inefficiency, abuses, and opacity of the Vietnamese command economy and political system; and part of it arose from a shared hope for improvement in the lives of ordinary Vietnamese people.

The United Nations, New York

Whereas very little is generally expected of the diplomatic corps as a collective entity in bilateral capitals, a great deal is expected of the collective diplomatic corps accredited to the UN in New York – at least in the UN's formal incarnations, such as the Security Council and the General Assembly. I have identified what I see as seven characteristics that distinguish the UN diplomatic corps from bilateral diplomatic corps, (such as those in Stockholm and Hanoi) and, in some cases, from other major multilateral corps.[26]

The first distinguishing characteristic is the perception of universality. With 192 member states, the UN represents – in varying degrees and ways – a good deal of international society. There is little doubt that most states value membership in international society.[27] Moreover, since 1945, membership in international society has been uniquely ceremonialized and legitimized at the UN, which has, in effect, become international society's membership committee, a role once performed more loosely through the international legal and diplomatic norms of recognition and the exchange of embassies in bilateral capitals.

Outside the conference rooms where debates and voting take place, a set of practices and procedures has evolved that makes this system of nearly 200 members work reasonably efficiently and without undue ceremony. *The Manual of Protocol of the United Nations* reflects the diplomatic profession's highly developed code, or norms, of appropriate behaviour and is designed to not cause offence to any member state and 'to ensure the safety and convenience of the diplomatic community'. UN member states establish a permanent mission led by a 'permanent representative' (PR), who traditionally holds the rank of ambassador extraordinary and plenipotentiary. As for the collective whole, the manual does not mention a diplomatic corps but, rather, speaks of the activities of the diplomatic community accredited to United Nations Headquarters (UNHQ). In UN terms, then, the diplomatic community in New York is narrowly defined as the UNHQ and the permanent missions, as well as observer missions accredited to it and specialized agencies.[28] While the Protocol and Liaison Service treats the diplomatic community as a collective group, there is no dean. Instead, the role of dean is assumed by the chairs of the regional groups making up the UN membership, underscoring the strong regional substructure of the universal body.

The second distinguishing characteristic of the UN diplomatic corps is the unique role of the UN secretariat and secretary-general. The 6,000-strong New York secretariat, led by the secretary-general – who is formally at the service of the UN Charter and member states – has no ostensible, formal foreign policy interests of its own. Arguably, the secretariat and secretary-general are an amalgam of the interests of all member states expressed through resolutions and practices over 60 years. Their actual role is contested by commentators: some see the UN as a 'building' in which sovereign member states go about their national business; others see it as an 'actor' in its own right.[29] The role of the secretary-general is unique and especially difficult to generalize, partly because each incumbent interprets the relevant charter provisions differently and international circumstances are always changing.[30] When the secretary-general travels overseas, he is normally accorded protocol appropriate to a head of state, even though he is not a head of state. In another contrast, the 1961 Vienna Convention on Diplomatic Relations requires that a receiving state approve an individual nominated as head of mission, but it is (very sensibly) not necessary for member states to secure the secretary-general's *agrément*. The secretary-general can, however, influence the level of formality; for example, the presentation of credentials became more formal and business-like under Kofi Annan than it had been under his predecessor.

One symbolic practice that also differs, and that demonstrates the UN's larger purpose, has to do with official photographs: they show the secretary-general standing in front of the national flag of a visiting head of state or government while the visitor stands in front of the UN flag. This practice is intended to reinforce the interdependent relationship between the member state and the UN itself.[31] Finally, since there is no UN 'government,' members of the UN diplomatic community devote more time than do members of bilateral corps to representing national policies and perspectives to each other.

A third characteristic, and one that is closely related to the first two, is the UN's platform as a world stage. While UN negotiating and deal-making are primarily conducted in private, much UN activity is conducted in public.[32] For most diplomats, this is unusual. Unlike the members of any other corps, UN diplomats are often 'performing' in plenary and committees, for each other and for wider world publics through television coverage, the press corps, and even visitors in the gallery. Stanley Meisler described Security Council debates at the time of the Cuban Missile Crisis as 'theatre'. This role as performers is also a feature of the General Assembly, a notable historical case being Soviet leader Nikita Khrushchev's famous 1960 shoe-banging to protest what he believed were the West's and Dag Hammarskjöld's anti-Soviet policies.[33]

Also in this vein were Venezuelan president Hugo Chavez's *ad hominem* remarks about US president George W. Bush during the 2006 Annual General Debate. The reaction of UN diplomats to Chavez's speech illustrates how deeply the norm of civility runs in diplomatic culture in general and in the UN corps in particular. Many linked Venezuela's subsequent failure to win a coveted two-year term on the Security Council to that speech. As one Latin American ambassador told *The New York Times*: 'The speech really hurt [Chavez's] case. Most members don't want this place turned into a mockery. In the General Assembly, there are limits, and he went beyond them.'[34] These notable breaches of decorum aside, the UN is perhaps less a stage than a unique global forum for dialogue in which norms of rational discourse generally apply: all sides are given a chance to speak, the tone is expected to be civil and restrained, and there is a right of reply. In short, even when disagreement is intense, the normative expectation at the UN is one of restraint and civility.

A fourth distinguishing characteristic of the UN corps is the generally high quality of its diplomats. Countries are widely thought to send their best diplomats to Washington D.C. and other postings seen as being the most important. Similarly, a UN posting is regarded as a prize for the most-skilled diplomats at the peak of their careers. The sense of having high-quality colleagues produces a community self-image of diplomatic professionalism and political clout back home. This is especially true in the case of ambassadors representing the Permanent Five members of the Security Council. One good example is Thomas Pickering, a US career foreign service officer who served impressively as US ambassador during the Persian Gulf War, 1990–91. Also, Russian foreign minister Sergei Lavrov had previously served as

Russia's UN ambassador, and French prime minister Dominique de Villepin was France's ambassador to the UN during the crisis concerning the 2003 Iraq War. The perceived importance of the UN corps is underlined by the charter provision permitting missions to have up to five national representatives and thus allowing some (for example, the US mission) to have five senior diplomats at the ambassadorial level.[35]

The fifth distinguishing characteristic that I have identified is the UN's unique relationship with the host country. The UN's location in New York and in the US produces a social and political dynamic more complex than that of any comparable multilateral capital, such as Vienna or Geneva, where host countries unreservedly welcome the UN's presence. Formally, the UN–US relationship is described in the Headquarters Agreement between the UN and the US. The 19-member Committee on Relations with the Host Country deals *inter alia* with security issues of missions accredited to the UN and with diplomatic parking. As host country, the US is accorded certain privileges, such as the custom of speaking second, after Brazil, at the Annual General Debate.

Politically, the US–UN relationship has been a mixed one since 1945, complicated by the fact that the US, as the host country, is the biggest financial contributor to the world body and is often its biggest critic.[36] One of the practical difficulties in having the US as host country is that Washington does not recognize all of the UN's member states, a problem not encountered in other countries, such as neutral Switzerland and Austria, which also host major UN institutions. To get around this problem, the US created a special visa status for diplomats from countries that are not recognized by the US (or whose governments are not members of the UN). Still, there have been disputes over visas, the best-known case involving the denial of a request for a US visa for Palestinian Liberation Organization leader Yasser Arafat to address the UN General Assembly. Two General Assembly resolutions were adopted 'deploring' the host government's actions and calling for a special session of the Assembly to be convened in Geneva to hear Arafat.[37]

The political sensitivity of the US's role as host country to the UN is somewhat mirrored in New York City's role as host city. New York City mayors officially welcome the UN presence, as they do the presence of the 105 consulates that make up what is the largest consular community in the world.[38] And secretaries-general reinforce the UN-city connection with such words as 'New Yorkers should be proud of their longstanding record of support for the UN'.[39] According to a 2004 study by New York City's Economic Development Corporation, the UN 'generates 18,000 jobs and gives the local economy a \$2.5 billion jolt'.[40] However, '[m]ayors periodically try scoring political points by thumping the United Nations, even urging it to get out of town'.[41] Historically, the reasons for the negativity have ranged from UN positions on Israel to the non-payment of diplomatic parking fines.[42] The UN's lack of a 'bilateral' representative to a specific government in New York City is reflected in the 'architecture' of the permanent missions. Most of them are functionally located in, and dwarfed by, Manhattan's skyscrapers, a situation very unlike that in many bilateral capitals, where individual embassy buildings are constructed to showcase, or symbolize in some way, the unique identities of the sending countries.[43] After the September 11, 2001 terrorist attacks on the World Trade Centre in New York City, the UN's relations with both the host country (and host city) warmed, only to turn, according to a Gallup poll, 'sharply negative following the organization's failure to authorize the United States' use of force in Iraq at the outset of the war in 2003'. The same poll also found that the UN's image among Americans had dropped to its lowest level since 1953, when it was first measured.[44]

The sixth difference is that the UN corps experiences a relatively high degree of 'cross-fertilization' and 'recycling'. By cross-fertilization, I mean the mixing of diplomats from at least two different corps at any given moment. A good example of this process is the UN's First Committee on International Security and Disarmament. Each year in October, many delegations to the month-long session in New York are led by an ambassador from Geneva (where the UN's Conference on Disarmament is). In some cases, the Geneva ambassador is supported by a mid-level diplomat who is also from Geneva. This is an interesting, regularized case of inter-corps relations and operational compatibility. Another form of cross-fertilization occurs when missions are reinforced with diplomats from other capitals when their country is a member of the Security Council or when special General Assembly debates are held. Such cross-fertilization between corps is not unusual (as described from a different perspective by Joyce Leader in this volume), but at the UN it is a systematic practice.

Additionally, a relatively high number of diplomats at the UN are recycled, by which I mean they are assigned to a post they held earlier in their careers. The concept of recycling might also be expanded to include diplomats who join the secretariat following a posting to the UN. One hears of many cases of diplomats being recycled in New York; it is a sensible practice that provides missions with instant expertise and experience. It also likely enhances an already strong 'epistemic sensibility' and the cooperation that is widely assumed to arise from direct personal contact, although such enhancement is far from proven from a social science perspective.

My seventh, and final, distinguishing characteristic is that the UN diplomatic corps operates simultaneously at three levels: the 'multilateral', which typically involves three or more states at permanent or *ad hoc* international conferences; the 'bilateral', which is between two states; and the 'polylateral', by which I mean between states and non-state entities.[45] Under Article 71 of the UN Charter, non-governmental organizations (NGOs) obtain consultative status with the UN's Economic and Social Council (ECOSOC) – interestingly, through formal accreditation arrangements. In 1948, there were 40 accredited NGOs with consultative status at the UN; by 2006, there were 2,719. In addition, the NGO section of the UN's Department of Public Information liaises with approximately 1,500 NGOs that are associated with the department, while the UN's Non-Governmental Liaison Service does liaison work with over 9,000 NGOs.[46]

These numbers are impressive, and, as Paul Wapner has argued, 'accredited NGOs have left their signatures … on almost all significant UN policymaking' since the 1990s.[47] Most secretariat departments and entities work in varying ways, formally and informally, with NGOs. One additional noteworthy aspect of these working relationships is the now commonplace use – by missions and the secretariat – of not only NGOs, but universities, think-tanks, and foundations as well, to convene meetings outside the formal UN rules and structures. Further, since the late 1990s, the UN has reached out to the private sector, notably through the innovative Global Compact on corporate responsibility.[48] Although there are variations among the departments, the UN secretariat is perhaps more open than foreign ministries are to non-governmental, academic, and other public contacts, especially concerning 'soft power' policy issues. In sum, such interactions between state agents and non-state representatives – encouraged notably by Kofi Annan – are perhaps more prevalent at the UN than they are in most bilateral capitals and, with the possible exception of Brussels, in other multilateral cities.

Conclusions

I have attempted to show that there are significant variations between the diplomatic corps in Stockholm, in Hanoi, and at the UN in New York. One important variation is the extent to which the MFA plays a gatekeeping role for diplomats in bilateral corps. Other differences between diplomatic corps arise from such determinants as the host country's political and economic system and the size and the relative isolation of the country's capital. These conclusions highlight the need for a method of classifying the nearly 200 diplomatic corps in world capitals (let alone the even greater number that would result from including consular corps in non-capital cities).

I have identified seven characteristics that distinguish the UN diplomatic corps from bilateral corps, and even from other multilateral corps. These distinguishing characteristics are (1) the universality of the UN corps; (2) the special role of the secretary-general and secretariat; (3) the UN's function as a world stage; (4) the relatively high quality of the diplomats in the UN corps; (5) the UN's relationship with the host country; (6) the UN's cross-fertilization and recycling of diplomats; and (7) the UN's relative openness to non-governmental interactions. With respect to this last characteristic, the cosmopolitan pressures appear to arise (with some honourable exceptions) not from within the corps itself, but from non-governmental entities that support the higher principles of the UN and that expect UN member states and their diplomats to have purposes beyond themselves. The UN as a body has indeed notably responded to this expectation on many occasions.

In sum, there are important differences between the diplomatic corps in Stockholm, in Hanoi, and at the UN in New York, and these differences must be taken into consideration in any attempt to categorize diplomatic corps. Also true, however, is that strong elements of a common diplomatic culture – even if taken for granted – are clearly at play.

Notes

1 I was posted to the Australian embassy in Stockholm from 1975–78 and to the Australian embassy in Hanoi from 1981–83. My third overseas diplomatic posting was in Brussels from 1983–86. In 2006–07, I worked in the Strategic Planning Unit, Executive Office of the United Nations Secretary-General. I am grateful for comments on earlier versions of this chapter from Edward Luck, Donna Roberts, and Paul Sharp, as well as from several currently serving diplomats and UN officials. The views expressed herein are mine and do not necessarily reflect the views of the United Nations. I wish to thank the Center for International Studies at the University of Southern California for its support, as well as Christina Gray and Abigail Ruane for their research assistance.

2 Lawrence Durrell, *Esprit de Corps: Sketches from Diplomatic Life* (London: Faber and Faber, 1957).

3 Geoffrey Berridge's account can be found in this volume. Garrett Mattingly's account is in his *Renaissance Diplomacy* (London: Jonathan Cape, 1955). See also Keith Hamilton and Richard Langhorne, *The Practice of Diplomacy: Its Evolution, Theory and Administration* (London: Routledge, 1995), p. 90.

4 R. H. Jackson, *The Global Covenant: Human Conduct in a World of States* (Oxford: Oxford University Press, 2000), p. 97.

5 On diplomatic culture, see Geoffrey Wiseman, 'Pax Americana: Bumping into Diplomatic Culture', *International Studies Perspectives*, vol. 6, no. 4 (November 2005), pp. 409–430.

6 G. R. Berridge and Alan James, *A Dictionary of Diplomacy* (Basingstoke: Palgrave Macmillan, 2001), p. 65. Berridge and Nadia Gallo refer to the corps' sense of 'professional collegiality' in 'The Role of the Diplomatic Corps: the US–North Korea Talks in Beijing, 1988–94', in Jan Melissen (ed.), *Innovation in Diplomatic Practice* (London: Macmillan, 1999), p. 226.

7 Kishan S. Rana, *Bilateral Diplomacy* (Geneva: DiploHandbooks, 2002), p. 42.

8 Hedley Bull, *The Anarchical Society*, 3rd edn. (New York: Columbia University Press), 2002, pp. 176, 166.

9 Adam Watson *Diplomacy: The Dialogue Between States*, rev. edn. (London: Routledge, 2004), p. 128.

10 Hedley Bull and Adam Watson (eds), *The Expansion of International Society* (Oxford: Clarendon Press, 1984).

11 John Shaw, *The Ambassador: Inside the Life of a Working Diplomat* (Sterling, Virginia: Capital Books, 2006), pp. 24, 36. Diplomatic relations reached a low point in December 1972 following public comments by Palme comparing the US's Christmas air bombing of Hanoi with other major atrocities of modern history.

12 Shaw, *The Ambassador*, p. 55. Today, Stockholm has nearly 100 embassies.

13 See, for example, Adam Roberts, *Nations in Arms*, 2nd edn. (London: Macmillan/IISS, 1986).

14 Brian Hocking, 'Catalytic Diplomacy: Beyond "Newness" and "Decline"', in Melissen (ed.), *Innovation in Diplomatic Practice*, pp. 21–42.

15 For details, go to www.sweden.gov.se.

16 Prime minister Fraser also offered Barnard a knighthood. The press speculated that the offer was designed to split Barnard off from the Labor party, which opposed the British honours system for Australians. Barnard declined the knighthood and completed his full term as ambassador.

17 My posting to the Australian embassy in Hanoi, in 1981, followed Vietnamese language training, part of it at the University of Hanoi. This assignment was regarded as a hardship because of Hanoi's isolation and difficult, post-war living conditions. Before this posting, I had worked in the Indochina Section of the Department of Foreign Affairs.

18 For two contemporaneous, pro-Vietnamese accounts of both Vietnam and Hanoi from an Indian perspective, see T. N. Kaul, *India, China and Indochina: Reflections of a 'Liberated' Diplomat* (New Delhi: Allied Publishers, 1980); and K. N. Raj, *Hanoi Diary* (Bombay: Oxford University Press, 1975).

19 In addition to the ambassador, there was one political officer (me), an immigration officer, and five administrative, secretarial, and communications staff members.

20 The US and Vietnam did not establish full diplomatic relations, exchanging embassies and ambassadors, until 1995. See Martin Bell, 'A Bilateral Dialogue Regime: US–Vietnamese Relations after the Fall of Saigon', in Melissen (ed.), *Innovation in Diplomatic Practice.*

21 The dean's role evidently varies under different circumstances. The current dean convenes a lunch on average every two months, discussing matters of mutual concern (e.g., taxes, airport procedures, security). He also organizes farewell receptions for departing colleagues on a less regular basis. (Author's e-mail correspondence with Ambassador Tomas Ferrari, 22 January 2007.)

22 The Australian ambassador had earlier in his career been posted to Washington and so was sensitized to US domestic politics. In Hanoi, we briefed a visiting US delegation representing the families of MIAs.

23 Bell, 'A Bilateral Dialogue Regime', p. 196.

24 Berridge and James, *A Dictionary of Diplomacy*, p. 151.

25 On this general theme, see Iver B. Neumann, 'To Be a Diplomat', *International Studies Perspectives*, vol. 6, no. 1 (February 2005).

26 Other UN centres are in Geneva, Vienna, Nairobi, Addis Ababa, Bangkok, Beirut, and Santiago. Arguably, there are only a few truly multilateral cities (e.g., Geneva and Vienna), as distinct from cities, some of which are capitals, that host major international organizations but generally are not identified as multilateral cities (e.g., Washington D.C. and Rome).

27 See Watson, *Diplomacy*, p. 169.

28 Twice yearly, the UN publishes the book 'Permanent Missions to the United Nations', also known as the 'Blue Book'. The transfer of UN diplomats in and out of New York City is closely recorded. A weekly addendum to the Blue Book shows 'interim movements of diplomatic personnel'. The UN Protocol consists of only some 11 staff members, which makes it small compared to the protocol departments of some mid-sized foreign ministries.

29 This distinction is neatly drawn by Samantha Power in 'United It Wobbles: Should We Blame the UN for Its Shortcomings, or the Countries That Make up the World Body?' www.washingtonpost.com, 7 January 2007, accessed on 10 January 2007. For an interesting comment on the actor-stage metaphor by a senior United Nations official, Robert Orr, see James Traub, *The Best Intentions: Kofi Annan and the UN in the Era of American World Power* (New York: Farrar, Straus and Giroux), 2006, p. 266.

30 For a discussion of the relevant UN Charter provisions, see Edward Newman, 'Secretary-General', in Thomas G. Weiss and Sam Daws (eds), *The Oxford Handbook on the United Nations* (Oxford: Oxford University Press, 2007), esp. pp. 176–79. See also Simon Chesterman (ed.), *Secretary or General? The UN Secretary-General in World Politics* (Cambridge: Cambridge University Press, 2007); Brian Urquhart, *Hammarskjöld* (New York: Norton, 1994); and James Traub, *The Best Intentions.*

31 Another protocol difference, this one stemming from the sheer size of the UN corps, is that seniority is not an issue in determining diplomatic precedence or seating at meetings or social occasions. Such matters are determined alphabetically.

32 This idea is captured in the title of Paul Kennedy's book about the UN, *The Parliament of Man* (New York: Random House, 2006), although one

should not infer from this title a legislative role for the UN that was never intended.

33 Stanley Meisler, *United Nations: The First Fifty Years* (New York: The Atlantic Monthly Press, 1995), chapter 8; pp. 116, 121, 360.

34 Warren Hoge, 'Venezuelan's Diatribe Seen as Fatal to U.N. Council Bid', *The New York Times*, 25 October 2006. nytimes.com, accessed 27 January 2007.

35 For average-sized missions, the custom is to have two ambassadorial-level representatives, the PR and the deputy permanent representative (Deputy PR). The quantitative dimension still counts at the UN. In contrast to the newest member, Montenegro, which has one accredited diplomat, the US has some 130 diplomatic personnel listed. See *Permanent Missions to the United Nations*, No. 296, October 2006 (New York: United Nations). The sole diplomat listed for Montenegro was the former PR of Serbia-Montenegro before Montenegro declared its independence in 2006. See Catherine Elton, 'The Saturday Profile: A One-Man Embassy Adjusts to a Smaller Portfolio', *The New York Times*, 5 August 2006.

36 See Linda Fasulo, *An Insider's Guide to the UN* (Yale University Press: New Haven, 2004), pp. 33–8. See also Edward C. Luck, *Mixed Messages: American Politics and International Organizations, 1919–1999* (Washington DC: Brookings Institution Press, 1999).

37 Mohamed Rabie, 'The US-PLO Dialogue: The Swedish Connection', *Journal of Palestine Studies*, vol. 21, no. 4 (Summer 1992), p. 61.

38 See, for example, the *Register of Foreign Consulates and Other Associated Government Offices in New York*, 2006–2007 edn. (New York: Office of the Mayor, City of New York Commission for the United Nations, Consular Corps and Protocol, 2006), pp. 4–5.

39 UN Secretary-General Ban Ki-moon, address to UNA-USA Business Council (SG/SM/10836), 10 January 2007.

40 Clyde Haberman, 'New UN Chief Steps Gingerly Into the City', *The New York Times*, 12 January 2007.

41 Haberman, 'New UN Chief'. For a view of the UN–New York City relationship in the early 1970s, see Eric Clark, *Diplomat: The World of International Diplomacy* (New York: Taplinger Publishing Company, 1974).

42 For an intriguing academic study suggesting that 'diplomats from high corruption countries ... have significantly more parking violations' and that diplomats from countries with 'less favourable popular views' of the US 'commit significantly more parking violations', see Ray Fisman and Edward Miguel, 'Cultures of Corruption: Evidence from Diplomatic Parking Tickets', National Bureau of Economic Research Working Paper No. 12312, July 2006 (www.nber.org/paper/w12312).

43 The diplomatic suburb of Red Hill in Canberra, Australia, provides some good examples of showcase embassies in a bilateral capital.

44 Lydia Saad, 'United Nations Ratings Remain at Lowest Ebb', The Gallup Poll, 8 February 2007, www.galluppoll.com, accessed 12 February 2007. See also Traub, *The Best Intentions*, e.g., pp. 369–72 and chapter 22.

45 Geoffrey Wiseman, '"Polylateralism" and New Modes of Global Dialogue', in Christer Jönsson and Richard Langhorne (eds), *Diplomacy Vol. III, Problems and Issues in Contemporary Diplomacy* (London: Sage, 2004), pp. 36–57.

Polylateral diplomacy differs from *plurilateralism,* a form of multilateralism involving two or more, but not all, states from a given region or from across regions.

46   The UN's Non-Governmental Liaison Service provided these figures. For a useful compendium, including details of the UN's accreditation arrangements, see UN Non-Governmental Liaison Service, *UN System Engagement with NGOs, Civil Society, the Private Sector, and Other Actors* (New York: United Nations, 2005).

47   Paul Wapner, 'Civil Society', in Weiss and Daws, *The Oxford Handbook on the United Nations*, p. 258. See also the 'Cardosa Report', which is formally entitled, *We the Peoples: Civil Society, the United Nations and Global Governance*, UN General Assembly A/58/817, 2004.

48   Malcolm McIntosh, Sandra Waddock, and Georg Kell (eds), *Learning to Talk: Corporate Citizenship and the Development of the UN Global Compact* (Greenleaf Publishing: Sheffield, UK, 2004).

13
Conclusion: The Diplomatic Corps' Role in Constituting International Society

Paul Sharp and Geoffrey Wiseman

> 'Few political thinkers have made it their business to study the states-system, the diplomatic community *itself.*' – Martin Wight, 'Why Is There No International Theory?'

The main impetus for this study was the editors' shared sense that the diplomatic corps was important and insufficiently studied. The preceding chapters provide evidence for our original sense of the corps' importance and have made a useful contribution to enriching our understanding of it. Nevertheless, they have raised more questions than they have answered and posed a set of empirical, theoretical and conceptual puzzles which cry out for further investigation. To put it simply, neither diplomatic theory's own account of the diplomatic corps nor international theory's attempts to capture its broader significance are easily squared with what some of our practitioner colleagues are fond of calling the 'facts on the ground'.[1]

From within diplomatic theory we get a straightforward, if largely implied, account of the corps. In this view, we should not be surprised if people in a similar predicament, with a similar way of seeing things and similar sorts of interests become aware of one another as such and develop a collective sense of themselves. Early envoys might face similar problems but usually were not together for any length of time since they were usually only sent on specific missions. Once residencies are established, however, this changes and, as Berridge notes, rivals in Renaissance Italy and, later, Constantinople begin to see themselves as colleagues in a corps, at least up to a point and for some purposes. With the passage of time, this collective sense is strengthened and its purposes facilitated by processes of increasing institutional and cultural refinement until the modern corps emerges as a universal institution in the 20th century, bestowing its benediction on the state occasions of its hosts and safeguarding the local terms and conditions on which its members go about their business.

Nor should we be surprised at the particular representative form of the diplomatic corps. Certain aspects of it may seem archaic at times – although much of what is old has been done away with and diplomatic spectacle lends itself very well to the invented traditions of state ceremony which modern societies seem to need.[2] Whether one regards these occasions for dressing up and being seen as 'a bit of fun' or a nuisance is very much up to the individual. Nevertheless, we live in a world of states and it is hard to imagine alternatives to the flag ceremonies, march-pasts, and national day receptions of expressing the fact that this is so. The thing to remember is that the cloak of state and diplomatic ceremony is worn lightly and provides shelter for what is going on beneath. To be sure, much of what the diplomatic corps actually does as a collective body may seem low key and unexciting. It is, however, important. Without diplomatic immunities and privileges, for example, diplomacy would become very difficult, and without a corps to act as watchdog over those immunities and privileges, governments might steadily encroach upon them. Similarly, without the sharing of information with colleagues, the familiarization of new arrivals and the subsequent socialization of junior officers that the corps facilitates, the wheels of diplomacy – what Adam Watson calls the diplomatic dialogue – would turn far more slowly. Thus diplomatic theory presents the corps as the guardian of the little, but vital details that make international life possible.

The problem with diplomatic theory's account of the corps, however, is that it is often not borne out by the facts. As many of the chapters above demonstrate, diplomats often do not think about the corps much. Ask foreign ministries who currently serves as the doyen of the corps accredited to their country and the answer is not always readily forthcoming. Ask doyens about their role and functions and a similar hesitation may follow. Above all, ask retired or senior diplomats what the diplomatic corps did at their former postings, and they will struggle to recall much, even about situations in which diplomatic theory would lead us to believe that the corps had an important part to play. Thus, for example, Hoare maintains above that the Seoul diplomatic corps had little to do because the South Korean government looked after the diplomats accredited to it and posed them few problems. The Bejing corps, in contrast, was powerless in the face of attacks on the privileges and immunities of some of its members during the

Great Cultural Revolution precisely because the Chinese government was a very poor host. Relief from this pressure was thus obtained primarily through individual, informal efforts, rather than formal, collective representations. Sometimes the corps does not function because it does not need to, therefore, and sometimes it does not function because it cannot.

It seems that it is only when the countries represented in a diplomatic corps value their relations with each other more than with their mutual host, and do so to the extent that this commitment filters down to their representation on the spot, that the collective road to seeking redress or exercising influence becomes salient. And it is more likely to filter down when the governments concerned are members of common associations or alliances like the EU or NATO, as in Sharp's account of the Macedonian case. Only where there was no such common association, or multiple and potentially antagonistic associations are present in the background, as in Kabir's account of Nepal, does a universal identity like the UN, or a particular articulation of it, in this case the Kathmandu corps, provide the framework for collective representations towards a weak host.

As the forgoing suggests, what diplomats tend to think in terms of is not the diplomatic corps so much as diplomatic communities – with their attendant and evolving sub-groups and currents. Invariably, after some brief anecdotes about particular doyens or a state ceremony when something improbable, and generally humorous, deflates the occasion, reflections on the diplomatic corps drift into accounts of the communities within which diplomats live and work. The idea of a diplomatic community is, of course, far less formal and far more nebulous than that of the diplomatic corps. It can involve all sorts of actors, both private and public, individual and collective, and it rarely functions as a whole in any capacity other than a putative audience before which the formulation of foreign policy, the conduct of negotiations or the attempt to exert influence are carried out. While diplomatic corps consist of accredited foreigners representing states and international organizations, diplomatic communities may consist of people from both home and abroad, and diplomats find themselves working with parts of, or currents in, such communities as they seek to build and exert influence for themselves, their governments and those aligned with both. At its broadest, the diplomatic community in a capital could, in principle, consist of just about everybody as when, for example, the local newspapers carry stories of crimes committed by diplomats in a private capacity and the public becomes engaged. At its narrowest, a diplomatic community or, more properly, a subsection of it, may coincide, may claim to coincide or be declared by others (often locals) to coincide with the diplomatic corps. Such claims are more likely to be made when the host is in conflict with all or part of the international world represented in its capital. They are more likely to be effective in the small capitals of states whose links – both public and private – with the outside world are relatively limited. It is easier for elements in the diplomatic communities of cities like Kathmandu or Kigali, for example, to claim to be the diplomatic corps (or be accused of the same), than it is for similar elements operating in Washington, London or Moscow. Interestingly, when the UN secretary-general announced that a fact-finding mission was to be dispatched to Fiji in April 2007, the statement noted that the mission would consult with a range of political authorities and with 'the resident diplomatic community', suggesting that even in a small state setting the idea of a 'community' is more palatable than that of a 'corps'.[3]

How then is this gap between what diplomatic theory tells us to expect about the diplomatic corps and the complexities of actual practice to be explained? What can broader theoretical orientations to understanding international relations tell us about why the diplomatic corps exerts what might best be described as a ghostly presence haunting the diplomatic background? Why does it often fail to materialize when it might reasonably be expected to put in an appearance, yet sometimes affect the most surprising, if frustratingly imprecise, manifestations? At least three possible explanations suggest themselves, each of which involves sweeping judgements about diplomats in general which are derived from distinct sets of theoretical assumptions about international relations:

a) Deception: the diplomats are having us on;
b) Anachronism: the diplomats have been left behind; and,
c) Lack of self-awareness: the diplomats do not (or effect not to) understand their own business

The *deception explanation* – that the diplomats are having us on – implies two arguments. The first is that, superficial appearances notwithstanding, international politics remain dominated by relations between states, and that diplomats with their political masters still dominate the conduct of those. The second is that because of the exceptional and disturbing moral character of relations between states, their conduct remains a secretive and esoteric business. Thus, diplomats still prefer to operate in the shadow of power, rather than in the spotlight. Power, in Morgenthau's phrase, has always been depreciated, and the more populist, democratic and consumer-oriented domestic political relations become, the more hidden and esoteric the real international action has to be. Ordinary people living according to the precepts of community-derived moral codes simply cannot understand the imperatives, both moral and other, which drive relations between communities. Behind the facade of professed ordinariness and openness with which many contemporary diplomats present themselves as just one class of participants among many in organizing and managing the common affairs of an emerging global civil society, therefore, the old game proceeds apace. The diplomatic corps, like some secret fraternity of masons, choreographs, directs and sometimes even produces the whole show, while the world looks (and talks) on.

On occasions, we obtain glimpses of a world which accords with such a view. The weak and powerless easily seek an explanation of their circumstances in the agency of others, and diplomatic corps provide convenient embodiments of that agency and, as we have seen, actual expressions of it on occasions. Political leaders at home can become exhausted, distracted and demoralized by effort, complexity and failure respectively, and when they do, they may actively or passively turn a difficult matter over to the professionals to handle. It is not that hard to imagine a world in which the centre of gravity for much policy initiation and innovation is to be found in the diplomatic corps at national capitals, rather than in the governments of the countries to which they are accredited. Diplomats themselves, on occasions, like to imply that this may be the case and, thus, that both as individuals and as a breed, they may be more important than most of us have been given to understand. And diplomatic historians encourage this view by providing narratives of the international past explaining how things came to be which go beyond recording 'one damn thing after another' (and often many things happening all at once).

The purposes of statesmen and diplomats, as recorded by themselves, provide a salient starting point for these exercises, and the shapes given to the past by their efforts certainly encourage our propensity to look for meaning and purpose in the present and to read the sort of glimpses above as evidence that someone is running the show. On the whole, however, the idea that diplomats are running the show on the quiet through institutions like the diplomatic corps is not persuasive. This explanation for the gap between what diplomatic theory suggests the corps does and the little which diplomats actually have to say about it violates Okham's razor and ignores a great deal of readily available evidence for simpler explanations.

What this weight of evidence does seem to bear out is the *anachronism explanation*. It suggests that diplomats – acting individually, in communities, or as corps – have very little to do with a great many international relations which we regard as important. As globalization gathers pace, diplomats and diplomacy are said to become irrelevant. International relations increasingly involve peoples and, indeed, people, rather than states. They are increasingly focused on what people as a whole care about, and every important technological development in the last century or so reinforces the trends in this direction. If one wants confirmation of this, look no further than the diplomats themselves. The bad ones – those who act as the possessors of secret knowledge about the game properly played – look increasingly irrelevant, while the ambitious ones look increasingly concerned (or at least affect concern) about the possibility that their profession is being left behind by a changing world and has a great deal of catching up and modernizing to do.

To the modernizers and those they have recruited, of course, the idea of the diplomatic corps is little help. It is doubly harmful, for its connotations of exclusivity and privileged influence are out of step with the times and, worse, the corps does not work in the way that people imagine it might. Like an old manual typewriter sitting in the corner of the office and employed to put addresses on awkwardly-sized envelopes, the diplomatic corps is still there, has its occasional uses, but has lost its pride of place as a source of the notes, minutes and memoranda which frame what is going on. Please, the diplomats seem to say, 'don't mention the corps'. The diplomatic community, in contrast, is a far more open idea reflecting all the changes in what international relations are supposed to be about, and whom they are supposed to be between. And yet it accomplishes all this while, presumably, retaining a favoured place for actual diplomats amidst the new networks and their attendant bustle. Thus the formal diplomatic corps may be seen as but one manifestations of the diplomatic community, existing to undertake the pieties and low key, but important, tasks implied by diplomatic theory as well as, on occasions, rising up to confirm the order of things amongst the weak, the troubled and the inadequately socialized.

There is much to commend this view both as a description of the way things currently are believed to be in international affairs, and as an explanation of the discrepancy between, on the one hand, what diplomats have to say about the diplomatic corps and, on the other, how it seems to operate. However, there are still some problems with it. Most importantly, while it gives us a pretty good idea of why the corps is pushed into the background of most diplomats' operational consciousness, it does not give us a clear understanding of why it continues to exist more-or-less unchanged in essentials, how it can motor quietly on doing what it has always done in some settings very effectively, and how, on occasions, it is even capable of taking on a prominent role and acting effectively.

The *lack of self-awareness explanation*, in the sense that diplomats take for granted or ignore the constitutive elements of their work, is helpful here. It may be dangerously, yet plausibly, suggested that diplomats taken as a whole are an unreflective group of people. This is true of all professions, including – indeed one might say especially – the academic one. Diplomats, however, seem to go out of their way to present themselves as ordinary, useful and, above all, busy people. Their days, to hear them tell it to outsiders, are filled by meetings, appointments, travel and committee assignments, rather than the romantic and glamorous activities in which the popular imagination assumes them to be engaged. Doubtless this is so, as it is in the law, medicine, the military, finance, trade and, even, academia. This sort of busyness is intrinsic to working in large organizations within and between which conversations have to be conducted if anything is to be accomplished. Yet lawyers, doctors, bankers, traders and professors are less willing than diplomats to allow themselves to be defined by what they spend (too) much of their time doing, rather than by the important, distinctive, one might say essential, aspects of what they do. Even the best diplomats seem to go out of their way to suppress the reflective impulse. It is very rarely that you can get them to talk about what they do in anything but a very direct manner, anecdotally detailing and illustrating their daily lives or, in their memoirs, describing the events which they were privileged to witness and the routines which made this possible.

In part, this is so because they *are* exceptionally busy people (even if they violate the code of the exceptionally busy never to say that this is so). It may also be so because they are members of a profession that is often said to be in decline and can certainly be said to have been on the defensive in recent years. Let no one doubt for a moment, they seem to say, that we have work to do and plenty of it. A much more important explanation for this reticence, however, is to be found in the tenuous nature of the very basis of absolutely everything they do, the idea that we live in a world of sovereign states which somehow represent effectively and authentically the plural character of human existence and constitute a society by which this is accomplished. To be sure, all professions rest to some extent on foundational myths which do not stand up to too much close empirical scrutiny, but which organize the meaning of their constitutive practices. However, lawyers, doctors, teachers and the members of other professions all function within a world which appears solid. The world of states appears as an anchor for the vast majority of people who live and work within them, but even for the still relatively few non-diplomats who work between and, sometimes, in spite of them. Everyone can take this world for granted even as they complain about its premises and object to their consequences. The world of states provides a notional safety net on which we can still rely to orient ourselves. Not so the diplomats. They have no foundational world other than their own, and this is constituted in great part by their own practice. Just like mountain-climbers, the members of any profession should not 'look down' too much if they want to remain effective, but diplomats cannot 'look down' because 'below' them is nothing but a notional void. The social world they constitute is the 'solid ground' for other social worlds. Diplomats have nowhere else to look when the bearings of their own world become confused because it is the social world of 'last resort' for everybody else. Diplomats may not have a full understanding of their own world, therefore, because they cannot afford to have one. If they did not take their world as real, they could not function.

It was for this reason that we referred, not entirely whimsically, at an earlier stage of our project to the idea of the diplomatic corps as 'constituting the constitutive.' That is to say, if the idea of an international society serves as an organizing principle that gives meaning to our international relations, then the diplomatic corps gives an important measure of concrete expression to that idea. It is one of the ways in which the claim that we live in an international society can be substantiated, and by the way in which it operates we gain important insights into the society to which it gives expression. It should come as no surprise, therefore, that, as these essays suggest, the diplomatic corps is a different thing and operates in different ways at different times and places in the contemporary international society. As in the political crises of Kigali and Kathmandu, it can take on the character of an agent: teaching, cajoling, ordering, and even pleading on occasions, about what the locals must do to play their part in the great scheme of things. In more stable, but nevertheless difficult, circumstances such as isolated capitals like Hanoi and Pyongyang, it can absorb itself in the creation and maintenance of the local terms and conditions of its members' employment. And when things are well understood and well run, as in Washington or London, what the corps does becomes less important than the fact that, in all its geographical, architectural and historical richness, it is there. It exists as a world in itself and, as such, gives a visual, certainly, and tangible, possibly, expression to the international world, together with the host's formal and political standing in it. As Henrikson makes clear, there can be few diplomats in Washington DC that doubt that they work in the world's most powerful national capital.

Even in the more apparently settled parts of the world, however, the diplomatic corps can also give expression to uncertainty and change. Can we view the communities of diplomats in New York and Brussels as they have been presented here as diplomatic corps, for example? In some respects, they function as such in their daily operations. Their members pay calls on one another, appear together on the appropriate occasions, and may act collectively, or at least in ubiquitous sub-groups to defend their privileges and immunities. Yet, who do they represent, and to whom? A diplomatic corps, as a body of diplomats accredited to a country and situated in its capital, represents, in R. B. J. Walker's terms, an outside world to, and within, an inside world.[4] Both the UN and the Brussels 'corps' (as the latter is presented here) render the inside/outside conception incoherent. In Wiseman's account, members of the UN 'corps', taken as a whole, might be said to represent themselves to the UN Secretariat and, rather less significantly, to the City of New York, but most of all they seem to represent themselves – in the sense of their respective countries – to themselves as a whole.

The Brussels 'corps' in Cross's chapter takes the puzzle to a new level. It is hard to tell what this group represents other than themselves as an epistemic community applying its expertise, not only to the acquisition and exercise of influence, but also to the generation of policy. And, whatever they represent, it is not to Belgium (there is a conventional Brussels corps which does that), nor to 'Europe' (in the form of the EU institutions located there) for, in effect, they are an expression of that notion of Europe. Perhaps the most we can say is that they represent one iteration of Europe (the EU) to another, *L' Europe de Pays*. However, just as we get a glimpse of that nirvana for enthusiasts of diplomacy, a body of men and women who know better acting independently on the basis of their expertise to achieve what is best for those they represent, they threaten to become something else. They shed, or may shed, the commitment to *la raison de système* which is the hallmark of professional diplomatic culture, and begin to acquire the preoccupations of agency with interest, getting one's way and being obeyed.

The diplomatic corps is then as contradictory, variable and, at times, ephemeral as the international society to which it gives expression. This poses problems for any attempt at a final word in terms of a response to that dreadful, but important, question '...so what should we do?' One does very little knowingly, and even less intentionally with the desired consequences, to constitutive entities. Since we are inside them and they frame our understandings of what is going on, it is terribly difficult to get a view of them from the outside upon which we can act with confidence. They are neither more nor less than what people do and think, but they develop, change and fade as if they have lives of their own. Therefore, while it might be tempting to launch into an argument about how the diplomatic corps should be strengthened and diplomats made more aware of the wonderful institution of which they are members and its potentials, or the reverse, that the corps should be retired and the diplomatic community allowed to take centre stage, there is not much point. Indeed, it is not entirely clear what injunctions of either sort might mean in practical terms. However, the chapters above do suggest at least one point worthy of further investigation, and they provide *prima facie* evidence for an important claim about the usefulness of thinking in terms of the international society of states and international societies generally.

The point is that the institution of the diplomatic corps, like so much else, has been profoundly affected by the great changes international relations have been undergoing over at least the last century. These changes, primarily in what international relations are about, who participates in them, and how they are conducted, are presenting an ever-sharpening choice about what the corps may look like in the future. Two possibilities suggest themselves. The one, in line with Rosenau's powerful image of a state system of severed heads which continue to talk to one another while the real action in international relations swirls above, below and around them, holds out what appears to be a gloomy future. The diplomatic corps, like its members, fades into increasing irrelevance like those gentlemen's clubs for people in organizations and activities no longer regarded as important. More optimistically, although within the same scenario, the corps might increasingly take on the functions of a lobbying group, professional association, or even trade union for its members. If capitals are, indeed, now full of new actors of increasingly greater diplomatic significance, then corps might grow from bodies concerned with collective representations towards their hosts, into bodies also concerned with collective representations towards these new diplomatic actors. To date, we have images of diplomats making both individual and collective representations towards their hosts, yet only individual representations towards the new actors with whom they are enjoined to talk, build alliances, and engage in common projects. The subject of these collective representations might be defensive, an assertion of rights regarding who may talk, when and with what authority, for example. It might be collaborative, in the sense of the corps as a whole, or diplomats claiming to act for the corps, working with domestic stakeholders or foreign private actors towards shared goals. And joint actions might well be in support of a noble cause – to protect dissidents, minorities and refugees; to denounce acts of genocide; to respond to a major humanitarian disaster such as a tsunami; and to prevent civil war.[5] Finally, such joint activity might be transformative, in the sense that the corps could work with others regarding informal and even formal membership of it by those who do not represent states or their international organizations.

Hence, the second possibility. Rather than fading from sight or shrinking into defensive organizations for the representatives of states within diplomatic communities broadly defined, diplomatic corps might find themselves at the forefront of a campaign to expand the formal membership categories of an international society. Certain international organizations enjoy a standing as members of international society that appears to be state-derived in name only, and this status is reflected in the presence of their representatives towards the end of the diplomatic lists of many countries. In daily practice, at least, it would seem a short step from this state of affairs to including other sorts of representatives in the formal diplomatic collective in any capital. *Pace* Barry Buzan,[6] there seems no reason why we cannot imagine a mixed international society populated by states, international organizations and possibly even private enterprises that are all sovereign and functionally differentiated only by degree, not by definition. To offer some intentionally odd couplings, trading states organized along theocratic lines; interest-driven international and non-governmental organizations motivated by the desire for profit and power; and armed, confessional merchant trading companies with public responsibilities, could all rub shoulders with one another while enjoying full equality and full membership. Indeed, formalities notwithstanding, it might be claimed that something like this is already coming into existence.

Imaginable though such a world might be, however, establishing the legal, moral and theoretical organizing principles of it would be a much more difficult matter. And this brings us, finally, to the big claim above for which these studies of the diplomatic corps provide *prima facie* evidence. It is that a world primarily constituted as and by a society of states remains a critical anchor and organizing principle of all the other organizing principles in terms of which we think about social life. We all ultimately live within this international society of states. The diplomatic corps – to take one manifestation of this international society – may fade into the background, may seem irrelevant to the great issues of the day, and may even seem forgotten on occasion by its immediate beneficiaries, the diplomats themselves. However, it has not gone away nor has it changed in terms of its membership principles and basic functions. As such, it continues to provide a primary backdrop in front of which the drama of international affairs is played out and, on occasions, like the scenery in a pantomime, it can come to life becoming at once both actor and stage. That it does so on its own relatively unchanging terms is testimony to the resilience of the idea of an international society of states and to the enormous difficulties we still get into when we attempt to think of the international relations of a plural world in terms of alternative organizing principles.

Alternatives cannot and should not be ruled out. The stresses and strains of stuffing the world in which we live into the international society of states idea are clear, and becoming clearer, for all to see. Nevertheless, and as Wiseman's and Cross's attempts above to apply the diplomatic corps idea in new ways in the settings of international and regional organizations strongly suggest, alternatives to the international society of states idea still seem to court high levels of conceptual incoherence and practical confusion. With what levels of such incoherence and confusion international life can carry on, it is difficult to say. We suspect they are higher than most of us would imagine. We also suspect, however, for all the old reasons, that order and coherence hold out the possibility of a better international life than does their absence. The diplomatic corps, it should be noted, remains a source of this order and coherence in ways in which other ideas, for example, the diplomatic community and global civil society, do not at least for now. Not only does it remain a source of order and coherence in the present, however. On the basis of the wide range of evidence presented in these studies, we suspect that the idea of a diplomatic corps will continue to be important in the future. If globalization is, indeed, transforming the world, and if we are, in fact, somewhere along the road on which the international society of states is becoming a world society, then at some point, the contours of that world will have to be constituted, the identities of its new participants stabilized, and the terms on which they participate established. The idea of a diplomatic corps, or something very like it, will become very useful once again if that point is reached.

Notes

1 By 'diplomatic theory', we mean here the body of principles and rules by which modern diplomacy and diplomats are regulated, and not International Relations theories which purport to understand or explain diplomacy.

2 See, for example, Eric Hobsbawm and Terence Ranger (eds), *The Invention of Tradition*, reprint (Cambridge: Cambridge University Press, 1992).

3 Statement Attributable to the Spokesperson for the Secretary-General – Fact-Finding Mission to Fiji, United Nations: New York, 20 April 2007.

4 R. B. J. Walker, *Inside/Outside: International Relations as Political Theory* (Cambridge: Cambridge University Press, 1993).

5 The diplomatic, and indeed consular, corps, will continue to serve as a cover for individual acts of courage and heroism. On this theme, see Richard Holbrooke, 'Defying Orders, Saving Lives: Heroic Diplomats of the Holocaust', *Foreign Affairs*, vol. 86, no. 3 (May/June 2007), pp. 135–8.

6 Barry Buzan, *From International Society to World Society? English School Theory and the Social Structure of Globalisation* (Cambridge: Cambridge University Press, 2004), p. 91.

Index

Note: 'n' following a page number indicates a reference from the notes